Music in Everyday Life

The power of music to influence mood and create scenes, routines and occasions is widely recognized and this is reflected in a strand of social theory from Plato to Adorno that portrays music as an influence on character, social structure and action. There have, however, been few attempts to specify this power empirically and to provide theoretically grounded accounts of music's structuring properties in everyday experience. *Music in Everyday Life* uses a series of ethnographic studies – an aerobics class, karaoke evenings, music therapy sessions and the use of background music in the retail sector – as well as in-depth interviews to show how music is a constitutive feature of human agency. Drawing together concepts from psychology, sociology and socio-linguistics, it develops a theory of music's active role in the construction of personal and social life and highlights the aesthetic dimension of social order and organization in late modern societies.

TIA DENORA is senior lecturer at the University of Exeter. She received the International Sociological Association's 'Young Sociologist' award in 1994 and is the author of *Beethoven and the Construction of Genius* (1995) as well as numerous journal articles.

Music in Everyday Life

Tia DeNora

CAMBRIDGE
UNIVERSITY PRESS

PUBLISHED BY THE PRESS SYNDICATE OF THE UNIVERSITY OF CAMBRIDGE
The Pitt Building, Trumpington Street, Cambridge, United Kingdom

CAMBRIDGE UNIVERSITY PRESS
The Edinburgh Building, Cambridge CB2 2RU, UK
40 West 20th Street, New York, NY 10011-4211, USA
477 Williamstown Road, Port Melbourne, VIC 3207, Australia
Ruiz de Alarcón 13, 28014 Madrid, Spain
Dock House, The Waterfront, Cape Town 8001, South Africa

http://www.cambridge.org

First published 2000
Fifth printing 2006

Printed in the United Kingdom at the University Press, Cambridge

Typeset in Plantin 10/12 pt in QuarkXPress™ [SE]

A catalogue record for this book is available from the British Library

Library of Congress Cataloguing in Publication data

DeNora, Tia, 1958–
Music in everyday life / Tia DeNora.
  p. cm.
Includes bibliographical references and index.
ISBN 0 521 62206 9 – ISBN 0 521 62732 X (pb)
1. Music and society. 2. Music – Psychology. I. Title.
ML3795.D343 2000
781'.11 – dc21   00-052606

ISBN 0 521 62206 9 hardback
ISBN 0 521 62732 X paperback

To my parents

John DeNora and Shirley Wood Smith DeNora

Contents

Figures

Preface and acknowledgements

On a drizzly Saturday morning in July 1998, I was sheltering under a tree in a North London market, conducting a series of impromptu interviews with women on the topic of 'music in their lives'. A contact had agreed to let me attach myself to her record stall and to vouch for me if questions arose. During a lull, the market manager wandered over to ask what I was doing. He told me he was originally from Nigeria, where, he said with emphasis, they 'really knew' how to use music. The situation was different in the United Kingdom, he said, where people did not seem to be aware of music's powers, and did not respect its social and physiological force. As he saw it, Europeans merely *listened* to music, whereas in Africa people *made* music as an integral element of social life. His mother, for example, sang certain songs as a regular part of her tasks and chores, even culinary operations, and she made use of different rhythms for different things. In Nigeria, he concluded, people had a richer and more overt understanding of music's powers, and a knowledge of how to harness those powers was considered to be an important part of common sense. By contrast, in the cold and over-cognitive climate of pre-millennium Britain, people were considerably less reflexive about music as a 'force' in social life.

For me, this encounter was deeply significant. It seemed to encapsulate so many of the issues I had been thinking about and the themes that undergird this book. It is certainly true that music's social effects have been underestimated in Western societies, despite the long-standing tradition from Plato to the Parents' Music Resource Centre devoted to just that theme, and despite the plethora of music's uses in daily life. Within modern societies, music's powers are – albeit strongly 'felt' – typically invisible and difficult to specify empirically. I believe, as I shall argue throughout this book, that this invisibility derives from a far more general neglect of the aesthetic dimension of human agency. This neglect is as common in the social sciences (with its cognitivist bias) as in the arts and humanities (with their emphases on text-objects).

But even if its official profile is not high, music's unofficial recognition as a powerful medium is strong. Over the past two years, nearly everyone I have spoken with about my research has had something to say on the subject of music's powers in their own lives, even when they were sometimes bemused by my interest in such picayune matters as whether or not people listen to music while washing the dishes. Their comments, taken as a whole, point to music as a dynamic material, a medium for making, sustaining and changing social worlds and social activities. Perhaps socio-musical scholarship's failure to recognize music's powers is due more to the use of inappropriate models for conceptualizing the nature of those powers – too often, music is thought of as a stimulus capable of working independently of its circumstances of production, distribution and consumption.

In this book I take a different tack. I suggest that it is probably impossible to speak of music's 'powers' abstracted from their contexts of use, though, within certain settings and in relation to particular types of actors, music's effects on action may be anticipated to varying degrees. Indeed, thinking about the nature of musical power can help to enrich the ways we think about other types of 'human–non-human' relations and the role played by other kinds of objects and materials within social life.

The question of *how* music works remains opaque. Perhaps because it is rarely pursued from the 'ground level' of social action, too much writing within the sociology of music – and cultural studies more widely – is abstract and ephemeral; there are very few close studies of how music is used and works as an ordering material in social life. In the course of conducting the research detailed in this book, I was struck repeatedly by just how much of what I observed in relation to music's powers could simply not have been imagined in advance. It is ironic that, nearly without exception, discussions of music's affect have had little association with interactionist sociology's abiding commitment to the fine-grained, exquisitely practical detail of everyday life, and its focus on lived experience and lay knowledge. A focus on music 'in action', as a dynamic material of structuration, has yet to be developed. Within the social sciences, as I discuss in the following chapters, it has been the psychologists who have led the way to an environmental approach for socio-musical studies. Within sociology, perhaps only Antoine Hennion's studies of amateur musical practices (through in-depth interviews) come close.

In short, we have very little sense of how music features within social process and next to no data on how real people actually press music into action in particular social spaces and temporal settings. These are large issues, but are probably best advanced through attention to the so-called 'small' details illuminated by ethnographic and ethnohistorical research. Accordingly, the arguments developed in this book draw upon a series of ethnographic investigations of music in daily life. This work included in-depth interviews with women of different age groups in metropolitan areas and small towns in the United States and United Kingdom, and four ethnographies of music 'in action' within specific social settings. (These included participant observation in aerobic exercise classes, karaoke evenings and music therapy sessions, unobtrusive observation of music in the retail sector and interviews with personnel in all these settings.)

Referring to these studies, the first aim of this book is to document some of the many uses to which music is and can be put, and to describe a range of strategies through which music is mobilized as a resource for producing the scenes, routines, assumptions and occasions that consti-tute 'social life'. Building upon these tasks, the second aim is to relocate music – as a type of aesthetic material – in relation to sociology's project, to bring it closer to the discipline's core concerns. Chapter 1 highlights music's active role in social life and proposes a way of drawing together perspectives from the American production of culture tradition, British cultural studies and sub-cultural theory, and the so-called 'grand' approach to socio-musical studies as exemplified by Adorno. Developing the grounded perspective outlined in chapter 1, the second chapter out-lines an interactionist conception of musical affect that moves beyond conundrums concerning whether music's affect is 'immanent' or 'attrib-uted'. Chapter 3 begins to put this perspective into practice by examin-ing music's role in relation to the construction of the self, centring on music's role as a technology of identity, emotion and memory. Chapter 4 considers the reflexive relationship between music and embodiment and develops an interdisciplinary perspective for investigating many of the ways in which the body – i.e., its physiological, micro-behavioural and motivational processes – may be understood to be 'musically composed'. Chapter 5 considers the role played by music within social scenes and situations, and describes how music may be used and inadvertently serve to draw otherwise disparate individuals into temporary (albeit often recurrent) configurations of social order – situations, scenes and institu-tional relations. Finally, chapter 6 weaves together these different strands and argues that socio-musical studies deserve far greater prominence within the social sciences, where they may be of considerable assistance in articulating a theory of agency and its relation to culture. In the twenty-first century, at a time when aesthetic forms of ordering are increasingly prominent, and as organizations are increasingly concerned with producing agents as well as products, the aesthetic bases of social life are – or at least should be – relocated at the heart of sociology's paradigm.

Doing ethnographic research is always dependent upon the good will and help of others. I would therefore like to begin by thanking the fifty-two women who were kind enough to let me interview them in the United States and United Kingdom. I have promised them anonymity and have changed identifying details. But I hope none the less that they will recognize themselves in the discussions and transcripts and I hope I have been as true as I could be to the spirit of what they told me when we met.

I am also deeply grateful to the retail managers and staff (who must remain anonymous) who allowed their stores to be used as a setting for research and to the instructors and students in the various aerobics classes studied (in particular to Kate Burnison) for the generous help they gave. Creative music therapist Hazel Bailey kindly took time out from her busy schedule to give advice and talk about her work with mental-health and learning-disabled clients and Helen Tyler of the Nordoff Robbins Music Therapy Centre in London graciously offered advice and the use of the Centre's library. Near the end of the project, conversations with staff nurse Helen Kirby of the Derriford Neonatal Intensive Care Unit got me thinking about music's role in neonatology and I have taken inspiration from her ongoing practical work in that area. Thanks are due as well to 'Karaoke Bob', Exeter's well-known karaoke M.C., who recounted a range of practical observations based on his long experience in the karaoke world.

I would like to thank my American academic 'hosts' during the fieldwork phase, James Webster of Cornell University's Music Department and Vera Zolberg of the Sociology Department, the Graduate Faculty of the New School for Social Research. Jim and Vera not only made it possible for me to be based at their institutions while I conducted the American interviews described in this book, but were instrumental in helping me to connect with contacts and potential interviewees. For further help at the fieldwork stage I would like to thank Robert Alford, Judith Balfe, Lenore Coral, Carol Krumhansl, Trevor Pinch, David Rosen, Margaret Webster, Neil Zazlaw, Ellen Zazlaw and the members of the Music Colloquium, Cornell University for thoughtful comments and discussions. I would also like to thank the members of the Science Studies Seminar and the Project on Culture and Society at the University of California, San Diego. In particular I am grateful to Bennett Berger, Richard Madsen, Hugh Mehan, Chandra Mukerji and Jann Pasler for very stimulating discussions.

During the year of the project on music and daily life I had the pleasure of working with an exceptional research assistant, Sophie Belcher. I would like to record my thanks to Sophie and note that the presentation of empirical work used to illustrate the argument of this book, particularly the section on aerobic exercise, was originally hammered out in our project meetings. I am also grateful to Sophie's family members who offered ideas and support and even, on one occasion, allowed us to study their 'shopping behaviour'. Thanks to: Perry Belcher, Kate and Simon Shattuck and Michele Anning. I would also like to thank Tessa Stone for help in contacting interviewees in London.

I am also grateful to the following for discussion and comments on the manuscript and for practical help at different stages in the research process: Paul Atkinson, Sara Delamont, Simon Frith, Sharon Hays, Antoine Hennion, Stevi Jackson, Pete Martin, Jo McDonagh, Sharon Macdonald, Frankie Peroni, Susan C. Scott, Robin Wagner-Pacifici, Kees van Rees, John Sloboda, Paul Sweetman, Anna Lisa Tota and my sociology of art collaborator here at Exeter, Robert Witkin. In addition, two anonymous reviewers for Cambridge University Press were very helpful, and I am grateful to the second reviewer who, at the last stages of writing, directed me to newly translated essays by Adorno on the sociology of music. I would also like to thank my editor at Cambridge, Sarah Caro, for her help and enthusiasm for the project, and the copy-editor, Katy Cooper, for her impeccable talent for producing clarity. I also wish to thank Catherine Max, who was involved with the project at Cambridge University Press in its early stages. Finally, I am, as ever, deeply grateful to my husband, Douglas Tudhope, who read and discussed the manuscript with me and helped me to see the relevance to the sociology of the arts of his own area of research, 'Human–computer Interaction'. Thanks, too, to audiences at the BSA, ASA, ESA and ISA meetings and to seminar groups at the universities of Cardiff, York, Surrey, Southampton and Milan.

The research for this book was supported by the Economic and Social Research Council of Great Britain ('Human–music Interaction – Music's "Effects" on Feeling, Embodiment and Temporality' (R000237013)). I would like to thank my colleagues in the Department of Sociology at the University of Exeter for the rotating study-leave plan that allowed me to complete this book, and Mary Guy, Nicki Barwick and Linda Tolly for their meticulous transcriptions of the taped interviews. Parts of chapters 3 and 5 draw on material previously published in *Poetics* and *Sociological Review*.

1 Formulating questions – the 'music and society' nexus

Music and society – the 'grand' tradition

When Howard Becker published *Art Worlds* in 1982, his 'art as a form of work' perspective publicized a trend that had been developing in American scholarship since the 1970s. Known as the 'production of culture' approach, and developed by scholars such as Richard Peterson (1976), Lewis Coser (1978), Janet Wolff (1981) and Vera Zolberg (1990), this new perspective provided an antidote to the brand of cultural sociology that Bennett Berger cheerfully referred to as 'culturology' (Berger 1995). By this, Berger meant a kind of sociology devoted to the 'reading' of works or styles so as to 'uncover' or decode their social content. In Berger's eyes, the great virtue of the production approach was its ability to unhook the study of art works from the grand but often imprecise matter of associating styles of art with styles of social being and with patterns of perception and thought.

In relation to music, the most notable exponent of this 'grand' approach was T.W. Adorno. For Adorno, music was linked to cognitive habits, modes of consciousness and historical developments. While on the one hand, he refers to music that 'trains the unconscious for conditioned reflexes' (Adorno 1976:53), on the other hand, he speaks of music that 'aid[ed] enlightenment' (1973:15). For example, the music of Arnold Schoenberg:

demands from the very beginning active and concentrated participation, the most acute attention to simultaneous multiplicity, the renunciation of the customary crutches of a listening which always knows what to expect . . . it requires the listener to spontaneously compose its inner movement and demands of him not mere contemplation but praxis. (1967:149)

Music such as Schoenberg's, Adorno believed, had the capacity to foster critical consciousness because its materials were organized in ways that countered convention and habit. By avoiding musical cliché, and by preserving dissonance instead of offering musical resolution and gratification, progressive music had the power to challenge cognitive,

perceptual and emotional habits associated with the rise of 'total socia-
tion', habits that reinforced, as a matter of reflex, relations of power and
administration in ways that made those relations seem natural, inevitable
and real.

For Adorno, modern music stood at the end of an historical trajectory,
one that began with Beethoven. With its idiosyncratic late style and,
in particular, the manner in which it organized musical material,
Beethoven's music exemplified or held 'truth-value' for, as Witkin
describes it:

> the subject confronted with the monolithic administrative force of modernity, of
> bureaucracy. From this point on, a music that had truth-value could no longer be
> governed by the illusion of harmony, but would have to recognise the true nature
> of force in the condition of the subject dominated and even overwhelmed by it.
> From now on, for the serious modern artist, there could be no more pretence that
> individual and society were reconciled or that the sensuous life of the subject
> could find its fulfilment and expression in society; the authentic work of art would
> henceforth have to reproduce the rupture of subject and object, of individual and
> society, within itself. (Witkin 1998:67)

As one can glean from this brief description, Adorno's work is exciting
and addressed to fundamentally critical issues in the human sciences.
Dedicated to exploring the hypothesis that musical organization is a simulacrum for social organization, Adorno's work conceives of music as formative of social consciousness. In this regard, Adorno's work represents
the most significant development in the twentieth century of the idea that
music is a 'force' in social life, a building material of consciousness and
social structure. But because it provides no machinery for viewing these
matters as they actually take place, Adorno's work also has the power to
frustrate; his work offers no conceptual scaffolding from which to view
music in the act of training unconsciousness, no consideration of how
music gets into action. The weakness of Adorno's approach thus lies in its
failure to provide some means by which its tantalizing claims can be
evaluated.

This criticism may be regarded as unfair, since Adorno never claimed
to offer a grounded theory of music's effects. None the less, the absence of
this grounding was certainly linked to the rejection of Adorno by musicologists of the late 1970s and 1980s (with the lone exception of Rose
Subotnik 1976; 1978; 1983; 1990, who, as McClary notes (1991:175n),
was 'severely chastised for having thus brought Continental criticism into
the discipline'), a time when his work was otherwise enjoying a resurgence
within the human sciences (Buck-Morss 1977; DeNora 1986a; Greisman
1976; 1986; Held 1984; Jay 1984; Middleton 1990; Witkin 1998). As one
writer within musicology bemoaned, 'one cannot say a Zeitgeist reached a

composer or other artist unless one can show the means by which it did'
(Lenneberg 1988:419).

Though today the terms are less hostile, less fraught with occupational
politics, the debate about Adorno's project is very much alive. From the
viewpoint of the empirical historian, the strategy of divining social
significance from the work itself (Berger's 'culturology') is fraught with
difficulty. This is because it does not account, in any extensive manner,
for how the genie of Zeitgeist originally got into the bottle of music or,
conversely, how music's organizing properties come to be decanted into
society. Here, quoted at length, is Peter Martin (quoting in turn Simon
Frith) on the problems associated with Adorno's 'grand' approach to the
matter of music's presence in social life:

As Frith puts it, the sociology of music, 'has usually rested on more or less crude
reflection theories: the music is taken to reflect, to be "homologous" to, the
society or social group that makes it'.
    As Frith's remark implies, however, there are problematic aspects of the claim
that there are close connections between sound structures and social structures.
Durkheim's notion of the conscience collective, for example, was developed in the
context of an analysis of simple, undifferentiated societies, and, as I have suggested, is not easy to reconcile with modern complex ones where a plurality of
contrasting cultures may coexist. Indeed, serious doubts have been expressed
about the usefulness of regarding *any* culture as a system, a relatively integrated
totality; there is, too, the associated danger of reifying such concepts as 'culture'
and 'society', treating them as if they were real entities. And the attempt to explain
any social activities – such as the production of music – in terms of the general
characteristics of society entails a further set of difficulties concerning the nature
of human action. (Martin 1995:79–80)

Martin is certainly correct about the levels of difficulty entailed. For
example, how are we to conceive of the temporal relationship between
music and Zeitgeist? Is music merely a passive receptacle of social spirit?
Or may it take the lead in the formation of social – that is, non-musical –
constructions? Or are both music and 'the social' generated by some
(mysterious and perhaps mythological) generative force? It is important
to address these questions of *process*, to try to specify how the social comes
to be inscribed in the musical, if one is to spell out an account of how
structural affinities or homologies between music and social formations
might arise and change over time. At best these issues are usually ignored;
at worst, they are fudged through some version of what Donna Haraway
(1991) calls 'the God trick', by which she means that the analyst poses as
if in possession of an omniscient vantage point from which to know the
social world (see also Hetherington 1998:11). And, as with early models
within the social study of science, the music-is-parallel-to-society
approach is best suited to static analytical frames – to the analysis of

particular composers or works – and to the description of shifts in musical styles (from polyphony to homophony, for example). It is less equipped to address the subtler matter of music stylistic change, moment-to-moment, year-to-year, and within specifically circumscribed social worlds. Yet without a descriptively informed theory of the music–society nexus, the sociology of music, however grand its ambitions, is in peril of being marooned, as the poet Ed Dorn once so eloquently expressed it, in 'that great Zero/Resting eternally between parallels' (1978:73). The French sociologist Antoine Hennion makes this point even more tersely: 'it must be strictly forbidden to create links when this is not done by an identifiable intermediary' (1995:248). Hennion's point is eminently reasonable: while music may be, seems to be, or is, interlinked to 'social' matters – patterns of cognition, styles of action, ideologies, institutional arrangements – these should not be presumed. Rather, their mechanisms of operation need to be demonstrated. If this demonstration cannot be achieved, then analysis may blend into academic fantasy and the music–society nexus rendered 'visionary' rather than 'visible'. Indeed, a grounded theory of the music–society nexus allows conventional distinctions between musical and social materials to be dissolved; in their place, musical and social matters are understood to be reflexively linked and co-produced. This matter is dealt with further in chapter 2.

Music and society – the 'little' tradition

In contrast to Adorno and the problems associated with his 'grand' approach, the production of culture or art worlds perspective established a secure empirical footing through its focus on artistic production within art worlds (Becker), realms (Peterson) or 'meso' structures (Gilmore 1987; Clarke 1990). Poised between large-scale notions such as social structure or ideology and individual art producers, the approach made a virtue of following 'links' as they were forged at the ground level of action. As Becker put it in his 1989 'Letter to Charles Seeger':

Sociologists working in this [the Art Worlds] mode aren't much interested in 'decoding' art works, in finding the work's secret meanings as reflections of society. They prefer to see those works as the result of what a lot of people have done jointly. (1989a:282; see also Becker 1989b)

In emphasizing local social contexts of arts production, the sociologists to whom Becker alludes were reacting against long-distance relationships with their research material. Their perspectives helped to specify many of the ways that art works were shaped by social organizations, interests, conventions and capacities available within their realms of production.

The art worlds approach thus showed its greatest potential when it addressed the question of how society got into art in much the same way that studies of the laboratory have illuminated scientific knowledge as a human product (Barnes and Shapin 1979; Latour and Woolgar 1986 [1979]; Knorr-Cetina 1981; Lynch 1982). Bringing the sociology of music closer to musicology's traditional interest in historical detail and to the then-burgeoning interest, within music scholarship, of 'context studies' was thus one of the production of culture perspective's greatest strengths.

But the perspective suited some questions better than others. Its weakness lay in its appellation, 'production *of* culture', where the realm of the aesthetic was implicitly treated as an object of explanation but not as an active and dynamic material in social life. Paradoxically, then, the journey into context was also a journey away from a concern with the social *presence* of aesthetic materials, a journey away from the original concerns of Adorno and others who focused on the ways in which music was active in – and not merely determined by – social life. More recently, the sociology of the arts has begun to return to this concern (cf. Bowler 1994; DeNora 1995a; Hennion and Grenier 1998; Witkin 1995; Born 1995; Frith 1990a; Tota 1997a). As Shepherd and Wicke have remarked, 'a viable understanding of culture requires an understanding of its articulation through music just as much as a viable understanding of music requires an understanding of its place in culture' (1997:34).

The challenge, in making this return, lay in how to articulate the concern with music as an active ingredient without reverting to the mythological realm of the 'great Zero', to show, symmetrically, how music articulates social life and social life articulates music. As Simon Frith has put it (1987:137), 'the question we should be asking is not what does popular music reveal about "the people" but how does it construct them'. It is here that the originally British tradition of cultural studies, ethnographically conceived, can be seen to provide excellent tools for the job.

Within the classic studies of young people and their intimate involvement with music, in books such as Paul Willis's *Profane Culture* (1978), and Frith's early monographs, *Sound Effects* (1981) and *The Sociology of Rock* (1978), music's social presence was illuminated. Rereading these works, we can see music providing a resource in and through which agency and identity are produced. Indeed, these studies can be seen to be compatible with Adorno's focus on music's link to social being. But this time, the music–social structure nexus was specified in a manner amenable to observation. Music's structuring properties were understood as actualized in and through the practices of musical use, through the ways music was used and referred to by actors during their ongoing attempts to produce their social situations and themselves *as* selves.

For example, in his report on the culture of the 'bikeboys', Willis noted that the boys' preferred songs were fast-paced and characterized by a strong beat, a pulsating rhythm. Willis resorted to the concept of homology or 'resonance' to explain the relation of this music to bikeboy culture, but his study effectively evaded the 'great Zero' of parallelism by showing the reader how not *he*, Willis, but the boys *themselves* established this connection between music and social life. In *Profane Culture*, structural similarities between music and social behaviour – in this case small group culture – were forged through the cultural practices and lay classifications of the group members – the boys – themselves. They were never analysts' constructs. As Willis put it, 'objects, artifacts and institutions do not, as it were, have a single valency. It is the act of social engagement with a cultural item which activates and brings out particular meanings' (1978:193). The boys, as Willis describes them, are active interpreters whose group values were, 'almost literally seen in the qualities of their preferred music' (1978:63). The focus is directed at the question of how particular actors make connections or, as Stuart Hall later put it, 'articulations' (1980; 1986) between music and social formations. Here, then, at least for working purposes, is an interactionist and grounded 'worlds' version of Adorno's original vision. The subsequent history of the development of this perspective is, arguably, one of sociology's greatest contributions to the understanding of culture, in so far as it has provided concepts and descriptions of how aesthetic materials come to have social 'valency' in and through their circumstances of use.

The observation that agents attach connotations to things and orient to things on the basis of perceived meanings is a basic tenet of interpretivist sociology. But its implications for theorizing the nexus between aesthetic materials and society were profound. It signalled a shift in focus from aesthetic objects and their content (static) to the cultural practices in and through which aesthetic materials were appropriated and used (dynamic) to produce social life.

In the two decades that have followed the publication of *Profane Culture*, the field of audience and reception studies has advanced considerably. But the early interactionist promise of these classic works is too-often muted in favour of a preoccupation with 'what' people think about particular cultural works. The great contribution of Willis, Frith and Hall was their focus not on what can be 'said' about cultural forms, but on what the appropriation of cultural materials achieves *in action*, what culture 'does' for its consumers within the contexts of their lives. Thus, one of the most striking (and usually underplayed) aspects of *Profane*

Culture is its conception of music as an active ingredient of social formation. The bikeboys' preferred music did not leave its recipients 'just
sit[ting] there moping all night' (1978:69). It invited, perhaps incited,
movement. As one of the boys put it, 'if you hear a fast record you've got
to get up and do something, I think. If you can't dance any more, or if the
dance is over, you've just got to go for a burn-up [motorcycle ride]'
(1978:73). Willis's work was pioneering in its demonstration of how
music does much more than 'depict' or embody values. It portrayed
music as active and dynamic, as constitutive not merely of values but of
trajectories and styles of conduct in real time. It reminded us of how we
do things to music and we do things with music – dance and ride in the
case of the bikeboys, but, beyond this, work, eat, fall asleep, dance,
romance, daydream, exercise, celebrate, protest, worship, mediate and
procreate with music playing. As one of Willis's informants put it, 'you
can hear the beat in your head, don't you . . . you go with the beat, don't
you?' (1978:72). As it is used, both as it plays in real time and as it is
replayed in memory, music also serves to organize its users.

If we take them at their word, the bikeboys tell us that they enter *into* the
music and 'go with it'. Music takes them from one state (sitting around)
to another (dancing as the music plays) to another (riding as the music
plays in memory). In this sense, music is a cultural vehicle, one that can be
ridden like a bike or boarded like a train. This description is metaphorical
(and the boys' metaphors of 'going' and physical transformation are
themselves cultural resources for holding on to a mode of being and a set
of procedural commitments – in this case, to movement) but it is worth
noting that one of the most common metaphors for musical experience in
post-nineteenth-century Western culture is the metaphor of 'transport',
in the sense of being carried from one (emotional) place to another (and
indeed, at times, being 'carried away'). Viewed in this way, music can be
conceived of as a kind of aesthetic technology, an instrument of social
ordering. As Sarah Cohen suggests, 'focus upon people and their musical
practices and processes rather than upon structures, texts or products
illuminates the ways in which music is used and the important role that it
plays in everyday life and in society generally' (1993:127). And, as
Georgina Born puts it in her ethnography of IRCAM, it is necessary to
focus on 'the actual uses of technologies [she could just as well have said
"musics"], which are often depicted in idealized, unproblematic, and
normative ways' (1995:15). In common with all instruments and
technological devices, music needs to be understood in terms of its (non-
verbal) capacities for enabling and constraining its user(s). How, then,
can this idea be developed and how can music's structuring powers be
illuminated at the level of social experience?

Getting into the music

I begin with a simple, highly mundane and apparently trivial case. A few years ago, when it was still a novelty to use a modem to access email from home, I was writing a book review of Susan McClary's *Feminine Endings* (see chapter 2, below). Normally, I would dial up the mainframe computer at the end of a work session, and there would be a short delay before the connection to the terminal server was established. Though the delay is only a few seconds, I tended to experience the wait as taking a long time, probably because of my eagerness to read my mail and my up-until-then rapid typing (and the expectation that when you press a key you get a response). When initially instructed on how to log on, I had been told to press the 'enter' key once or twice as a kind of prompt, and so, for a number of months when logging on, I pressed the key, somewhat impatiently, as fast as I could. Then one day, after I had been reading McClary's essay about Georges Bizet's opera, *Carmen*, I found myself pressing the enter key to the Habanera's opening rhythm, while simultaneously replaying the music in my head (see figure 1); and even before Carmen had begun to sing the words, 'L'amour est un oiseau rebelle', I was on the mainframe, impressed by the way time had flown. Somehow, this particular use of the Habanera became a habit. For some months after, as I logged on to the computer, I thought of the music and tapped the enter key to the opening rhythm, each time feeling, as I reached my email, slight regret that I had to 'interrupt' the aria to read my mail.

This simple example helps to introduce just a few of the ways in which music can 'get into action', so as to organize subjects in real time. The first way music does this concerns the body. *My* body, in this example (my index finger anyway), visibly slowed. Not only was the number of times I tapped the 'enter' key reduced, the action of my finger was realigned, or musically entrained with the Habanera's rhythm. In direct contrast to the case of the bikeboys, whose music speeded them up ('you've got to get up and do something'), here, music slowed down embodied action by enlisting the body into rhythm. But the Habanera's effects extended beyond bodily movement. The introduction of music changed the way I experienced a five-second interval. It redefined that temporal situation, translated it from 'long time' into 'short time'. The music did not simply fill in the time of waiting; it reconstructed the ongoing aim of my action such that the very thing I had been awaiting so eagerly (access to my email) was redefined in the real-time situation, as something that was interrupting the pleasure of the music. Defined in relation to the interrupted musical phrase, the email was then re-experienced as arriving 'too soon'. Here

Figure 1. Georges Bizet, *Carmen*, 'Habanera'

then, is the first in a series of examples of music's power to 'compose' situations. Consider now a second and distinctly less trivial one.

The 'art' of feeling secure – aesthetics of risk assessment

A transatlantic flight epitomizes a peculiarly modern requirement, namely the need to place one's trust in technological systems. The prospect of putting a few hundred strangers together in a hermetically sealed, crowded and, for at least some, potentially frightening, space is, of necessity, a prospect that confronts the problem of social order. Aware of this, airlines attempt to mould their consumers, to form them into 'ideal' users, into individuals who exhibit 'preferred' forms of passenger behaviour. Understandably, the airlines want no terrorists; they want passengers to remain mostly seated; they want passengers to obey requests from crew and to appear calm. Accordingly, carriers deploy a range of socio-technical devices to discipline passengers – security checks, passports, metal detectors, x-ray machines, overhead lighted signs and instructions from the flight crew, for example. Some of these devices are quite primitive – physical barriers, for example, of varying strength. No one is allowed through security without a passport and ticket, or with a weapon if it is detected in carry-on luggage. More subtly, passengers may be less likely to try to get up from their seats when a meal cart is blocking the aisle or the remains of a meal occupy a tray-table. Other disciplining devices appeal to passengers as 'rational actors', willing and able to participate in a rule-governed basis for social order and placing their trust in the superior knowledge claims of system professionals. When the captain announces the possibility of forthcoming turbulence, for example, and asks passengers to return to their seats, it is expected that everyone – even those who had wished to go to the lavatory – will obey, on the assumption that the airline and the flight crew know what is best.

Trust in the face of contingency is a key component of any expert system, and, as Anthony Giddens has observed, such trust 'is inevitably in part an article of "faith"'(1990:29). The literature on risk and risk cultures has documented how faith, as the foundation of trust in expert systems, is constituted from a 'pragmatic element' – for example, 'the experience that such systems generally work as they are supposed to do' (1990:29), and from the manner in which expert systems are embedded within external regulatory systems, and statistical representations of 'safety'.

These literatures excel when they address the construction of faith in expert systems from the point of view of *general* risk perception – the safety of air travel as a general concept, for example – as spoken about in the subjunctive (for instance, 'would you say that air travel is safe?'). But they are on weaker ground when they are called upon to account for the construction of trust in particular experiences of travel ('how do you feel about *this* flight?'). To ask about how individuals – atomized as passengers in seats – come to apply their generally held precepts about safety and security to the here-and-now of being on an aircraft is to ask about how social order and its attendant beliefs, habits and authority structures get instantiated in real-time circumstances. At the same time, this is a question about how modes of agency are constructed in and through a temporal dimension, across time and space.

What, then, does it take to inculcate trust in a local sense, to instantiate faith? What are the materials passengers use to make an interpretive connection between the typically 'safe' features of 'most flights' and 'this' flight? For it is in and through the nature of this interpretative activity that faith is renewed and trust established. And how are reminders of this propositional knowledge – flying is, in general, safe – woven into the texture of intra-aircraft culture so that the ontological security of the pre-ferred passenger and his or her faith is sustained throughout the course of the flight? In relation to these questions, research on risk cultures needs to address non-cognitive aspects of risk assessment. Within that area, a key topic would revolve around the non-cognitive, aesthetic dimensions of risk perception hitherto absent from the risk literatures (see Lash and Urry 1994:5, 31–44 on this point). With regard to Giddens's notion of 'faith' in expert systems, throughout history and across culture, aesthetic materials have been used to instil and inspire faith, as a part of the cere-monial occasions and settings in which faith is renewed. In this sense, the concern with the aesthetic dimension of risk perception is a species of a far more general matter within sociology – the cultural foundations of belief, co-ordination, conformity and subjectivity; and so, with respect to air travel, the social sciences have missed what the airlines have known for some time, that the here-and-now of travel depends as well on subtler ordering devices. Among these, music is key.

Music 'in flight'

In March 1997 I flew from London to California. I made note of the musical accompaniment of my in-flight experience. The hassle of board-ing was musically underpinned with an 'ambient music video' – some-thing called, 'True North', in which images of lakes and glaciers – cool and muted greys, greens and blues – were accompanied by slow, low pitched melodies and whale song. Just before take-off the mood changed. Trumpets heralded the safety video (see figure 2). This decisive, upward-sweeping and definite-sounding brass then faded to the background as the firm but friendly (male) voice described what we should do in the event of a water landing, etc. The brass returned full volume at the close of the presentation and the plane taxied out to the runway for take-off.

There are many things that could be said about the use of brass, the use of a piece by an American composer (by an American airline), the fanfare genre, of instruments associated with heraldry and the military (precision, technology, expertise) and (thinking about gender and class (I flew economy)) about a piece by Copland entitled 'Fanfare for the common man'. Music is active in defining situations because, like all devices or tech-nologies, it is often linked, through convention, to social scenarios, often according to the social uses for which it was initially produced – waltz music for dancing, march music for marching and so on. Genre and conventional

Figure 2. Aaron Copland, 'Fanfare for the common man'

formulations as they accrue over time in musical practice can in turn be used to impart conventional understandings to the settings in which they occur. They are part of the materials with which scenic specificity is constructed and perceived. Music can be used, in other words, as a resource for making sense of situations, as something of which people may become aware when they are trying to determine or tune into an ongoing situation.

Nearly all music exists in intertextual relation to compositional conventions and works (for example, genres such as a mass, a symphony or dance music, material procedures of harmony, melody, rhythm and so on, and gestures of various kinds). It also exists in relation to sound structures in the social natural worlds outside of music (sudden falling movement, tense climbing, gently stroked keys, volume and energy levels) and in relation to its past association with social situations, from its social patterns of employment. Music comes to have recognizable social 'content' in and through its perceived participation in these (and other) realms. The idea that music makes use of figures, gestures, styles, sonorities, rhythms and genre, and that these are to varying degrees part of a public stock of musical 'understanding', was a common part of music theory in Bach's day and in Mozart's (Allanbrook 1983). In Mozart's Vienna, composers employed conventional music *topoi* of rhythmic gesture, melodic and tonal material. Indeed, Bach's project of instigating and reinstigating religious faith through the aesthetic means of music (and drawing upon a shared conventional vocabulary of musical gesture in order to do so) is, in operational terms, not so different from what an airline does when it enlists music to instil faith in its expert systems. Bach's contemporary, Mattheson, produced a catalogue of musical affect (1981 [1739]). In our own day, despite the range of compositional and reception practices, music is still used to signal plot and mood within the film and television industries and, there, catalogues of musical materials are still employed. If anything, these industries have only multiplied the kinaesthetic music–image associations to which we are exposed, and which the advertising industry draws upon to sell us everything from cars to bars of chocolate.

The musical materials of the airline's safety video, for example, have been used for centuries to imply – with a quick, relatively loud, tonally centred and upward-sweeping gesture – a message along the lines of, 'sit up and pay attention, something important is about to happen'. They may thus be understood as an attention-seeking gesture. At the same time, the Copland fanfare moves at a stately moderato pace. There is nothing agitated in its manner; to the contrary, it may be read as commensurate with a graceful 'lift-off'; it embodies the very activity it is used to signify.

Of course, other music may be equally able to command *attention*. And no music is guaranteed to invoke 'preferred' or appropriate action frames (music can be received with irony, naively, alternatively). What does seem clear, however, is that there are some musical materials that would under-mine preferred or appropriate action frames. Would an airline consider using the ravaged atonality of Schoenberg's *Erwartung* or Strauss's *Tales from the Vienna Woods* to underpin its safety video? Would the former inculcate further passenger anxiety and the latter trivialize or possibly perplex? Neither would convey the combination of organizational control, formality, ceremonial gravitas, attention seeking and (musical-tonal) security associated with the genre to which their chosen composition by Copland is oriented, the generic musical materials of which it partakes. But if the Copland were to be performed imprecisely, with unusual phras-ing or dynamics, might it too be counterproductive? There is, however, probably no music that would engender trust in the face of an aircraft filling with smoke! Trust is kindled through gesture, both through the choice of this – musical – gesture *and* through the way it is instantiated. In addition, as Antoine Hennion has shown in relation to controversies over baroque authenticity, works into which values are invested and which become articles of faith (Bach's St Matthew Passion, for example) can be undermined according to how they are performed since 'authenticity' is constructed in and through the mobilization of human and material 'mediators' – anything from who performs a work, to how a double-dotted rhythm is executed, to instrument choice (Hennion 1997).

In fact, there are a good many known examples of music that have failed in relation to air travel. According to Joseph Lanza, when Pittsburgh Airport decided to play Brian Eno's eerily ambiguous opus, 'Music for airports', over its public address system, performances were quickly cancelled when travellers complained that the 'background music' made them feel nervous. Similarly, certain numbers were deleted from in-flight radio programmes because they were associated with, *reminders* of, the very matters that both passengers and crew typically attempt to forget. 'Stormy weather', 'I have a terrible feeling I'm falling [in love with you]' and 'I don't stand a ghost of a chance' all had to go. As Lanza observes, 'Music tinged with the slightest disagreeable song content, altered tempo, stray key, or change in order can cause "the Comfort Zone" to slip into "the Twilight Zone" '(Lanza 1994:195).

Music as a medium of social relation

Consider a third example of how music can get into social life. Gary is in his early twenties. He is unable to see or speak in words. He exhibits dis-tress in the form of shrieks and screams when taken to (no doubt fright-ening) public places such as shops, and sometimes he bites or scratches other people if they come too close. He was referred by a local health authority for music therapy, often used as a 'last resort' for clients when previous, more conventional, therapeutic strategies have been tried and are deemed to have failed.

Gary is sitting in the music room with his carer, waiting for the music therapy session to begin. He is very still. His child's body is knotted up, his head bent over, his legs are crossed. As the music therapist begins to play, Gary shouts, and rocks backwards and forwards in his chair. The therapist responds to whatever noises he makes, imitating them but also modulating them into softer, more 'musical' forms. The therapist then picks up a drum and bangs out a steady beat in sync with Gary's cries. She begins to sing, 'Gary is rocking', after which Gary's rocking becomes so intense that his carer has to hold on to Gary's chair (he has toppled himself over before). The therapist then holds the drum closer to Gary and he takes her hand (the first time he had ever done so). He then uses her hand as a beater, and bangs the drum with it. Later, the therapist returns to the piano and plays a low-pitched, 'eastern'-sounding (pentatonic) melody. Gary is still rocking, but gently now. His noises are gentler too. At the end of the session he is smiling, making sounds that his carer identifies as 'happy'.

  After the session, Gary's therapist describes the progress he has made over months of attending music therapy sessions. At first, he would not allow the therapist to come near him; if she did, he would bite and lash out. Now he is calmer during sessions, more interactive, even allowing himself to touch or be touched. (Belcher n.d.)

The therapy begins with the premise that, unlike most people, Gary is cut off from most media of interaction. He has few tools for world-making, for imprinting 'himself' on the environment and for stabilizing that environment (which most of us do through our everyday words and other cultural practices such as decoration or gesture). Accordingly, the session provides Gary with an environment in which he can interact, and it provides him with media to which can relate and which he can influence. It is possible that, for Gary, there is no other realm nor media in or with which he can interact to this degree, no other environment that he is able to structure as much as this one. It provides an environment that Gary can query and control through musical acts, a ground against which his own musical acts are reflected back to him, and a medium with which he can be and do things with another. For Gary, music is a vehicle that brings him into closer co-ordinated activity with another person. It is a device that enables him to act in (social) concert, one with which Gary may develop his sense of self, his presence to self and other(s). The therapist, through her musical-interactive skills – her considerable improvisational abilities – is providing what Gary cannot provide for himself: an aesthetic environment and forms of aesthetic interaction capable of producing pleasure, security and, perhaps most fundamentally, that allow for the demonstration and self-perception of one's self in an aesthetic medium. Is it any wonder, then, that Gary appears to be more contented at the end of the session?

Using music as a resource for creating and sustaining ontological security, and for entraining and modulating mood and levels of distress, is by no means unique to the purview of the professional music therapeutic encounter. In the course of daily life, many of us resort to music, often in highly reflexive ways. Building and deploying musical montages is part of a repertory of strategies for coping and for generating pleasure, creating occasion, and affirming self- and group identity. Consider, for example, Lucy, who is in her fifties and works as an administrator for an international academic organization. In the following excerpt, she is describing her use of music in the face of the stresses and strains of daily life. On the morning of the interview, she used music to foster a sense of inner 'calm'. She turned to some of the Schubert *Impromptus*.

Q. Can you describe the situation of listening in the front room, like maybe the last time you listened to music in the front room?
A. This morning in fact [laughs].
Q. Oh. Excellent [laughs]. Can you just tell me it in fairly detailed, just what made you go in there to listen, like was it a choice or . . . ?
A. It was a choice because I was feeling very stressed this morning because we're in the throes of moving house and it's, you know, we're not, we haven't sold our house yet, and it's moving, you know, and so I actively decided to put on Schubert's *Impromptus* because they were my father's favourite – you might want to come along to that again, because Schubert's *Impromptus* have a long history with my life – and I thought, my husband had just gone off to work and I thought well, about half an hour before I come up here [to her place of paid work], I'll just listen to them. So, the speakers are [she gestures] there and there on either side of what used to be the fireplace and I sit in a rocking chair facing them, so I get the sound in between the speakers, and I just sat there and listened [sighs, gentle laugh]. But I needed it. It was only ten minutes or so, you know, I didn't listen to them all. I just listened to the bits I wanted to listen to.

Lucy goes on to describe how she entered the front room of her house feeling 'very stressed'. Ten minutes or so later she left feeling different, calmer. Here, self-administered music was a catalyst, a device that enabled Lucy to move from one set of feelings to another over a relatively short time span. Through reference to music, Lucy reconfigured herself as a social-emotional agent. This matter is taken up in depth in chapter 3.

Conceptualizing music as a force

Music is not merely a 'meaningful' or 'communicative' medium. It does much more than convey signification through non-verbal means. At the level of daily life, music has power. It is implicated in every dimension of social agency, as shown through the previous examples. Music may influence how people compose their bodies, how they conduct themselves, how they experience the passage of time, how they feel – in terms of energy and emotion – about themselves, about others, and about situations. In this respect, music may imply and, in some cases, elicit associated modes of conduct. To be in control, then, of the soundtrack of social action is to provide a framework for the organization of social agency, a framework for how people perceive (consciously or subconsciously) potential avenues of conduct. This perception is often converted into conduct *per se*.

The ability to exploit music's social powers is fundamental to any disc jockey's craft. Indeed, one of the best natural laboratories for observing soundtracks as they are converted into social and social psychological tracks, into action–feeling trajectories, modes of agency, is the humble karaoke evening. Within such an event, the style and tempo of musical numbers changes quickly; each number is chosen by performers individually. At a karaoke event, there is no preordained schedule of musical numbers, no attempt to create a 'grammar' or sets of musical numbers over the course of an evening, such as a disc jockey might seek to do. However, at least in Britain, karaoke is often hosted by a 'master of ceremonies', who may interject one or more of his own performances to tide things over, get things going, and so on. In the course of our study of music and everyday life we met up with one of the United Kingdom's most active karaoke hosts, 'Karaoke Bob', who was based in Exeter. Bob – who currently holds the *Guinness Book of Records* title for the longest karaoke impersonation of Elvis Presley – explained, as he saw them, the ins and outs of karaoke as a social occupation. Here is part of what he had to say about how quickly – from song to song (the order is usually random, the result of who signs up for what, though Bob may interject one or two of his own numbers at any time) – his audience adapts to and begins to adopt musical stylistic trajectories, adjusting conduct style and energy levels, such as when the music of Oasis encourages young men to adopt a 'cool' stance and reach for a cigarette:

Like when they bring out Oasis everybody is standing there with cigarette smoke in the eyes [one of the most popular Oasis numbers for Bob's karaoke evenings is entitled, 'Cigarettes and alcohol'], they tend to love that sort of thing as much as the Beatles. In the Beatles' day they used to sort of stand there doing this, standing at the bar . . . whatever music we play they tend to react as different individuals [i.e., through the adoption of different personae].

[They] put on a lot of love songs and then it gets a bit boring so then I slip a couple of rock 'n' roll songs in or line dancing – stuff like that, basically stuff in the charts – then it starts to come back up again and at the end of the night if there's too many drunks shouting around and that then I say, 'right, I'm going to put some ballads on now to quiet it down again.' So we look at the audience.

At the level of practice, music's social effects – of the kind that Bob describes – are familiar to marketeers and social planners. In chapter 5, music's burgeoning role in relation to 'social control' and the structuring of conduct in public is discussed. For example, clearly audible classical music in the New York Port Authority Bus Terminal and Tyneside railway station has been associated with major reductions in hooligan activities (MAIL 1998; TEL 1998; NYT 1996; see also Lanza 1994:226). In-store experiments suggest that background music can be used to structure a range of consumer behaviour and choices – the time it takes to eat and drink (Milliman 1986; Roballey et al. 1985), the average length of stay in a shop (Milliman 1982), the choice of one brand or style over another (North and Hargreaves 1997b) and the amount of money spent (Areni and Kim 1993). In the commercial sector, where results are assessed in the cool light of profit margins, considerable investment has been devoted to finding out just what music can 'make' people do. Consider these excerpts from brochures from background music companies:

Creating a happy and relaxed environment through the imaginative use of music is a vital element in securing maximum turnover and ensuring that your business has optimum appeal. Used correctly, music can influence customer buying behaviour by creating or enhancing the image, mood and style you wish to achieve. (Candy Rock n.d.)

Music is a powerful factor in creating your image . . . and one of the most cost-effective ways to change it. (AEI Music n.d.)

There is little doubt that music is experienced by its recipients as a dynamic material. In interviews with music users, the psychologist of music John Sloboda has shown that users highlight repeatedly the ways in which they view music as having power over them ('music relaxes me', 'disturbs me', 'motivates and inspires me' (Sloboda 1992)). Similarly, in the United States, in the 'Music in Daily Life Project', conducted by Susan Crafts, Daniel Cavicchi and Charles Keil (1993), respondents offered a range of narratives about what music 'did' for them, albeit with little description of their mundane musical practices and the contexts of these practices.

The challenge is to unpack those narratives, and to resituate them as musical practices occurring within ethnographic contexts. Just how does music work to achieve its diverse ends? Does music make people do things? Is it like a physical force or a drug? Will it affect all its recipients in similar ways? Is it possible, not only to document music's effects, but to begin to explain how music comes to achieve these effects? And, finally, what part does a focus on music's mechanisms of operation form within sociology's core and critical concerns with order, power, and domination or control? It is time to reclaim the matter of music's powers for sociology.

Relations of music production, distribution and use

One of the first issues this project needs to face is the matter of how music is produced and distributed within environments – the who, where, when, what and how of sonic production and reproduction. This matter is critical in modern times where mechanically reproduced, mass-distributed music is as ubiquitous as temperature control and lighting. As Lash and Urry have observed (1994:54), the concept of 'expert systems' is applicable beyond the realms of social science, techniques of self-therapy and the environment. It applies as well to the aesthetic realm, where 'the use of film, quality television, poetry, travel and painting as mediators in the reflexive regulation of everyday life' is also pertinent. The salience of such systems can be seen perhaps most acutely in relation to particular social groups. During an ethnography of high street retail shops I was intrigued to learn that the larger of the national and global outlets not only play the same music at precisely the same times of day, but they do so in order to structure the energy levels of staff and clientele. In principle, one should be able to enter any one of these stores at any moment in any branch in the United Kingdom and the music playing should be (or at least is intended to be) identical. At a time when public spaces are increasingly being privatized, and when 'people management' principles from McDonald's and Disneyland are increasingly applied to shopping precincts, sociologists need to focus much more closely on music's social role. Here, the concern with music as a social 'force' – and with the relation of music's production and deployment in specific circumstances – merges with a fundamental concern within sociology with the interface between the topography of material cultural environments, social action, power and subjectivity. This literature and the contribution it can make to socio-musical studies is discussed in chapter 2 and again in chapters 5 and 6.

Consider again the examples discussed so far. In one, an individual (myself) replayed in memory a popular aria in a way that reconfigured the experience of a temporal interval. In another, a group of individuals on an aircraft are exposed to music chosen expressly for its perceived ability to promote a particular image and to structure social mood. In a third, a therapeutic client makes whatever 'music' he can while a music therapist weaves that music into a larger musical tapestry and mode of interaction. In a fourth example, an individual engages in a kind of do-it-yourself music therapy, locating and listening to a desired recording as part of her everyday regulation and care of herself. In a fifth example, a karaoke host alters the energy levels and social inclinations in a pub by interjecting strategically chosen numbers of his own. In the final examples, transport stations and shops draw upon 'expert'-designed music systems to encourage organizationally preferred forms of conduct. In all of these examples, music is in dynamic relation with social life, helping to invoke, stabilize and change the parameters of agency, collective and individual. By the term 'agency' here, I mean feeling, perception, cognition and consciousness, identity, energy, perceived situation and scene, embodied conduct and comportment.

If music can affect the shape of social agency, then control over music in social settings is a source of social power; it is an opportunity to structure the parameters of action. To be sure, there are occasions when music is perceived as something to be resisted. The degree of participation in the production of a 'soundtrack' for ongoing (and future) action, the relations of music production, distribution and consumption, is thus a key topic for the study of music's link to human agency. This hitherto-ignored topic is focused on the social distribution of access to and control over the sonic dimension of social settings.

The second topic for a sociology of musical power is less straightforward, despite the attention it has received within cultural theory. It concerns the matter of how to specify music's semiotic force. In what way should we specify music's link to social and embodied meanings and to forms of feeling? How much of music's power to affect the shape of human agency can be attributed to music alone? And to what extent are these questions about music affiliated with more general social science concerns with the power of artefacts and their ability to interest, enrol and transform their users?

2   Musical affect in practice

What we have said makes it clear that music possesses the power of producing an effect on the character of the soul.

(Aristotle, The Politics, 1340a)

It is a pervasive idea in Western culture that music possesses social and
emotional content, or that its semiotic codes are linked to modes of subjective awareness, and in turn, social structures. Equally pervasive,
however, is the view that music's social force and social implications are
intractable to empirical analysis. At the level of the listening experience,
for example, music seems imbued with affect while, at the level of analysis, it seems perpetually capable of eluding attempts to specify just what
kind of meaning music holds and just how it will affect its hearers. The
point of this chapter is to explore the 'gap', as John Rahn once put it
(1972:255), 'between structure and feeling', and to derive from it an
ethnographically oriented, pragmatic theory of musical meaning and
affect, one located on an overtly sociological plane. Such a theory emphasizes music's semiotic force as the product of what can be called
'human–music interaction'.

The interactionist critique of semiotics – overview

This chapter considers musicological readings of works, socio-linguistic
conceptions of meaning in use, and social science perspectives on
material culture. Its aim is to draw these perspectives together and to
propose a theory of musical affect in practice. The argument can be
summarized as follows: implicit in much work devoted to the question of
musical affect is an epistemological premise. This premise consists of the
idea (albeit unacknowledged) that the semiotic force of musical works
can be decoded or read, and that, through this decoding, semiotic analysis may specify how given musical examples will 'work' in social life, how,
for example, they will imply, constrain, or enable certain modes of
conduct, evaluative judgements, social scenes and certain emotional
conditions. Following this premise, the logical role for socio-musical

analysis is semiotics, and the analyst's task may be confined to the consideration of aesthetic forms; music's users thus hardly need to be consulted. There is no need, in other words, for (time-consuming) ethnographic research. This semiotic conception of socio-musical analysis is what Bennett Berger (1995) (discussed in chapter 1) described as 'culturology'. It also underpins Adorno's way of working, and helps to explain why he felt qualified to disparage jazz, for example, and why he so exasperated Bertolt Brecht, who once observed, 'he never took a trip in order to see' (quoted in Blomster 1977:200). This semiotic protocol is prevalent in socio-musical studies. It is usually devoted to what is often referred to as 'the works themselves'.

In what follows, it is argued that semiotic approaches, conceived in this manner, possess limitations. Their limits derive from a particular type of theoretical shortcut taken by semiotic analysts as they slide from readings of works to discussions of the social impact of those works. This shortcut uses the analyst's interpretations of music's social meanings as a resource instead of a topic. That is, they often conflate ideas about music's affect with the ways that music actually works for and is used by its recipients instead of exploring how such links are forged by situated actors (particular audiences or recipients as, for example, in Willis's study of the bike-boys described in chapter 1). From the comfort of an ergonomically designed armchair, poised in front of a lap-top computer in an office with a view, the analyst duly 'informs' readers about music and what it will do – for example, the forms of feeling it may engender, or the social structures to which it gives rise or from which it emanates.

To be sure, not all semioticians envisioned such analytical powers for themselves; as Barthes once observed, his own responses to Vivaldi might (but need not necessarily) align with the responses of others; they were 'his' responses, visceral, proximate, and bound up with the temporal weft of his being. In this sense, Barthes captures the way in which 'good' semiotics is akin to criticism and appreciation but may not have the power to tell us about how music works in social life. When it exceeds these bounds, semiotics risks a kind of covert objectivism, a presumption that music's meanings are immanent, inherent in musical forms as opposed to being brought to life in and through the interplay of forms and interpretations.

This tendency – to hypostatize the meaning and social consequences of aesthetic forms, as discussed by Morley in relation to media studies (1980:162) – is deeply ironic given that semiotic work within the arts often aligns itself with 'postmodern' conceptions of meaning-as-constructed, meaning-as-emergent, and with deconstructions of knower–known, subject–object relations. One of the hallmarks of these conceptions is the idea that the meanings of things are made manifest in and through attempts to interpret and describe them, in and through the ways actors orient themselves in relation to them. The ethnomusicologist Henry Kingsbury makes this point clearly when he says, 'musicological discourse is not simply talk and writing "about music", but is also constitutive of music' (1991:201). He suggests that objects we describe may lend themselves to being framed in a variety of ways; describing or defining an object is therefore an act of selecting, honing and filtering a particular version of that object's implications. The act of description thus *co-produces* itself and the meaning of its object. With regard to music, then, the matter of its social significance is not pregiven, but is rather the result of how that music is apprehended within specific circumstances. While these points are by now commonplace within literary theory, ethnomethodology and constructivist perspectives (as, for example, in science studies), they are curiously often abandoned when analysis is applied to art 'objects'.

Within certain and more traditionally grounded segments of musicology, a concern with reception is often misconstrued as a disinclination to address music's 'intrinsic' properties, whether these concern structures, values or connotations. For example, it is often suggested that by turning the analytical lens on to music consumption one abandons the 'music itself' (note again that phrase, 'the music itself', as if under the specialist's analytical razor we would arrive at the 'core' or essence of music's semiotic force). On the contrary, a reflexive conception of music's force as something that is constituted in relation to its reception by no means ignores music's properties; rather, it considers how particular aspects of the music come to be significant in relation to particular recipients at particular moments, and under particular circumstances. The point, then, to be developed below, is that music analysis, traditionally conceived as an exercise that 'tells' us about the 'music itself', is insufficient as a means for understanding musical affect, for describing music's semiotic force in social life. For that task we shall need new ways of attending to music, ones that are overtly interdisciplinary, that conjoin the hitherto separate tasks of music scholars and social scientists.

Popular music studies have always been concerned with the matter of how music is experienced by real people (see Frith 1990b). Indeed, the very reason pop music culture is, in Willis's terminology, 'profane' is that it has traditionally been appropriatable, open to reinterpretation and determination in and through use; it has possessed all the attributes of the non-sacred (despite various attempts by fans and critics to canonize particular pop music works and performers, and to specify ritual appropriations). Because of this, the emphasis within popular music studies on the experience and appropriation of music has flowed more naturally (see Shepherd and Wicke 1997:18; Frith 1990b); such an emphasis has neither had to deal with, nor been regarded as hostile to, canonic discourse and the idea of musical 'autonomy', both of which are products of late-eighteenth-century cultural practice (W. Weber 1984; 1992; DiMaggio 1982; DeNora 1995b).

The project proposed here, in this chapter and beyond, differs markedly from musicology's traditional professional concerns. It is to conceptualize musical forms as devices for the organization of experience, as referents for action, feeling and knowledge formulation. Such a project begins with concerns outlined by thinkers such as Aristotle and Adorno and seeks to convert them into a set of researchable questions. This project differs fundamentally from a concern with what music signifies, what it may inculcate. It also sidesteps the perennial wrangle, recently summarized adroitly by Shepherd and Wicke (1997), concerning whether musical meanings are 'immanent' or 'arbitrary'. Drawing inspiration from recent work in science and technology studies and from socio-linguistic theory, it seeks to circumvent the dichotomous manner in which questions of music's affect have been posed ('music' on the one side, 'affect' on the other) and to evade the various forms of reductionism these interrogative formulations presuppose of their answers (for instance, 'music plays no role in determining affect' versus 'music prescripts affect'). For while music's semiotic force can be seen to be constructed in and through listener appropriations, a focus on how people interact with music should also be concerned with, as I have already suggested, the role music's *specific properties* may play in this construction process. Thus, even though they cannot be 'read' for the forms of social life that issue from or within them, music's materials provide *resources* that can be harnessed in and for imagination, awareness, consciousness, action, for all manner of social formation.

To begin to illustrate this point I draw on Susan McClary's classic discussion of *Carmen* (1991; 1992), which exemplifies the virtues of semiotic analysis but which also helps to bring into relief the point at which attention to 'the music itself' is insufficient as a means of accounting for music's semiotic force, for its affect and power in social life. McClary is by no means the only semiotician within musicology; there are many excellent works concerned with musical representation (for example, Charles Ford (1991); Lawrence Kramer (1990; 1997); Philip Tagg (1991); Gretchen Wheelock (1992)). Her work is dealt with here only because it makes what are probably the boldest claims for musicology's intervention in wider socio-cultural and epistemological issues.

Mapping gender on to music and music on to gender – the case of *Carmen*

Georges Bizet's opera *Carmen*, first performed in Paris in 1874, is about a soldier's infatuation with a gypsy. The plot revolves around a nineteenth-century, patriarchal obsession – 'licentious' woman leads 'respectable' man to ruin and, in the denouement, becomes his victim. According to McClary's pioneering mode of analysis, the music of *Carmen* helps to underscore, make manifest or enhance certain sexual stereotypes in circulation at the time of the opera's production and developed through the opera's libretto. McClary shows, for example, how the libretto is musically enhanced in a manner that is by no means obvious to the opera's audience but that works, none the less, subliminally upon hearers and their ability to respond, in non-cognitive ways, to musical material.

McClary focuses upon the allocation of musical material and the ways in which this material is mapped, within *Carmen*, on to the opera's characters or roles. This musical division of labour helps the opera's recipients to identify characters socially and – equally importantly – social-psychologically. Throughout the opera, for example, Carmen's arias are cast in dance formats (Habanera; Seguidilla), ones that give priority to musical pulse and, accordingly, Carmen's body (in the Seguidilla and elsewhere she vocalizes, dispensing with words – the idea being to signify her embodiment over and above her rational faculties). Within the canonic paradigm of nineteenth-century music aesthetics and its ideological excision of the body in 'absolute' music, dance forms are constituted as 'lower' order genre. In addition, Carmen's musical material is highly chromatic (using the notes in between the do-re-mi notes of the scale – see figure 1) and is therefore unstable because it creates tonal ambiguity (recall that the 'Fanfare' discussed in chapter 1 – used by an airline as the theme for its safety video – employed a musical discourse that reaffirmed the tonal centre and hence was an embodiment of tonal stability).

Musically, then, the character of Carmen may be construed as low status, deviant, sensual and disorderly. The aesthetic material of music – crucial to her embodiment as a character within the opera's plot – can be seen as active in the construction of her imagined forms of agency; she is cut off, musically, from the discourses of high culture and musical respectability. Her position here is further consolidated against the musical foil of a second female character, Michaela, the demure 'good girl' from Don Jose's village, who plays the role of his potential saviour. A soprano to Carmen's lower mezzo voice, Michaela's melodies are full of tonal certainty; indeed, they rarely stray far from the 'home' or tonic tone. They are also rhythmically straightforward, their pulse unemphasized (few dotted rhythms, no syncopation). Her accompaniment consists of arpeggios (the harp is a traditionally feminine instrument and also the instrument conventionally associated with angels). Comparing the two female parts in terms of musical material alone, it is possible to see how the distinction between nice, steady girl and unpredictable and slippery woman is established through the medium of sound.

McClary's brilliance, her great achievement in the work on *Carmen*, was to show her readers how music is produced and consumed as a resource with which to elaborate interpretations about extra-musical matters. Her work shows us how music is by no means inert, how it helps to construct our perception and imagination of non-musical matters – social character and status, pleasure, longing and so forth. The question of how a composer – in this case, Bizet – draws upon conventional musical materials to frame or comment upon a text is not dissimilar from the way in which music may be used by other types of actors or agents as a framing device (as, for example, in the airline safety video). In both types of use, music is employed as a way of enhancing its recipients' sense of what is happening; in both types of use, music provides a potential map for making sense of the thing(s) to which it is attached. In this way, music can be understood as providing non-cognitive resources to which actors may orient and that they may mobilize as they engage in interpretive action, as they formulate knowledge and aesthetic stance in real time. It is worth repeating that this process is by no means always conscious.

Thus, by describing the ways in which conventional musical gestures and devices are enfolded into particular works and then mapped on to non-musical matters, critical analysts such as McClary have illuminated some of the ways in which musical works stand in intertextual relation to the history of conventional musical practices and how these practices may be mobilized to non-musical effect. This musical discourse analysis provides the groundwork to more overtly sociological programmes of research, dealing with the question of how listeners draw upon musical elements as resources for organizing and elaborating their own perceptions of non-musical things, whether these things are the perception of an opera's characters or the perception of a particular plane journey as 'safe'. We may infer, according to McClary, that Michaela is 'good' (albeit also perhaps slightly boring) because her musical material is highly predictable, and that Carmen is 'base' because her musical material is tethered to bodily pulse and dance rhythms. In short, music provides a resource for interpretation, one that can be referred to for the ongoing creation and sustenance of non-musical matters.

This matter harks back to Hall's concern with how articulations are made between cultural and social formations, and to Willis's description of links between music and social values. Just as Willis's bikeboys looked to music in order to map or elaborate their values and activities over the course of an evening (see chapter 1), so we, as recipients of *Carmen*, may take account of Bizet's deployment of music to reach an understanding of the opera's characters and storyline. In both cases, musical materials provide parameters (stylistic, physical, conventional) that are used to frame dimensions of experience (interpretation, perception, valuation, comportment, feeling, energy). This framing is central to the way in which music comes to serve as a device for the constitution of human agency. Musical framing occurs when music's properties are somehow projected or mapped on to something else, when music's properties are applied to and come to organize something outside themselves. Using the notion of framing as a starting point, it is possible to investigate how actors of all kinds forge links between musical materials and non-musical matters, whether at the level of musical production (for example, composition – Bizet's mapping of music and gender) or at the level of consumption (for example, interpretation – our impressions of the opera's characters).

There is a good deal more to this project, however, than is comprised by musicology's conventional concern with the musical 'object'. Indeed, exclusive focus on the music itself is problematic. The problems associated with such a strategy highlight why semiotic analysis is not sufficient as a means of addressing the question of music's affect in practice, music's role in daily life. This argument can be advanced by considering two related issues.

First, focus on music's ability to make manifest or clarify an opera's libretto cannot ignore, if it is to be a balanced view, the related topic of how the music's meaning or force is simultaneously made manifest through its intertextual relationship with (a variety of) non-musical things, for example, the opera's libretto. As Shaun Moores puts it in his survey of audience research (quoting Richard Johnson): 'the reality of reading is inter-discursive' (Moores 1990:15). Sociologists Kees van Rees (1987) and Anna Lisa Tota (1997a; 1999) have made similar arguments regarding the construction of an art work's identity (meaning, value and so on). In case studies of, respectively, literary and theatrical value, they show how the constitution of an art work's social meanings proceeds in relation to a range of interpretive resources, nearly all of which later come to be hidden as the 'work itself' is hailed as giving rise to the very things

that were attributed to it. Among the resources for interpretation of
musical works are textual documents (for example, programme notes and
libretto in the case of opera), critical reception, ongoing discussions and a
variety of reappropriations at the levels of production and reception (Tota
1997a; 1997b; 1999). These resources may provide maps or grounds
of their own, against which music's meaning and force are in turn
configured. To put this simply, when we are confronted with a kinaesthetic medium such as opera, we may look to the music for cues about
how to interpret character and plot, and, simultaneously, look to the plot
and characterization to make sense of the music. (We may also look to any
number of other things such as programme notes, particular production
qualities, location of performance and so forth (DeNora 1986b).)
Examples of musical self-borrowing, where the same music is used to
signify different things (when it is located against the ground of different
contexts), make this point quite clear (see Barzun 1980 and throughout
this book for examples of self-borrowing). Musical and textual meaning
are interrelated, co-productive; the specific properties of each may be
used – by a sense-making observer – to clarify the other. The 'restful'
tones of the Barcarolle from Offenbach's *The Tales of Hoffmann* were originally conceived as the 'Goblin's song' in *Die Rheinnixen*, for example
(Barzun 1980:17). It is therefore not possible to speak of and decode the
'music itself', for music's semiotic capacity results from its intertextual
relation to many other things. One of these things is the framework plied
upon music by the analyst her/himself.

   It is therefore necessary to consider the matter of how an analyst comes
to identify music's significance and affect. Considering this point helps to
highlight again why semiotic analysis is not sufficient as a means of
addressing music's affect in practice. For example, just how far may the
analyst go in determining music's semiotic force, its affect and its social
effect? And what methods may he or she use, legitimately, for this task?
There is a tacit shift in many semiotic 'readings' of music, McClary's
included, from description of musical material and its social allocation to
the theorization of that material's 'wider' significance and cultural
impact. This is an epistemologically naive move. It occurs when an
analyst substitutes his or her own interpretations or responses to the
music for more systematic evidence that the music's semiotic properties
and its affects 'pre-exist' analysis, that they are 'out there', waiting to be
perceived or uncovered. In this regard, McClary is much more careful
than many; she would appear to conceive of her task as consisting of the
observation of conventions and codes tapped by composers for the
musical rendering of social and social psychological matters. The danger,
however, of this approach is always present; it lies in a tendency to slide

between, on the one hand, the analyst's personal responses to music and, on the other, reference to catalogues of musical devices – a musical equivalent of speech act theory. This slippage is problematic because the ways in which music partakes of patterns and conventions at the moment of production (even assuming such a matter can be specified) by no means guarantees the ways in which it is appropriated and so comes to be meaningful in particular social circumstances. (The moment of production is never automatically isomorphic with the moment(s) of consumption.) Hence, and despite the brilliance of her observations (for McClary's powers to illuminate music against the ground of her own interpretations are considerable), even McClary exceeds the musicologist's remit. This transgression is clearest in statements such as the following:

> The aspects of *Carmen* I have just discussed – namely these particular constructions of gender, the ejaculatory quality of many so-called transcendental moments, the titillating yet carefully contained presentation of the feminine 'threat', the apparent necessity of violent closure – are all central to the great tradition of nineteenth-century 'Absolute Music'. We can easily find both the characterizations and plot lines of *Carmen*, *Salome*, or *Samson et Dalila* exquisitely concealed in the presumably abstract, word-less context of many a symphony. (1999:67)

The mode of explication becomes dangerously attenuated when moments are specified where such matters as 'violent closure' are disclosed in these 'presumably abstract' contexts. For example, consider the following, which draws inspiration from the Adrienne Rich poem, 'The Ninth Symphony of Beethoven understood at last as a sexual message' (Rich 1994 [1973]:43):

> The point of recapitulation in the first movement of Beethoven's Ninth Symphony unleashes one of the most horrifyingly violent episodes in the history of music . . . The entire first key area in the recapitulation is pockmarked with explosions. It is the consequent juxtaposition of desire and unspeakable violence in the moment that creates its unparalleled fusion of murderous rage and yet a kind of pleasure in its fulfilment of formal demands. (McClary 1991:128)

This reading is attenuated because it is not anchored in anything beyond the analyst's identification of connotations. Identifying abstractions such as 'the feminine' or 'the masculine', 'violence' or sadistic 'pleasure' (or for that matter any type of non-musical content) and perceiving these things 'in' the music has no ground outside of what the analyst says. It is therefore indistinguishable from simple assertion, from an 'I'm telling you, it's there' form of analysis. Such a strategy is impossible to validate and impossible to refine. We may agree or disagree with it; we may, depending upon the analyst's rhetorical skill, come to perceive what the analyst perceives (that it is 'horrifying' or 'pockmarked with explosions').

To be sure, McClary's rhetorical skills are considerable. In the discussion of Beethoven, she brings into the vortex of 'analysis' linguistic resources for perceiving Beethoven's work, ones that map on to his work certain analogies and metaphors that are particular 'ways of seeing' the musical object, that provide a frame for the music and so offer the reader a discourse location, a perspective for viewing the musical works. This strategy, which consists of a kind of linguistic legerdemain, helps to frame the reader's perception of her analytical object, so that the qualities perceived in the music itself are in fact ones that have been attributed to it. This is what Agatha Christie's Miss Marple meant when she uttered the phrase, 'they do it with mirrors'.

By this I mean that McClary 'tells' us what the music connotes, 'tells' us the structures of consciousness and practical habits to which it is homologous, but fails to locate the mechanism that 'permits' her (as Hennion puts it – see chapter 1, above) to claim that this is so. Apart from her own recognition (that is, articulation) or mapping of Beethoven's misogynous musical practice, she identifies no 'mediator' or accountant for her claim. Instead, her 'analysis' provides a prescription through which the musical object may be perceived. In light of her framework, we also may perceive what she perceives and, fallaciously, make the assumption that it was 'there all along'. This strategy has been ably described by sociologists of epistemology such as Dorothy Smith in her famous 1978 essay, 'K is mentally ill' (in Smith (1992)), by Steve Woolgar in his work on the production of scientific knowledge (1988) and by Hugh Mehan on oracular reasoning in the context of a psychiatric exam (1990). Such a strategy may occasionally win over readers since it prepackages their interpretive work – it provides a guide for finding in the 'music itself' the very things analysis has reflexively brought to bear upon it.

As Antoine Hennion (1990; 1993; 1995) suggests it is impossible to speak of music 'itself' since, as observed by Kingsbury (quoted above) all discourses 'about' the musical object help to constitute that object. The analyst exists in reflexive relation to the object of analysis. None the less, as Hennion suggests, this reflexivity need not provide a cause for analytical despair. It is still possible to speak about musical materials – if not 'works themselves' – in relation to matters of value, authenticity, meaning and effect. To do so, however, requires us to identify not what the work, as a bounded object, means, or does in itself, but rather, how it comes to be identified by others who refer to or attend to (and this includes non-discursive, corporeal forms of attention) its various properties so as to construct its symbolic, emotive or corporeal force. Such a strategy ensures that interpretation of music is not used as a resource for, but rather a topic of, investigation. Interpretive work and/or many other forms of mediation serve as accomplices to the work's meanings, to its effects. Thus, it is possible to speak of the content or effects of musical works, but never to speak of those matters in relation to (that standard phrase within arts sociology) 'the works themselves'. For the work 'itself' cannot be specified; it is anything, everything, nothing. The social identity of the work – like all social identities – emerges from its interaction and juxtaposition to others, people and things. It is underdetermined by 'the work'. Thus, McClary – and perhaps many listeners – *may* hear Beethoven in particular ways but these hearings are neither inevitable nor derived from 'the music itself'; they are the product of mediating discourses and the instructions these discourses provide for music's perception. When these instructions are followed, the phenomenon may come to appear real, authentic, true and so forth, for all practical purposes as an article of faith. This is what Hennion means when he refers to 'la passion musicale' (1993; Hennion and Gomart 1999).

Simply put, a sociology of musical affect cannot presume to know what music causes, or what semiotic force it will convey, at the level of reception, action, experience. Sociologists have shown how not even propositional social rules (of etiquette, for example) can be fully known and determining of actual social practice, since the very 'telling' of the rules is itself an interactive and world-making resource (Barnes 1982; Wieder 1974). This point applies with perhaps even greater force to music where the 'telling' of music's affect, its connotations and its implications for forms of social life may be understood as secured through the ways composers and listeners make connections between music's materials and other, non-musical things. To circumvent this project by pointing to what music represents and how it will structure perception, is to take the kind of theoretical short cut described above. That short cut consists of substituting an analyst's understanding of music's social meanings for an empirical investigation of how music is actually read and pressed into use by others, how music actually comes to work in specific situations and moments of appropriation. It is worth noting that, within current psychology of music, a similar critique has been launched against the idea that music's role in social life cannot be deduced by studying music reception within the white walls of the laboratory setting. Instead, there is a trend in favour of observing music appropriation *in situ* because, as described above, music's semiotic force cannot be derived from the music itself:

The relationship between music and the listening situation also has important theoretical consequences. If the situation mediates responses to music and vice versa, then it is only possible to arrive at a comprehensive explanation of music listening behaviour by carrying out investigations in the context of the everyday environments and activities in which we are conventionally exposed to music: the 'social vacuum' that typifies most laboratory research may indeed be inadequate. (North and Hargreaves 1997c:312)

How is music's social power generated? The sources of semiotic power

The tendency to take the short cut described above to account for music's social effects through reference to the music itself, is by no means unique to the discipline of musicology or experimental psychology. It is a staple within sociology too. For example, in their enthusiasm to examine musical affect, Catherine Harris and Clemens Sandresky argue that:

Music plays a remarkable role in communicating a notion of the 'character' or style of emotional expression of a particular people, nationalities and historical periods. It has symbolized collective feelings of grief and joy, excitement and despair . . . the list could go on. Some examples are in order . . . The exuberance of our national anthem, the 'Star-Spangled Banner', gives form to one aspect of patriotic feeling; the quieter radiance of 'America', another. When sung with conviction, who among us can resist a feeling of pride and community. (1985:296)

The popular music scholar Richard Middleton has intervened promisingly in this area with an institutional theory of meaning 'in' music, namely the idea that certain musical works may accumulate long-standing, widely accepted connotations, ones that, for all practical purposes, arise from the musical works 'themselves'. In this respect, Middleton comes closest, perhaps, of the writers considered so far in this chapter, to Hennion's notion that particular configurations of meaning (value, authenticity, affect) can be stabilized through ritual procedures and practices over time:

[H]owever arbitrary musical meanings and conventions are – rather than being 'natural', or determined by some human essence or by the needs of class expression – once particular musical elements are put together in particular ways, and acquire particular connotations, these can be hard to shift. It would be difficult, for instance, to move the 'Marseillaise' out of the set of meanings sedimented around it . . . which derive from the history of the revolutionary French bourgeoisie. (1990:10)

But there is still a short cut here. If we accept the idea that the process of the stabilization of meaning is itself a topic for research and not something that may be taken as read, then we cannot make assumptions about social responses to music without also offering a description of how those responses are actually produced. In Hennion's sense, we need to identify the mediators that make particular interpretations possible. So, are there mediators who might detract from the qualities of the 'Marseillaise' or 'The Star-Spangled Banner'? Are there ways of performing or hearing these works that would 'shift', as Middleton terms it, their meanings and empower rival appropriations? Might 'The Star-Spangled Banner' evade all feelings of 'pride and community' under some circumstances of performance and reception? Think, for example, of the Jimi Hendrix version of this piece as played at the Woodstock Festival in 1969 during the Vietnam War:

The ironies were murderous: a black man with a white guitar; a massive, almost exclusively white audience wallowing in a paddy field of its own making; the clear, pure, trumpet-like notes of the familiar melody struggling to pierce through clouds of tear-gas . . . One man with a guitar said more in three and a half minutes about that peculiarly disgusting war and its reverberations than all the novels, memoirs and movies put together. (Murry 1989, quoted in Martin 1995:262–3)

Think, too, of how certain renditions of 'The Star-Spangled Banner' at baseball games in the United States have had patriotic fans up in arms. Moreover, even 'sung with conviction' would any version of 'The Star-Spangled Banner' have evoked national pride and community spirit among seasoned Hendrix fans? Would it perhaps have been contested or heard ironically? With regard to the 'Marseillaise', could not the English schoolboy lyrics set to that tune ('A Frenchman went to the lavatory . . .') manage to shift its conventional connotations as evidenced if it makes us laugh when we hear it? All of these are hypothetical examples of how music may be reappropriated, reclaimed for different interpretive uses according to the configuration of its mediators. Indeed, only a few pages later in his book, Middleton himself discusses how musical works can be 'prised open' and rearticulated in new ways, for example in the football appropriation of 'Amazing Grace', where the melody is sung to one repeated word – 'Arsenal' (1990:16). He goes on to observe, later on in the book, that these matters 'must be referred to *listeners*, for the answers depend on what is heard and how it is heard' (1990:188).

These examples of musical mediation (or reappropriation) highlight how music's semiotic force – its affect upon hearing – cannot be fully specified in advance of actual reception. This is because musical affect is contingent upon the circumstances of music's appropriation; it is, as I wish to argue, the product of 'human–music interaction', by which I mean that musical affect is constituted reflexively, in and through the practice of articulating or connecting music with other things. The music analyst, in this view, does indeed occupy a significant place in the study of how music achieves its social, emotional and embodied effects. Her or his role is to specify a musical text's mobilization of conventional musical materials, gestures and devices, to specify its intertextual relationship with other musical works and the history of their reception. But the question of how these materials may be experienced by future recipients is well beyond the purview of semiotic analysis, and to develop a particular interpretation of a work is, however illuminating or persuasive, still to engage in the politics of representing that work. There are, however, ways of attending to music as an active ingredient in the construction of affect without eliding the empirical processes of musical consumption. Such a project, however, requires new tools, ones that have yet to be applied to the study of music in social life. In the remainder of this chapter I wish to develop this new perspective through discussions of the sociology of technology and the ethnomethodologically inspired analysis of conversation. Both these areas draw upon pragmatic theories of meaning in use, meaning in interaction, and both conceive of cultural products – technologies and utterances – as simultaneously determining and determined by the ways they come to be used or interpreted.

Artefacts and users

The sociology of technology in the 1990s has returned with vigour to Langdon Winner's classic (1980) question, 'Do artefacts have politics?' Winner's famous essay took, as its case in point, the parkway bridges connecting New York City to Long Island. Built by Robert Moses, one of New York's greatest public architects, between 1920 and 1970, the bridges had overpasses only twelve feet high. While this height limit posed no problem to automobiles, the bridges were too low for buses. Thus, they effectively structured the access to Jones Beach along class and racial lines (that is, those who had no access to travel by car – because they could not afford to keep one – had no access to Jones Beach). As technologies of transport, then, the bridges led to the – presumably – unanticipated consequence of social exclusion; in collaboration with other forms of transport technology, they constrained users. Many other scholars have also provided examples of how the political is embedded within the technical. Discussing Cynthia Cockburn's study of gender politics and the transformation of typesetting (Cockburn 1983), Judy Wajcman has observed that 'there is nothing natural about units of work. Whether it is hay bales or 50-kilo bags of cement or plaster, they are political in their design . . . Male workers use their bodily and technical efficiency to constitute themselves as the capable workers and women as inadequate' (1991:51).

In both of these examples, forms of social relations – patterns of working, images of workers, the social distribution of travel options – are prestructured by material culture. In no sense neutral, materiality is shown as a resource in and through which social regularities – production, segregation, imagination – are accomplished and sustained.

But to what extent do technologies structure social relations and social action? To what extent are users, in Steve Woolgar's famous term, technologically 'configured'? Winner's perspective left little space in which to consider an artefact's social properties as – ultimately – constituted in and through appropriation. His position may be (and often is) read as implying a form of determinism, from artefact to behaviour and social relations. More recent thinking on the subject (Akrich 1991; Latour 1991; Akrich and Latour 1991; Law 1994; Pinch and Bijker 1987; Woolgar 1997) has expanded the conceptual space around this issue. The arguments, however, are complex and, because they do not take the form of a discourse of cause and effect, may seem hard to follow.

They begin with the idea that artefacts 'prescribe' behaviour (Latour 1991) and 'configure' users (Woolgar 1997). This means that an object's design is oriented to particular scenarios of use and users (and designers may have attempted to elicit particular scenarios of use prior to the design process). For example, a car implies certain forms of driving – on paved roadways and at particular speeds. A book is produced to be read from front to back (jumping ahead to find out 'who did it' only deprives one of the pleasure of suspense). Artefacts may prescript, in other words, the ways they are incorporated into social life, and so they structure use and users. In Pelle Ehn's sense, they serve as 'reminders' of 'paradigm cases' of action (Ehn 1988:433).

But artefacts do not *compel* users to behave in preferred or prescripted ways. To argue along those lines is to succumb to what Bruno Latour calls 'technologism' – that is, a form of technological determinism as described with reference to Winner (above), one that elides the question of how artefacts can and are appropriated for use in a variety of ways. Artefacts are, in Pinch and Bijker's sense, 'interpretively flexible' (1987). A car may be driven in unconventional ways (for example, an elderly man in Pontypridd, South Wales, was once issued a ticket for driving too slowly) and a book may be 'read' by someone who is merely using it as a prop to signal intellectual orientation or – as on a train or plane – to avoid conversation. A gun, as Keith Grint once controversially stated (Grint and Woolgar 1997:140–68), may be used for purposes other than shooting. None the less, one only has to consider the statistics on gun ownership and murder rates to realize that artefacts do indeed come to be associated with conventional patterns of use, that they may, in Anthony Giddens's sense, enable forms of activity. This is to say that while artefacts are not determining, they may come, via use and always in retrospect, to be associated with descriptive patterns of use. They may place on offer courses of conduct. Artefacts, and the scenarios with which they come (through use) to be paired, provide means for enacting scenarios as motivation and opportunity arise. To argue that artefacts contribute *nothing* to the scenes in which they are used, that we pick up and 'name' the uses of objects solely according to local use and to whim (for example, that one would recognize no difference between a hammer and a gun when one wished to insert a nail into a piece of wood or to shoot at something) is merely the flip side of 'technologism' (Latour (1991) refers to it as 'sociologism'). Moreover, as John Law has observed (1994), some materials are more obdurate than others. Instead, and in common with much recent thinking on the matter of technology, Latour argues that neither technologism nor sociologism is sufficient as a way of accounting for the production of order, subjectivity and action. Rather, these matters issue from 'human–non-human' interaction. By contrast, new perspectives within the sociology of technology (and it is within this perspective that Hennion's work may be located) attempt to document the ways in which heterogeneous mixes of people and things are brought together, and to examine the interactive process whereby people and things are mutually structuring. Focus here – as it was in Willis's study of the bikeboys – is on the ways in which the specific properties of a material (an artefact) are accessed and implicated in some social or social psychological process. To illuminate this appropriation process – the mutual constitution of an artefact's prescriptions and the behaviours and scenes that cluster around it – is to illuminate the social-technical *mélange* through which forms of agency and social order(s) are produced and held in place. The final section of this chapter shows how such a perspective is useful in thinking about music's effects – for thinking about whether, how and to what extent we may be permitted to speak of music as 'prescribing' its uses or responses. But first, I wish to consider certain issues in the area of natural language use and the pragmatic character of verbal meaning. I wish to present the utterance as yet one more kind of cultural object or artefact.

Verbal meaning in naturally occurring speech situations

Consider the statement, 'The child picked up the tractor.' To make sense, context is required. Is this a giant child, such as had originally been planned for the Millennium Dome in Greenwich (where a real car had been planned to be set down as one of its toys)? Is it a superhuman child of normal size? Or is the child an ordinary child, but the tractor toy-sized? Or has the child – say aged fourteen – been sent down a farm lane to drive a tractor back to a farm house?

The example highlights a well-rehearsed line of thinking within socio-linguistic theory and research, namely the idea that verbal utterances and their meanings stand in interdependent relation to social contexts. This idea illuminates many of the ways in which we draw, into the vortex of our interpretive activities, a range of 'relevant' contextual features that help to clarify the meaning of what is going on or what is being said. When I first arrived in Scotland in 1982, my mother-in-law and I spent a pleasant interval chatting and looking at British cookbooks. She handed me Elizabeth David (with whom I was unfamiliar) and said something like, 'She is known for *haute cuisine*.' Because of her (correct) French pronunciation (and my ignorance), and because of the novelty of having only recently arrived in Scotland (which I associated with porridge), I heard what she said as 'oat cuisine'. I replied, as enthusiastically as I could muster, 'Imagine a whole cuisine devoted to the oat!'

Verbal meaning is by no means immanent. The utterance, 'It is cold in here' may be understood as a passive observation, an attempt at small talk, a polite reference to why the speaker has not bothered to remove his or her outdoor clothes, a sign of displeasure, an indirect request that a window be closed or a fire lit, and so on. A hearer's sense of what an utterance signifies will be linked to matters of style and social relations – voice tone, volume, phrasing, body language, the speaker's relation to the setting, what was said before, what these speakers have said to each other before and so on. But the significance of an utterance is dependent upon the equally crucial matter of how hearers respond. As Jurgen Streeck (1981) has observed in his critique of Searle's speech act theory, the meaning of an utterance is clarified by the hearer's response; it is assigned only in retrospect, in and through the response it receives. Moreover, its significance is recursively constituted and reconstituted as talk continues. The utterance, 'It is cold in here', for example, would function, retrospectively (that is, in effect) as a request to close a window if one or more hearers respond to it in that way. Otherwise, it may pass in that moment as signifying something else. Or it emerges as a coded form of complaint, or even a compliment (reply: 'Yes, the air conditioning works well, doesn't it?'). There is thus an array of received meanings that may be linked – articulated – to any utterance. An analyst of spoken interaction cannot therefore deduce meaning from a particular text object, whether that object is one utterance or an entire conversation, to which he or she was not party unless he or she is familiar with local circumstances that surround it. To do so is to ply an interpretation – the analyst's own account – upon that utterance. And in so doing, the analyst makes a fateful shift; he or she becomes party to the creation of meaning within that scene; his or her 'map' of conversational significance becomes, as it were, a comment upon or way of framing meaning within that scene (precisely the problem discussed above in relation to interpretations of the 'music itself' that do not identify a 'mediator'). To determine the meaning of an utterance from outside is thus to forgo an opportunity to investigate how particular actors produce indigenous maps and readings of the scene(s) in question and how to read them. Real actors engage in semiotic analysis as part of the reflexive project of context determination and context renewal. Telling what the meaning is, and deftly deflecting dispreferred meanings and readings, is part and parcel of the semiotic skills of daily life. We need to learn to see professional semioticians in a similar vein – as mobilizing particular features of utterances in order to produce meanings and ongoing scenic locations from within the interaction order, providing new 'versions' of reality, new assertions, new definitions of situations, new cultural materials. And, in particular, we need to consider and deconstruct their unexamined commitment to particular constructions and construals. They, like the speaker or hearers themselves, are 'doing things with words', using and deploying linguistic formulations in order to tell particular stories about social reality.

From inscription to affordance: the dual nature of semiotic materials

Meaning, or semiotic force, is not an inherent property of cultural materials, whether those materials are linguistic, technological or aesthetic. At the same time, materials are by no means empty semiotic spaces. Latour (1991) is correct to argue that the human sciences must avoid the twin explanatory errors of technologism and sociologism and to look instead at the ways in which people, things and meanings come to be clustered within particular socially located scenes. Such a perspective leaves space for the ongoing negotiation and renegotiation of the meanings of people, things and situations. Readings, even highly professional ones, become just that – particular interpretations, particular mobilizations of texts. Readings are thus a topic for the study of how 'artefacts have politics' (see Mulkay 1986); they are never resources in their own right. And to speak 'about' things is, as Kingsbury (1991) observed with regard to music, to constitute those things.

Our focus needs to move away from one or the other pole of the 'artefact–actor' divide to, as the sociologist Jürgen Streeck puts it (1996), the topic of 'how to do things with things'; this means a focus on the interactions between people and things. There is no short cut to this issue; only ethnographic research will do, and only ethnographic research has the power to elaborate our conceptualization of what such processes entail –

there is much work to be done before the mechanisms through which cultural materials 'work' are properly to be understood.

Streeck grounds this argument in an analysis of a business discussion between executives of a biscuit company. Sitting around a table, speakers are tasting and talking about *cookies* – their own brand and those of a rival firm. To underline certain points (for instance, the 'better' appearance and texture of their product and so on) the cookies themselves are used as props and arranged in contrasting geometric patterns. Here, the materiality of cookie arrangements is mapped on to utterances – rather as Bizet mapped music's material and stylistic properties on to the libretto in *Carmen*. The cookies are enrolled as, in Michel Callon's (1986) sense, allies of the speaker and his argument. It is as if they, like the scallops of St Brieuc Bay that Callon describes so beautifully (who have various requirements attributed to them by environmentalists, fishermen and so forth), can 'speak'. Their speech in these cases is in part ventriloquism such that, when they make their utterances, they 'say' through another means and therefore amplify points propounded by their spokesmen. But, unlike ventriloquists' puppets, they may also betray their spokespeople in the form of unruly and unanticipated conduct (for example, by not producing the requisite 'snap' when broken or bitten). Their materiality also constrains what can be said, 'in their name'. Streeck's analysis makes this clear. Thus, for example, if one's own product makes a loud snap and one's rival does not, then the criterion of 'snappiness when bitten' is invoked as a relevant category of value (as opposed to, say, 'chewiness').

Streeck argues that material objects – in this case, cookies – thus possess properties that that can be lent to some uses more easily than others (the biscuit texture, for example, and the criterion of 'crispness' versus 'chewiness'). To make this point, Streeck appropriates the psychologist J.J. Gibson's notion of affordances. Objects 'afford' actors certain things; a ball, for example, affords rolling, bouncing and kicking in a way that a cube of the same size, texture and weight would not. So, too, the particular materials of the cookies afford certain marketing ploys and will not afford others.

One of the most useful theoretical discussions of the notion of affordance – one that places the concept on an overtly sociological plane – comes from ethnomethodologically inspired studies of organizations. In 'Can Organizations Afford Knowledge?' Bob Anderson and Wes Sharrock begin with the premise that technologies are social as well as technical, 'in the sense that they are deployed and used in social settings and defined by social constructs' (1993:115). They develop the idea that perception is 'culturally provided'. This assumption is in line with what socio-musical analysts such as McClary or Adorno propound; that patterns of perception, modes of attention, structures of feeling and habits of mind are inculcated in and through musical media. But, unlike Adorno and McClary, Anderson and Sharrock navigate adroitly between technologism and sociologism; they do not fudge the issue of how artefacts 'get into' action either by resort to implicit determinism or by dismissing the idea that artefacts may possess specific and sometimes obdurate qualities, that they may be active ingredients in the constitution of agency. Moreover, they bring the idea of 'inscription' closer to the realm of what can be observed in real time.

They begin by contrasting their own conception of affordance with its originator, J.J. Gibson (1966). For Gibson, objects afford things independently of how users appropriate them. Within such a view, we are returned to the realm of Latour's technologism and objects are again sole 'authors' of their inscriptions (the object 'itself'), where they predetermine the responses that can be made to them. By contrast, for Anderson and Sharrock, an object's affordances are 'constituted and reconstituted in and through projected courses of action within settings' (1993:148–9). By this they refer to the reflexive process whereby users configure themselves as agents in and through the ways they relate to objects and configure objects in and through the ways they – as agents – behave towards those objects.

Ethnographic studies of the constitution of affordances show how actors often erase the work they do of configuring objects and their social implications (one of the best examples here is Moore 1997). Indeed, it would seem to be part of the natural attitude (or, in Adorno's sense, the 'ontological ideology') to 'forget', paraphrasing Marx, that we are oppressed by the things we have helped to produce. This 'forgetting' is the cognitive practice of reification. For this reason, the most interesting questions concerning the social implications of artefacts (whether these are technologies, utterances or aesthetic materials such as music) focus on the interactional level where articulations – links – between humans, scenes and environments are actually produced, and where frames of order come to be stabilized and destabilized in real time. With regard to the issue of musical affect, recognizing music as, in Anderson and Sharrock's sense, an affordance structure, allows for music to be understood, as I put it in earlier work, as a place or space for 'work' or meaning and lifeworld making (DeNora 1986b). Music can, in other words, be invoked as an ally for a variety of world-making activities, it is a workspace for semiotic activity, a resource for doing, being and naming the aspects of social reality, including the realities of subjectivity and self, as discussed in chapter 3, below. We are now, finally, at a place where we can begin to develop a theory of how music's semiotic force is generated, to consider how music comes to have social 'effects'.

Music is not a 'stimulus': semiotic force does not reside within its forms alone

Reconsider Lucy, introduced in chapter 1, whose morning encounter with some of Schubert's *Impromptus* was a catalyst for realigning her ongoing, local state of emotional being. Was it simple exposure to the stimulus of this music that calmed Lucy? According to Lucy, the musical material of the *Impromptus* was active in the process of her 'de-stressing'; it was a contributory factor, an accomplice to her mood shift. In the case of the *Impromptus*, the works are mostly quiet (see figure 3), they are highly melodic and songlike, they do not make a feature of sudden rhythmic or dynamic changes (they are 'peaceful') and they call for a pianist who is 'gentle', for nuanced rather than pyrotechnic virtuosity. The pieces also feature a kind of musical ambiguity and so may be associated with connotations of detachment or wistfulness, especially if heard in conjunction with most sleeve notes or critical documents. For example, they shift, unobtrusively, from minor (the conventional 'sad' or 'dark' modality) to major ('happy', 'light'). Lucy herself alludes to these features when she describes the *Impromptus* as 'sort of sad, but not completely'. The ways in which these pieces are phrased in performance serves to heighten this ambiguity, through slight hesitations at cadence points (points of tonal closure) and at the apex of melodic arches. The performative rendering of these works then tends to intensify what *might* be read as gentle acquiescence (harmonic, rhythmic, melodic) implicit in the score, the dissipation of tonal and rhythmic force through a variety of musical forms of reticence, or gentle 'pulling away' from (musical) exertion, exuberance and definition.

However, it would be wrong to say that the musical material 'acts' as sole agent or stimulus for Lucy's self-regulation. On the contrary, the music's powers are constituted by Lucy herself; they derive from the ways she interacts with them. The *Impromptus* are, for Lucy, carriers of much more than their conventional musical-stylistic connotations, however these are described. Their character as physical sound structures and their relation to a body of musical-stylistic convention is interpolated with, for Lucy, equally important biographical connotations and with a history of use such that the pieces calm her not only because they embody musical calm, but because they restore to Lucy a sense of her own identity. First, for Lucy, the works are associated with comfort; they are bound up with a complex of childhood memories and associations. Her late father, to

Figure 3. Franz Schubert, *Impromptu* in G flat major

whom she was close, used to play the piano after dinner and these works, wafting up the stairs, were ones Lucy used to hear as she was falling asleep. Secondly, the material culture of listening is also an accomplice, in this example, of music's power to shift Lucy's mood on the morning she describes. Lucy's listening is conducted in a quiet room. She sits in a rocking chair placed between the speakers and so is almost nestled in the, as she perceives it, calm and nurturing music. (The vocabulary of nurturing is Lucy's. As she puts it, music 'soothes me', 'I retreat into music when I can't bear the rest of the world', 'you can go into [music] and have it around you or be in it'.) The point is that music's power to 'soothe' derives not only from the musical 'stimulus' but from the ways in which Lucy appropriates that music, the things she brings to it, the context in which it is set. Lucy did not, for example, listen to this music while scrubbing the kitchen floor, or while working out on an exercise bike.

This process of appropriation is what consolidates and specifies music's force. In Lucy's case, music's effects are derived from the ways in which she is active in pulling together a range of things (furniture, speakers, memories, current emotional state, musical recordings, a temporal interval). There is nothing untowardly mysterious about this process. Music's effects are generated by a describable addition, whose sum is greater than its parts: music, plus the ways that the recipient (in this case, Lucy) attends to it, plus the memories and associations that are brought to it, plus the local circumstances of consumption. Through this alchemical process of pulling together a range of heterogeneous materials, Lucy herself is partner to the construction of music's semiotic force; she is a contributor to the constitution of the music's power over her, its ability to move her from one emotional location to another.

Music's interpretive flexibility was highlighted by nearly all the interviewees consulted in the music and daily life project, who described how music's semiotic force varied according to the circumstances of its reception. For example, here is a nineteen-year-old Vietnamese woman, a student at an American university. She was discussing music in connection with 'romantic' relationships:

Q. Is there some music that is romantic or some music that isn't romantic, or can any music be romantic?
A. I think it would have to be the mood when you listen to the music – but some music is – just the appropriate song, the tone of the song and the melody because of the music kind of puts you in a cheerful mood, it doesn't have to be romantic and may be that same song when you listen to it, like when you're in a really upset mood or angry it just seems very sad, but then another time when you listen to it among your friends when you have fun you may change your perception about the song – you know, your hearing can change even though it's the same song.
Q. Oh yes, even though it's the same song?
A. The same song can create a different atmosphere also, depending on the mood, I think.

Latoya, a twenty-five-year-old sales assistant at Manhattan's Tower Records, makes a similar point, in her discussion of the 'messages' she gets from music:

One day, I'll listen to the song and I'll, like, get one message out of it, like, 'Damn, that was messed up, maybe I shouldn't have gone bad or that shouldn't have happened.' And the next day I'll be like, 'No I shouldn't have done that, I should have done this,' you know, with the same song! You know, it'll be, it goes back to the mood thing, how I'm feeling during the day, and that moment, what the song will do for me.

These quotes from in-depth interviews illuminate music's interpretive flexibility, the way in which music's affordances – moods, messages, energy levels, situations – are constituted from within the circumstances of use. The idea that music's meanings are constituted in and through use in no way implies that music's meaning is entirely indeterminate. To the contrary, music may contribute, as is discussed below in chapter 3, to the sense that actors make of themselves and their social circumstances. Music is active within social life, it has 'effects' then, because it offers specific materials to which actors may turn when they engage in the work of organizing social life. Music is a resource – it provides affordances – for world building.

This last point emphasizes how, just as music's meaning may be constructed in relation to things outside it, so, too, things outside music may be constructed in relation to music. 'I hear music/when I look at you', run the lyrics of Hammerstein and Kern's 'The song is you', 'a beautiful theme/of every dream/I ever knew'. Here music is being used as a referent for the clarification of identity. A person is 'like' a particular type of musical material. In conversation with the daughter of a colleague who was describing a young man whom she thought looked too 'cool' for his role in some conventional, professional occupation, she said, 'he was like . . .' and here she paused as if searching for the right words. She then broke into a rhythmic execution to indicate the quality that she thought incongruous with his pinstriped suits. Here is an example where a conventional musical material – a rhythmic *topos* and its conventional connotations that I, as the recipient of this utterance, perceived (urban cool, drum and bass and so on) – serves as a framing device for the constitution of a portrayed identity. Indeed, there are times when only music will do, when a social situation is given over entirely to musical materials. Beethoven's friend and patron, Baroness Ertmann, for example, described to Felix Mendelssohn how Beethoven had consoled her on the death of her last child: 'We will now talk to each other in tones,' Beethoven had said, and through that exercise, she recalled, 'he told me everything, and at last brought me comfort' (Thayer and Forbes 1967:413). All of these examples show music as taking the lead in the world-clarification, world-building process of meaning-making. In all of these cases music serves as a kind of template against which feeling, perception, representation and social situation are created and sustained.

In sum, music is a referent (with varying degrees of conventional connotations, varying strengths of pre-established relations with non-musical matters) for clarifying the otherwise potentially polysemic character of non-musical phenomena (social circumstances, identities, moods and energy levels, for example). In this sense it is mythic, a resource against which other relationships can be mapped in Levi Strauss's sense. Middleton captures this point precisely when he observes:

music, too, considered as a structural-semantic system, offers a means of thinking relationships, both within a work and between works, and perhaps between these and non-musical structures. Musical patterns are saying: as this note is to that note, as tonic is to dominant, as ascent is to descent, as accent is to weak beat (and so on), so X is to Y. (1990:223)

The point is that it is music's *recipients* who make these connections manifest, who come to fill in the predicates, X and Y, that Middleton describes. Music's semiotic powers may, moreover, be 'stabilized' through the ways in which they are constituted and reinforced through discourse (*pace* the discussion of McClary, above), through consumption practice and through patterns of use over time (DeNora 1986b). Non-musical materials, such as situations, biographical matters, patterns of attention, assumptions, are all implicated in the clarification of music's semiotic force. Conversely, though, and simultaneously, music is used to clarify the very things that are used to clarify it. Focus on this 'co-productive' or two-way process provides a way around the twin poles of sociologism and technologism (or its corollary in socio-musical studies, musicologism) as they apply to the musical 'object'. Of interest then is the reflexive problem of how music and its effects are active in social life, and how music comes to afford a variety of resources for the constitution of human agency, the being, feeling, moving and doing of social life. To understand how music works as a device of social ordering, how its effects are reflexively achieved, we need actually to look at musical practice. This is the aim of the chapters that follow – to get closer to what Aristotle may have had in mind when he spoke of music as possessing 'the power of producing an effect on the character of the soul'. Accordingly the next chapter begins with three interconnected topics: the self and its regulation, the constitution of subjectivity, and the biographical work of self-identity. In relation to these things, music is a resource to which actors can be seen to turn for the project of constituting the self, and for the emotional, memory and biographical work that such a project entails.

3   Music as a technology of self

'I think everybody should listen to music. It helps you to be calm, relaxed, to see your life differently.'   (Mireille, contract cleaner, London)

The self and its accompanying narrative of the 'unitary individual' is a linchpin of modern social organization. More recently, and in line with various deconstructions of biography and identity, focus has turned to the 'reflexive project' of the self, whose care and cultivation rests upon a somewhat fragile conglomerate of social, material and discourse practices (Harré 1998; Giddens 1991). It is curious, then, that music – arguably the cultural material *par excellence* of emotion and the personal – has not been explored in relation to the constitution of self. As Shepherd and Wicke have recently observed, even in the realm of sub-cultural theory as it is applied to musical life, 'there has been little conceptual space created for a theorization of the private, internal world of an individual's awareness of existence and self' (1997:40). Focus on intimate musical practice, on the private or one-to-one forms of human–music interaction, offers an ideal vantage point for viewing music 'in action', for observing music as it comes to be implicated in the construction of the self as an aesthetic agent.

Here, the music psychologists have taken the empirical lead in their turn to music's role in so-called 'naturalistic' settings and their increasingly qualitative investigations of 'the mechanisms mediating between music and social influence' (Crozier 1997:74). At the Keele University Centre for the Study of Musical Development and Skill, for example, researchers have recently taken up the matter of how music is used by individuals in their daily lives. In a report on recent work within the Centre, John Sloboda (forthcoming) has described a range of investigative strategies that employ an individual 'case study' approach. In one of these (Neilly 1995), twenty respondents were asked to keep a diary of when they 'exposed themselves to music by their own choice'. In another (De Las Heras 1997), eighty-four respondents were asked to address forty-five Likert-scale items about musical use. In an earlier study

(Sloboda 1992), sixty-seven people were interviewed about their emotional responses to music. Of these, forty-one identified music as, in some way, a 'change agent' in their lives. A third investigation used the format of a 1997 'mass observation' mailing in the United Kingdom to learn about people's music uses. (The mass observation study (Sheridan 1998) involves a sample of 500 people in Britain who, two or three times a year, respond in writing but in open-ended fashion to sets of questions they have received in the post. The proportion of women to men in this sample is 3:1 and most correspondents are over forty years of age.) Sloboda (forthcoming) describes the investigative process as follows:

> The overarching question was 'Please could you tell us all about you and music.' All other questions were optional cues to focus correspondents on areas they might like to talk about. The key cue for this study was 'Do you use music in different ways? My mother used to play fast Greek music to get her going with the housework – do you have habits like this? Are they linked to particular times, places, activities or moods? For instance, you might use music in different ways at home, outdoors, or at work; in company or on your own; while you exercise, cook, study, make love, travel or sleep; to cheer you up or calm you down.'

In a preliminary analysis of the replies (Sloboda forthcoming), respondents reported using music in relation to six thematic categories: memory, spiritual matters, sensorial matters (for pleasure, for example), mood change, mood enhancement and activities (including things such as exercise, bathing, working, eating, socializing, engaging in intimate activity, reading, sleeping).

This research points clearly to the ways in which music is appropriated by individuals as a resource for the ongoing constitution of themselves and their social psychological, physiological and emotional states. As such it points the way to a more overtly sociological focus on individuals' self-regulatory strategies and socio-cultural practices for the construction and maintenance of mood, memory and identity.

This chapter draws upon ethnographic interview data to spotlight actors as they engage in musical practices that regulate, elaborate, and substantiate themselves as social agents. It is concerned with how music is implicated in the self-generation of social agency and how this process may be viewed as it happens, 'in action'. Viewed from the perspective of how music is used to regulate and constitute the self, the 'solitary and individualistic' practices described by Sloboda and his associates may be re-viewed as part of a fundamentally social process of self-structuration, the constitution and maintenance of the self. In this sense then, the ostensibly 'private' sphere of music use is part and parcel of the cultural constitution of subjectivity, part of how individuals are involved in constituting themselves as social agents. As such, private music consumption connects with recent discussions within sociology of 'aesthetic reflexivity' (Lash and Urry 1994) and with Attali's (originally utopian) vision (1985) of putting music 'in operation, to draw it towards an unknown practice', and with Giddens's (1991) notion of the self as a reflexive project, one that entails the active production of self-identity over time.

How, then, can we begin to understand music's powers with regard to the constitution of self and self-identity? And how may music's powers in relation to the self and to subjectivity be seen in the private, aesthetically reflexive musical practices of individuals? I begin by considering the very high degree of practical musical knowledge as exhibited by the respondents in our study.

Knowing what you need – self-programming and musical material

'Music helps me', says Lucy, who has been quoted in chapters 1 and 2. It, 'can inspire you', 'bring understanding', 'raise you to another plane'. With her own experiences in mind, Lucy expresses what nearly every interviewee has underlined – music has transformative powers, it 'does' things, changes things, makes things happen.

Lucy is but one of a sample of fifty-two British and American women interviewed between 1997 and 1998. These women were of different ages (between eighteen and seventy-seven). They lived in one of two small towns in the United States and United Kingdom, or in London or in New York City. The point of the research was exploratory – to investigate musical practice in daily life, and to examine music as an organizing force in social life. The study focused on women – as opposed to women and men – because it was concerned with redressing the gender imbalance characteristic of cultural studies of music and social life (see, for example, Wise 1990 [1984] on this issue). Questions were open-ended. They focused on respondents' music collections (if applicable) and daily routines. For example, 'Can you tell me about yesterday – from the moment you woke up to the moment you fell asleep – and about how music featured in your day, whether this was music you chose to listen to or that you overheard, for example in a shop?' Prompts were used to jog respondents' memories ('Did you listen to any music while you had your bath? Did you use a radio alarm to wake you up?'). The interviews did not aim to produce statistically 'representative' data about, for example, the links between musical taste and social standing; this work has been conducted ably by others (Bryson 1996; Lamont 1992; Peterson and Simkus 1992; DiMaggio, Useem and Brown 1978; DiMaggio and Useem 1979; Bourdieu 1984). They were, rather, oriented to exploring a so-far missing ethnographic dimension within music reception studies (cf. Radway 1988; Press 1994). They focused on the matter of how the consumption of a cultural product (music) is part of the reflexive and ongoing process of structuring social and social psychological existence. The aim was to move beyond respondents' bald statements of what music does to them in the abstract (for example, Lucy's comments about how music 'helps' her) and to arrive instead at a gallery of practices in and through which people mobilize music for the doing, being and feeling that is social existence. This strategy entailed an attendant shift from a concern with what music 'means' (a question for music criticism and music appreciation) to a concern with what it 'does' as a dynamic material of social existence.

Nearly all of these women were explicit about music's role as an order-ing device at the personal level, as a means for creating, enhancing, sus-taining and changing subjective, cognitive, bodily and self-conceptual states. Consider this quote from twenty-five-year-old Latoya, a sales assistant at Manhattan's Tower Records:

Like with my R&B, most of the time I listen to it when I'm, you know, trying to relax. I'm gonna sleep, sometimes I'll throw on a few tracks to wake me up, nice 'n' slow and then I'll throw on something else. And then, sometimes, you know, if I'm not really, not in that relaxed mood, I'm like, you know, 'I don't wanna listen to that' and I'll throw something fast on, or something fast is playing and I'm like 'That's too chaotic for me right now, I have to put something slow on.'

Here Latoya underlines one of the first things that became clear from the interviews with women about music 'in their lives' – nearly everyone with whom we spoke, levels of musical training notwithstanding, exhibited considerable awareness about the music they 'needed' to hear in different situations and at different times. They were often working – as Latoya's quote makes clear – like disc jockeys to themselves. They drew upon elab-orate repertoires of musical programming practice, and were sharply aware of how to mobilize music to arrive at, enhance and alter aspects of themselves and their self-concepts. This practical knowledge should be viewed as part of the (often tacit) practices in and through which respon-dents produced themselves as coherent social and socially disciplined beings. The use of music in private life and the study of this use turned out to be one of the most important features of the constitution and regu-lation of self. For example, Lucy explains why she chose to listen to the *Impromptus*, described in chapter 1:

Lucy: It's very difficult to explain. I mean, I knew I wanted to hear that particular tape, sometimes I wouldn't choose that because well, it would remind me of my dad *too* much. I know that that music all my life has helped me, has soothed me, and it's lovely. I never get tired of it so, I *knew* I wouldn't be disappointed in it and – even so, it's difficult to say why I chose it. Sometimes – I didn't have to think about it this morning. I mean I wanted to play that but other times I know that I want some music but I can't, I look at all the tapes and I think, 'No, that's not quite it, I don't want to hear that.'

Q. And you go through thinking, 'What seems right just now?'

Lucy: Yeah. And sometimes you just can't find the right thing, or you just want a particular bit and it's too difficult to find it in the tape, I mean a CD is a bit easier because you can just flick around.

Here, in another example, is Deborah, a twenty-five-year-old executive assistant to a New York literary agent:

Deborah: First thing in the morning, when I get up I have the clock radio set to music, it's a lot softer than having the alarm go off in the morning.

Q. What kind of music is likely to come on when your clock radio comes on?

Deborah: A lot of things, depending on what kind of mood I'm in. I usually set it the night before or something if I know I'm going to have a rough day the next morning, that kind of thing.

The vocabulary of using music to achieve what you 'need' is a common discourse of the self, part of the literary technology through which subjectivity is constituted as an object of self-knowledge. But the specific discourses that respondents invoke as descriptors of 'what they need' are not free floating; they are typically linked to practical exigencies of their appropriation and to interactions with others, as the discussion below of 'emotional work' makes clear. For example, Angela, an eighteen-year-old high school student in New York City says, 'If I need to really settle down and just like relax or something I'll put on slow music.'

Also with relaxation in mind, Monica, a twenty-one-year-old student at an English university, describes what she views as 'bath-time music':

Q. . . . How about having a bath or exercising; would you have any music on for either or both of those?

Monica: Having a bath, yeah I listen to Enya; it's really nice and peaceful.

Q. Do you think of Enya as 'the music you listen to when you're in the bath'? Is that particularly –

Monica: It tends to be.

Q. Why would that be as opposed to Blur [one of her favourite groups], say?

Monica: Because it's so peaceful and relaxing. Because quite often you can't hear the words so it's quite nice to not have to concentrate on it, but you can just let it wash over you if you are trying to relax.

Later in the interview, Monica restates this position, and explains in further detail the niche that Enya's music fits into within her life and her musical needs, namely for unwinding in the bath. She describes how she first encountered Enya's music in the context of a 'flotation tank' (which she regarded as a highly pleasurable experience). Now she associates it specifically with bathing. The context in which the music was first heard (the articulation between the music and the flotation experience was made by the Centre for Alternative Relaxation) came, in other words, to be strongly imprinted upon her sense of what Enya connotes and on her sense of how to 'use' that music such that Enya is reserved exclusively for bath-time.

Monica: . . . If we're having some lunch it'll probably be more up-beat music. If we're sitting huddled with a cup of tea it'll be slower stuff.

Q. Yeah, yeah. Would Enya be something you'd choose there or would that be inappropriate?

Monica: No. I never really put that on . . . I mean I wouldn't really put it on when people come round.

Respondents were also highly knowledgeable of musical materials that, in pursuit of self-regulation, they tended to avoid. For example, here, Lucy shows that she has given serious thought not only to the matter of what she 'needs' musically, but also to what she needs to steer clear of (rather as one might avoid certain foodstuffs). When she is in a sad frame of mind, for example, minor keys are more sorrowful than they would be otherwise; their effects are heightened:

Lucy: I do find that I have to be careful with music in a minor key, sometimes. I remember once when my mother died, and I must have put some music on and it made me cry – not that it was associated with her, but it was just – in a minor key and my husband said, 'Gosh, you should avoid the key for a little while,' and he was quite right because anything sad just dropped the mood a little bit lower. I wasn't able to cope with any more sadness at that time.

Q. At that time did you make any deliberate attempt then to turn to music that would lift you, or make you not sad? Did you change listening habits?

Lucy: I can't remember – this was years and years ago when she died, I can't remember that particular incident, but I think I've learned from that to be careful, and not to, if I am feeling really sad, not to wallow in it with music, it can make you, really, really, luxuriate in sadness. I think what's coming out of this is that music is so important to me that I have to be careful what it does to me, because it can do an awful lot.

Aesthetic reflexivity

Recent social theory concerned with 'modernity' has identified the ability to be reflexive about and mobilize cultural forms as a hallmark of being in so-called 'high' modern societies (Lash and Urry 1994; Giddens 1990; 1991). Following Simmel (1917), these writers conceive of the rise of aestheticization as a strategy for preserving identity and social boundaries under anonymous and often crowded conditions of existence. The modern 'self' is portrayed, within this perspective, as subject to heightened demands for flexibility and variation. Actors move, often at rapid pace, through the numerous and often crowded conditions that characterize daily existence. These writers portray the 'self' – depicted as emerging as a concept during the Renaissance but as incipient in the Christian theological conception of the soul (cf. Auerbach 1953) – as subject to heightened demands under advanced modernity. The self is called upon to be increasingly agile, to be able to manage perspectival and circumstantial incongruity, as happens, for example, when individuals move rapidly through numerous and often discrete worlds where personnel and values may clash. As incongruity escalates, and as actors experience alternation as they move between worlds, the machinery or 'work' required of social actors as they configure themselves as agents is made increasingly visible, as an object upon which actors can reflect (Witkin 1995). Heightened aesthetic reflexivity is thus conceived within current social theory as a function of the (often contradictory) demands made upon the self in the modern world. It is further fuelled by the rise of a post-production economy in the West, where 'service' and 'life-style' industries have created and continue to expand markets at nearly all socio-economic levels (Bocock 1993; Lash and Urry 1994; Belcher 1997). Individual actors thus not only engage in self-monitoring and self-regulation; they also seek out such 'goods' as space, relaxation, pleasure and so forth.

One need not accept the historicism of such arguments to be persuaded by their thesis concerning reflexivity and contradiction (see Barnes 1995). Under any historical conditions where tension between what an individual 'must' do and prefers to do, or between how he or she feels and how he or she wishes to feel, the problem of self-regulation arises and with it, the matter of how individuals negotiate between the poles of necessity and preference, between how they think they ought to feel and how they do feel. It is often unclear whether engaging in the regulatory work aimed at reconciling these tensions (through forms of cultural and aesthetic appropriation) is self-emancipatory or, as Adorno and other critical theorists have suggested (such as Giddens 1991), whether it is party to the 'prison house' of advanced capitalism with its reconfiguration of the subject as a 'good's desiring' entity. Such 'high-level' questions are perhaps best answered through specific reference to real actors. This chapter aims to contextualize issues such as these by considering some of the processes in and through which self-regulation transpires. Indeed, a focus on self-regulatory strategies can only enhance current concern within organizational sociology on the matter of how individuals manage to equip themselves as appropriate organizational agents, which is simultaneously a matter of how they configure themselves as aesthetic agents possessed of an 'incipient readiness' (Witkin 1995; Witkin and

DeNora 1997) for action modalities within specific social scenes and schedules. Hochschild's (1983) classic discussion of 'emotional work' speaks to this issue. Within organizationally sponsored circumstances, individuals may feel it incumbent upon themselves to configure themselves as certain kinds of agents, characterized and internalizing certain modalities of feeling. Hochschild describes, for instance, how flight attendants are called upon (in gender-biased ways) to engage not only in productive, contractually specified, activities, but also to engage in the non-contractually specified work of adopting and projecting modalities of emotional agency. Just as they must engage in 'body work' (Tyler and Abbot 1998), so too they must seem genuinely friendly, caring and so on, to produce themselves as human emblems of an airline's 'friendly skies'.

Musically reconfiguring agency – self-regulation, self-modulation

One of the first things music does is to help actors to shift mood or energy level, as perceived situations dictate, or as part of the 'care of self'. For Latoya, Lucy and Deborah, discussed above, music is an accomplice in attaining, enhancing and maintaining desired states of feeling and bodily energy (such as relaxation); it is a vehicle they use to move out of dispreferred states (such as stress or fatigue). It is a resource for modulating and structuring the parameters of aesthetic agency – feeling, motivation, desire, comportment, action style, energy. By this, what respondents often mean is that its specific properties – its rhythms, gestures, harmonies, styles and so on – are used as referents or representations of where they wish to be or go, emotionally, physically and so on. Respondents make, in other words, articulations between musical works, styles and materials on the one hand and modes of agency on the other, such that music is used, prospectively, to sketch aspired and partially imagined or felt states. When respondents are choosing music as part of this care of self, they are engaging in self-conscious articulation work, thinking ahead about the music that might 'work' for them. These articulations are made on the basis of what respondents perceive the music to afford, what, in Lucy's words above, will be 'the right thing', what will 'help'. This perception is in turn shaped by a range of matters, as alluded to in chapter 2: previous associations that respondents have made between particular musical materials and other things (biographical, situational), more generalized connotations respondents associate with the music (for example, its style), perceived parallels between musical materials/processes and social or physical materials/processes (for example, slow and quiet: relaxed) and so on.

For example here is Becky, describing how she uses music to motivate her on evenings when she is going out. The passage comes after a discussion of her 'ambient sounds' CDs that she uses for working, relaxing and meditating.

Q. One of the questions I was going to ask [was] . . . are there sounds apart from music that you particularly like . . . ?
Becky: . . . I love to listen to the sea. And I've also got dolphins, I like to listen to the sound of the dolphins. I find that quite peaceful. I find that very soothing, all of them are very, very relaxing. It makes me smile and when I find myself smiling I think what are you smiling for [laughs]. They have that effect.
Q. And that would be the dolphin sounds or the wave sounds or whatever, that would be something you would use if you needed to relax? How about like at bath-time, do you listen to music during bath-time?
Becky: I do yes, I tend to listen to these tapes unless I'm getting ready to go out [when] I tend to put something very loud, very heavy on [laughs]. Which again I use it to try and motivate me to get in the mood for where I'm going.
Q. If you were going out what kind of thing [would you listen to]? Would it be the radio?
Becky: No, it would probably be a CD. I don't know, I think it would depend on where I was going and how I was feeling at the time. If I was feeling particularly like I wasn't really looking forward to where I was going, then I would have to put something really lively on to try and get me in the mood.
Q. Where might you be going that you weren't really looking forward to?
Becky: Family gatherings [laughs]. Or some sort of meeting to do with the scouts, I tend to really not look forward to that.

Faced with the prospect of having to get into what she perceives as the appropriate energy and emotional mode for going out, Becky turns to different kinds of music to reconfigure herself, to get in the mood. Here, music is used as a catalyst that can shift reluctant actors into 'necessary' modes of agency, into modes of agency they perceive to be 'demanded' by particular circumstances. In this sense, interaction with music illustrates Hochschild's notion that emotion is 'bodily co-operation with an image, a thought, a memory – a co-operation of which the individual is aware' (1979:551, quoted in Williams 1996:129). This common musical strategy was described by many respondents in relation to getting ready to go to work or getting moving with household chores. For example, 'I typically play a country music station almost every morning coming in to work 'cause it is – I just enjoy the music, it's sort of sad, twangy, ballady music and there's that very lively stuff, but it's lively music at the first part of the day so that's what I almost always do,' says Elaine, a fifty-five-year-old psychotherapist in up-state New York. 'First thing in the morning I like quite – sort of music that will get you up and get you going, so something that's quite upbeat and cheerful,' says Nancy, 'And late at night as well if I'm going out, something similar.' '[Music] keeps you going – almost like nullifying in a way, because you don't think about what you're doing, you just listen to the music and get on with the routine of housework or whatever,' says Lesley.

In other cases, music is used by respondents to ease them on to courses of action and modes of aesthetic agency that they wish to achieve. It is, in Sloboda's terms, a thing that 'gets them going' (forthcoming). Fifty-two-year-old Vanessa, for example, uses precisely this term in describing how she uses music on summer afternoons as she prepares to host a barbecue.

Q. Have you ever tried to set a mood in any way, where you may have put things on in the background to get things livened up, or have some effect, in other words?

Vanessa: Yeah, in particular barbecues. A barbecue should be lively, shouldn't it?

Q. Yes.

Vanessa: Everyone talking – that's why I tend to put on Latin, which is really buzzy.

Q. Yes? This is during the day?

Vanessa: Yeah, in the afternoon – whatever. And if I wanted to cheer myself up I would play that type of music as well.

Q. OK – and what is it about that, that would cheer you up? I know that sounds like a stupid question . . .

Vanessa: I don't know – I just like Latin – it makes you feel good, I guess.

Q. Something to do with the music itself? Like the rhythm?

Vanessa: Yeah, it must be the rhythm.

Q. Or is it something to do with the association?

Vanessa: It's just a get-up-and-go type sound really. It sort of – instantly you hear it – you speed up a bit.

Q. Would you say then, that it has quite an effect on your energy?

Vanessa: I think so, music does definitely.

Q. When you put the Latin music on at the barbecue, do you put it on before anyone arrives?

Vanessa: Yeah, I tend to whilst I'm preparing the food.

Q. OK – why do you put it on at that stage?

Vanessa: Before?

Q. Yes.

Vanessa: Because it gets *me* going.

Q. When you say 'me', what do you mean?

Vanessa: Well, it gets you in the mood. When you're cooking and preparing it gets you in the mood.

Using music to 'get in the mood', 'get going' and so forth were referred to by nearly all respondents, particularly in reference to going out, or getting ready for a social event. 'I probably put a '70s disco album on and prance around and stuff [laughs]. Or I'd probably put – this is another sad thing I do – Gary Barlow,' says nineteen-year-old Imogen.

Conversely, music can be used to 'get out of moods' – bad moods in particular, but also to 'de-stress' or wind down. Beatrice, a soft-spoken twenty-year-old American university student who lives at home and likes to play Bach preludes and fugues on her piano, puts it this way: 'Whenever anyone gets angry we all tend to go to our rooms and turn on the music really loud.' She describes the process as 'venting' (that is, letting off steam) with music:

I just go to my room, slam the door, play my music and just sort of feel mad for a couple more minutes . . . When I turn the music up real loud it fills my room, it's like I can't hear anything outside my room and just me really mad.

As Beatrice describes this process, 'the act is parallel to – perhaps – punching a pillow or something. Because it really makes me feel that I'm taking the anger away. I don't know how that happens but it really works.' The music provides a simulacrum for a behavioural impulse – Beatrice makes an articulation between an alternate course of action ('punching a pillow'), her feelings ('angry') and a set of musical materials. Lesley, a thirty-nine-year-old mature student at an English university and mother of three teenage boys, makes this point explicitly: 'Sometimes, like with punk music or any sort of so-called anti-establishment music, you can identify with it but it can also diffuse your mood because you sort of listen it out, if you see what I mean – rather than just going and hitting someone or doing something like kicking the door.' Music gives respondents a medium in which to work through moods. It provides a way of transferring their means of expression from the 'real', physical realm ('hitting someone or doing something like kicking the door', 'punching a pillow') to the imagined, the virtual. Music thus provides a virtual reality within which respondents are able to express themselves in a (symbolically) violent manner, for example by choosing 'aggressive' or 'anti-establishment' music, or by playing music at full volume. This virtual realm is a haven for angry individuals; within this haven, they adopt the position of being in control of the symbolic and physical environment. For a few moments, the environment consists, virtually, of only music ('it fills my room . . .'), and the determination of this environment, within a bedroom in a house, can be controlled with the flick of a switch. One can thus recapture virtually, transposed to the medium of music, what one has had to concede interactionally; self-determination is re-established on a transposed level. It is no surprise then that headphones are strictly *not* employed for this process; for the point is to perpetrate a kind of aesthetic violence, to 'scream', 'punch' or 'kick' musically, and thus to have power over one's (aesthetic) environment. As discussed in chapter 5, below, it is also important to *feel* (and respond to) the *physical* character of this reality throughout one's body.

Typically, for the purpose of 'venting', as Beatrice calls it, respondents do not use music they associate with their regular routines, habits and normal courses of conduct and musical tastes. Unlike cases where respondents report on how they use music to 'get them going' prior to going out or to hosting a party, here music is used to express and then diffuse a particular interlude of intense, negative feeling. Karen, for example, a twenty-six-year-old postgraduate student in New York City, describes how she would never listen to her preferred music – Broadway musicals – 'because if I don't want my mood to change, if I'm just grumpy, I don't want to hear people singing about being happy . . . I just feel irritated more when I listen to it when I am in the wrong mood. Most of the time I'll know it and I won't even think about putting it on.' Karen goes on to describe how, if she is in a 'bad mood' she puts on rock music (which otherwise she does not listen to). And Monica describes how, living with her boyfriend's parents over the university summer vacation she used Radiohead's 'We hope you choke!' as a way of simultaneously diffusing her anger against her 'in-laws' and also as a message to them, played at full volume! (The use of music as virtual communication within a household or through giving music as a present and so on is discussed in chapter 5.)

'Anger' or 'rage' are, for these women, exceptional emotions; and the musical materials ('rock', 'anti-establishmentarian') and music consumption practices ('blasting') associated with these exceptional states are accordingly located on the margins of respondents' personal musical maps. Unlike the far more common practices associated with modulating and regulating mood and energy levels, here music's role as a virtual medium of self-expression, of letting off steam ('venting') is key. But it would be wrong to fall into an expressivist discourse of accounting for this practice. Music is not simply used to express some internal emotional state. Indeed, that music is part of the reflexive constitution of that state; it is a resource for the identification work of 'knowing how one feels' – a building material of 'subjectivity'. This is to say that a candidate simulacrum of feeling is also a template for fleshing out feeling, a material against which the aspects of 'how I feel' may be elaborated and made into an object of knowledge. One may say to one's self, 'this music is how I feel' and one may grow tense and relax as the music does, when the music does. Twenty-four-year-old Ellen, for example, describes how she uses music to induce and heighten a sad emotional state, in a way that is akin to 'looking at yourself in a mirror being sad', so as recursively to work herself up into an emotional state that reaches a plateau and then subsides. Henrietta, a seventy-year-old retired nurse, describes a similar process in relation to grieving:

The Verdi Requiem is one of my favourites. *That* is associated with losing a baby. And I'd got to know it through my husband and it was really quite a way of grieving – I'd shut myself away in a room [she begins to cry] . . . It's cathartic, I think.

When the music gathers itself into a climax and subsides, one may 'go with it', as Willis's bikeboys (described in chapter 1) aptly put it ('you go with the beat, don't you?' (Willis 1978:72)), to the extent one identifies one's emotional state with that musical structure. Over time, assuming one uses the same musical materials for these events, one may develop patterns or even styles to emotional states, and this issue is discussed in chapter 5. Thus, to play music as a virtual means of expressing or constructing emotion is also to define the temporal and qualitative structure of that emotion, to play it out in real time and then move on. In this sense music is both an instigator and a container of feeling – anger, sorrow and so forth. The natural history of the practices and processes in and through which feeling states are identified and 'expressed' (that is, enacted to self or other over time) is a key topic for the sociology and social psychology of subjectivity. It concerns the question of how aesthetic agency is configured in real time, as passion is choreographed and entrained. This question is taken up in relation to reliving past events at the end of this chapter, and again in chapter 5 which examines the socio-cultural ecology of music in public places and in that most private of aesthetic spaces – the intimate interaction. Meanwhile, what of music's role in establishing the seemingly 'passionless' state of focused mental concentration?

Getting into focus – music and mental concentration

If there's complete silence then my mind wanders and I just don't concentrate. (Monica)

[Music] keeps my mind working. (Yen)

I always have music on in my study. (Diana)

One of the most basic things music does is to block out other sounds. This was crucial in noisy urban spaces such as Manhattan ('I put my Walkman on sometimes just to drown out sound'). Music also serves as an alternative stimulus for some women when they look up from their work ('It's nice to have a background for something and it's nice to just sort of stop every so often and it refocuses you . . . You know how when you look at your computer screen a lot they tell you to stop every half hour and look away, well music does that for me, it sort of reminds me there is something there pleasant I'm doing').

But music for some respondents was intrinsic to producing environments that afford concentration, that help them to produce the kind of focus they needed to carry out mental work such as balancing a cheque-book, writing or studying; and there were certain musical materials that they hailed as conducive to producing focus. For example, Karen observes that music:

gives us both a distraction and a better focus. I find I can focus better when there's music on . . . I think that's why, it gives you something else that's going on in your head while you're doing whatever you're doing . . . um, if I'm doing like heavy contracts work or something that I have to focus on it would probably be classical. Sometimes it is Broadway music, but it's usually not pop or rock when I'm using it to try to concentrate or something. It's usually classical or stage music.

And Diana says:

Diana: [W]hen I was studying I would on the whole listen to something which I didn't have to think about, so I would be listening to Schubert, or Beethoven or um – a lot of Bach choral things. What else have I got up there? Quite a lot of Schubert, Sibelius – Mozart piano concertos, Mozart quartets, quintets, that sort of thing.

Q. You mentioned things with words, are there any other styles of music that you wouldn't listen to when you were working?

Diana: I could listen to jazz – but when I'm studying if it's something that, if you like, pulls at your heartstrings, or conjures up memories then I won't listen to it when I am studying.

'Classical' music or music without words was most frequently cited as aiding concentration. This did not appear to relate to the music's 'intrinsic' qualities *per se*. Rather, music's powers to promote concentration were derived from its relational position in respondents' map of tastes and practices of music consumption. For the respondents who hailed 'classical music' as a 'focuser', this was usually because such was least likely to be associated with aspects of their lives outside the realm of work or study – that is, music not strongly associated with specific aspects of their social or emotional lives or memories. (Indeed, they often did not know the actual composers or works they used for this purpose but rather made use of compilation CDs, such as baroque highlights and so forth.) Just as some respondents used music that lay on the margins of their normal music listening material to hold and diffuse anger, so, too, music for holding and concentrating focus was music on the margins of their musical-practical maps.

In addition, they were not the sorts of pieces that made them want to sing along. For example, here is Monica describing the sorts of CDs she had to turn off in order to get back to work:

I listened to Mick Drake actually, then I put on Madonna . . . the *Immaculate Collection*, which is one of my favourites, then I've stopped working you see because it's really – I just sung along to all the songs! So I completely lost really what I was doing. That's what I mean when there's a really good song I like to sing along to it.

The music that promoted concentration typically did not give prominence to lyrics – at least not in a language they could understand. They thus engaged in self-conditioning, associating familiar, focus-producing music with concentration such that, when the music was replayed, they were able to induce concentration. (For example, 'I wouldn't put something new on. If I am trying to work and have music, I would know the music already so I really don't have reactions to it.') Respondents described how they used music that they associated with the production of concentration and circumstances in which mental activity and focus were predominant. In short, music was used here to reproduce an aesthetic environment of 'working' and to circumscribe within that environment 'where the mind can go'. One literally stays tuned, through such practices, to a mode of concentrated focus, to the mental task at hand. For example, at the end of the interview with Karen (quoted above) I asked her if we could return to the issue of music and focus:

Karen: . . . Sometimes it holds my focus if I'm bored or something.

Q. It's interesting, you have brought up this issue quite a few times of music and focus. It sounds like you do use music to focus.

Karen: Yes, I do.

Q. And now I'm going to ask you something. I don't know if you will be able to help, but try. How do you think it helps you to focus?

Karen: Um.

Q. Whether you could describe it in terms of how you feel.

Karen: OK. I just – this is kind of why I use it for work, I'll try to describe it that way – I stop thinking about random thoughts, [they] just stop going through my head when I have music on, I won't think of what I'm doing or I'll be listening to the music, I won't just be thinking, 'Oh I have to do this, this, this, this, this. It kind of clears my head of all the random thoughts that may pop in and distract me otherwise. And that's how I've used it to focus.

Q. Can I ask you about random thoughts? Is there something about the rest of the environment that's maybe more conducive to bringing random thoughts to you?

Karen: . . . I just think I get distracted easily [laughs] and music helps me not to get distracted easily, so I'll focus on that and I will focus on what I am, the other thing I'm doing and not about the distraction.

As with the example of music for 'venting', here, too, music is used to seal off an environment, and to regularize that environment by predetermining the types of sonic stimuli it will contain. Music is thus a device with which to configure a space such that it affords some activities – concentration – more than others. And in these examples, music affords concentration because it structures the sonic environment, because it dispels random or idiosyncratic stimuli, aesthetic or otherwise. It places in the foreground sounds that respondents associate with mental work, sounds that are familiar and that recede to the background. With the addition of music, an environment comes to be configured for mental work.

To be sure, not all respondents used music to establish focus. Indeed, to most of the respondents over seventy and to those who were professionally trained musicians, the idea of music as 'background' to nearly anything was antithetical. Music is something one either makes or listens to intently. For example, seventy-five-year-old Eleanor, a church organist and highly active amateur musician, describes how she would *never* attempt to listen to music if she were doing paperwork, studying chess or otherwise needing to concentrate:

No. Because the music I have is not background music, the music that I love is something that is wonderful to me, you know, and when I listen to music I listen to the music and, well, I might sometimes put it on in breakfast time but then I can't really concentrate. I use the time during breakfast time doing two crossword puzzles, two cryptograms. It gets my brain going [laughs].

Relevant units of affect

In all of the above examples, music is an active ingredient in the organization of self, the shifting of mood, energy level, conduct style, mode of attention and engagement with the world. In none of these examples, however, does music simply *act upon* individuals, like a stimulus. Rather, music's 'effects' come from the ways in which individuals orient to it, how they interpret it and how they place it within their personal musical maps, within the semiotic web of music and extra-musical associations. Moreover – and this would be a grave disappointment for Adorno (see Adorno 1991) – the concept of the musical 'work', the total work as a, or indeed *the*, meaningful unit, is mostly irrelevant. Music takes its meaning from many things apart from its intertextual relationship with other musical works (and with the history of those works). While music-stylistic and historical matters may be relevant to the configuration of music's meaning and significance in some cases (especially with regard to music's conventional signifying materials such as genre, instrumentation, style and gesture), equally important to the matter of music's social 'effects' is the question of how musical materials relate to extra-musical matters such as occasions and circumstances of use, and personal associations, where the relevant semiotic unit is more likely to be a fragment or a phrase or some specific aspect of the music, such as its orchestration or tempo. The use of music as an organizing device in relation to subjectivity and self is, above all, a pragmatic affair and, although this practice may possess a logic, it also differs considerably from the practice of 'music appreciation' traditionally conceived. Respondents, particularly those without formal musical training, engage in various DIY activities with regard to music, mobilizing, picking and choosing, in magpie fashion, musical 'bits' or, as Keith Negus (1996:94–6) has aptly termed them, 'semiotic particles' that in turn provide cues for and parameters within which a respondent's modes of aesthetic agency come to be configured and transformed. This practice can be seen clearly in relation to music's role as a resource for identity construction.

Music and self-identity

The point of this chapter so far has been to illuminate music as an active ingredient in the care of the self and to introduce some of the ways in which music is employed for this purpose. Music is a device or resource to which people turn in order to regulate themselves as aesthetic agents, as feeling, thinking and acting beings in their day-to-day lives. Achieving this regulation requires a high degree of reflexivity; the perceived 'need' for regulation described by our respondents emerges with reference to the exigencies and situational 'demands' made upon them in and through their interactions with others. Such reflexivity can also been seen in relation to music's role as a building material of self-identity.

In light of recent social theory, the concepts of self-identity, personality and biography have undergone major redevelopment. No longer conceptualized as a fixed or unitary entity – as something that is an expression of inner 'essence' – identity has been recast conceptually as a product of social 'work' (Garfinkel 1967; Giddens 1991; DeNora 1995a; 1995c). Resituated, identity and its historical counterpart, biography, are conceptualized as an abiding trope of modern Western culture, realized in and through practices – textual and social (Atkinson 1990; Bertaux 1986; DeNora 1995b; Denzin 1989; Morgan and Stanley 1990). Looked at from this literary/pragmatic perspective, individuals engage in a range of mostly tacit identity work to construct, reinforce and repair the thread of self-identity. This work is what makes that thread appear continuous throughout the varied moments of day-to-day living whenever one formulates accounts of self to self and others. A great deal of identity work is produced as presentation of self to other(s) – which includes a micro-politics – through the enactment of a plethora of mini 'docu-dramas' over the course of a day (see Garfinkel 1967 on passing). But the 'projection' of biography is by no means the only basis for the construction of self-identity. Equally significant is a form of 'introjection', a presentation of self *to* self, the ability to mobilize and hold on to a coherent image of 'who one knows one is'. And this involves the social and cultural activity of remembering, the turning over of past experiences, for the cultivation of self-accountable imageries of self. Here music again comes to the fore, as part of the retinue of devices for memory retrieval (which is, simultaneously, memory construction). Music can be used as a device for the reflexive process of remembering/constructing who one is, a technology for spinning the apparently continuous tale of who one is. To the extent that music is used in this way it is not only, in Radley's sense, a device of artefactual memory (Radley 1990; Urry 1996); it is a device for the generation of future identity and action structures, a mediator of future existence.

'The song is you' – identity and relation through music

One of the first things respondents used music for was to remember key people in their lives, for example loved family members who had died. 'There's a piece of music that my grandad used to like very much', Monica says, 'and sometimes I'll be feeling a bit reminiscent about him because we were very close and I'd listen to that to remember him, but it wouldn't make me sad, it doesn't make me happy either, it's just sort of, "I've just remembered you today", sort of thing, you know.' Similarly, Lucy describes how, shortly after her father had died:

I was coming home from choir practice one evening, and I had the car radio on, switched it on as soon as I got going, and it was playing the [Brahms] Double Concerto and I just had to stop, and some friends were coming behind, you know, and I was just in floods of tears and they said, 'Why don't you turn it off' and I said, 'I can't' and that it was ages before I could listen to that or anything like it without thinking of him, it's only in the last year or so, because I know now that it meant so much to him and it means so much to me and I realize now how much like him I am. That's not to say my mother didn't have an important role in music as well . . .

The most frequent type of relationship respondents described in relation to music was romantic or intimate. Music helped them to recall lovers or former partners and, with these memories, emotionally heightened phases or moments in their lives. Diana, for example, described her listening habits and her tendency to listen to biographically key music in the 'late evening . . . I'm on my own with peace and quiet in my study and I'm often up 'til two in the morning. I regard this time as my own space.'

Diana: . . . I had an affair with a Londoner and we used to go out in the evenings, about twice a week, I don't know how I managed it, oh I know, because my husband was [working at home] and I would just say I was going out and we used to go to a [London] pub . . . and [there singers] used to sing to pop music of that era and 'A whiter shade of pale' was our tune and I just loved it and I suppose that affair went on for about two years, two and a half years.

Q. Can you tell me about how it came to be your tune? You heard it in that bar did you?

Diana: Yes, and of course it was on the radio all the time. Yes, we just sort of were absorbed in each other, or we'd hold hands or look at each other intently, something like that.

For many of the respondents, such as Diana, music was linked to a 'reliving' of an event or crucial time, linked often to a relationship. Even within the confines of the small, exploratory sample of fifty-two, certain works appeared more than once.

Lucy: There's the whole pop music of the sixties and all those hits which can instantly bring back memories . . . 'A whiter shade of pale' . . . I can say it's [German university town] *Hauptbahnhof*, in August 1967, you know! . . . [It] was the hit in summer '67, and I spent a semester in Germany as a student, and being there in the station, I was just leaving there to go to France, in fact, to meet up with [her future husband] . . . and we spent the summer, well, a couple of weeks, in France and that was the big record then, and . . . I suppose that was the start of our – just before we got engaged or whatever . . . but it was just, just culminated the sixties I think, there were a whole lot of songs like that. . . .

Q. Do you ever listen to that song now?

Lucy: Well I just heard it the other day. I was in a shop, buying something, and there was a woman about the same age as me [fifty-two] and I said, 'That takes you back, doesn't it?' and she said, 'Yeah' [laughs] and in fact, it was a CD, hits of the sixties, that they were playing in that shop.

Q. How did you feel, you said, 'It takes you back'?

Lucy: I just felt happy, you know, reminded me of [things] . . .

As Deborah puts it, 'I have relationship songs, everyone has their relationship songs, and then years later when I talk to somebody I go, "Oh my God, I totally related that with us, with you."' Maria, for example, describes an outdoor concert she heard on holiday. 'Now every time I hear a certain kind of new age music, I think of the sky that night and the moon, it was a hot summer, the tall trees, and standing there, arm next to arm with David, feeling electric, like part of a chain of being with him and our environment.' For Andrea, Rod Stewart's 'The first cut is the deepest' and 'Sailing' both 'have sad memories for me but I like listening to them. I suppose one likes to cry sometimes.' The songs are associated with a broken relationship and 'the happiness that went with it, as well'. Here, Andrea alludes to how, despite being a reminder of a happy time that has come to an end, music simultaneously helps to recapture or construct a sense of the capacity within which one once acted (one's aesthetic agency); in so doing, it helps dramatize to self a set of heightened life experiences. Through this vicarious review of past experience, this stock-taking of 'who one is' or 'where, interpersonally, one has been', one registers one's self to one's self as an object of self-knowledge, in the aesthetic construction that is memory.

For some respondents, such as Lucy above, music's power to evoke the emotional content of relationships is too painful; one does not 'like to cry'. Henrietta, for example, burst into tears and asked that the tape be stopped during the interview simply after mentioning the song she and her ex-husband shared when they were first courting ('Memories were made of this'). Becky avoids what she terms 'seventies' music because 'I have very bad memories, they remind me of my ex-husband and I dislike the music for that very reason.' Here, seventy-seven-year-old Bertie, who had recently moved, after her husband died, to an American 'life care center' in up-state New York, tries to explain why she cannot recall in any detail the contents of her record collection (which is stored just next to where we were sitting in her living room but which she avoids consulting, despite some gentle hints):

Bertie: . . . I haven't played my records now half as much as I used to.
Q. Yes, because you mentioned you listen to the radio.
Bertie: Yes. [Pause] And I think that has something to do with my husband dying.
Q. Yes.
Bertie: [Pause] All those records were so shaded with him and with our listening. I think that's why I don't listen as much as I used to.

For Lucy, Maria, Martha and Bertie, music brings back waves of emotion, the specificity of a time, an event, a relationship. For other people, music may evoke a more general era. As Judith puts it, 'Music does do it – brings back a certain time in your life. I don't think it makes me remember about specific things though, whereas photography does, it makes you remember specific things.' Psychologists refer to this process as priming, where, 'a network of associations that are linked by shared mood connections is activated by music' (Crozier 1997:79). As Deborah, thinking back to her student days and a pleasant semester abroad at Oxford, says:

Even if [I don't like the music] I'd buy the record because of its memories, things like Take That remind me of England [laughs]. Apart from the fact that I bought one album and spent far too much money on imports because of it reminds me of people I knew in England. Turning on Radio 1 in the morning, that kind of thing when I was there.

For Maria, Diana and Deborah, music reminds them of who they were at a certain time – a moment, a season, an era – and helps them to recapture the aesthetic agency they possessed (or which possessed them) at the time. Reliving experience through music is also (re)constituting past experience, it is making manifest within memory what may have been latent or even absent the first time through (Urry 1996) and music provides a device of prosthetic biography (Lury 1998). Indeed, the *telling* about the past in this way, and of music's ability to invoke past feelings and ways of being, is itself part of this reconstitution. The telling is part of the presentation of self to self and other(s). Such reliving, in so far as it is experienced as an identification with or of 'the past', is part of the work of producing one's self as a coherent being over time, part of producing a retrospection that is in turn a resource for projection into the future, a cueing in to how to proceed. In this sense, the past, musically conjured, is a resource for the reflexive movement from present to future, the moment-to-moment production of agency in real time. It serves also as a means of putting actors in touch with capacities, reminding them of their accomplished identities, which in turn fuels the ongoing projection of identity from past into future. Musically fostered memories thus produce past trajectories that contain momentum.

At the most general and most basic level, music is a medium that can be and often is simply paired or associated with aspects of past experience. It was part of the past and so becomes an emblem of a larger interactional, emotional complex. A good deal of music's affective powers come from its co-presence with other things – people, events, scenes. In some cases, music's semiotic power – here, its emblematic capacity – comes from its conditional presence; it was simply 'there at the time'. In such cases, music's specific meanings and its link to circumstances simply emerge from its association with the context in which it is heard. In such cases, the link, or articulation, that is made – and which is so often biographically indelible – is initially arbitrary but is rendered symbolic (and hence evocatory) from its relation to the wider retinue of the experience, to the moment in question.

To stop at this point, however, is to fail to appreciate the extent of music's semiotic powers in relation to the construction of memory and, indeed, to the experience that comes to be lodged and is 'retrievable' within autobiographical memory. These two issues are related. They need to be developed because they lead into the matter of how, as it is sometimes put, 'the music itself' is active in the constitution of the shape of subjectivity and self-identity.

Musical memories and the choreography of feeling

Music moves through time, it is a temporal medium. This is the first reason why it is a powerful *aide-mémoire*. Like an article of clothing or an aroma, music is part of the material and aesthetic environment in which it was once playing, in which the past, now an artefact of memory and its constitution, was once a present. Unlike material objects, however, music that is associated with past experience was, within that experience, heard over time. And when it is music that is associated with a particular moment and a particular space – as it was for Diana in a pub, Maria under the trees at an outdoor concert and Lucy in the German train station – music reheard and recalled provides a device for unfolding, for replaying, the temporal structure of that moment, its dynamism as emerging experience. This is why, for so many people, the past 'comes alive' to its soundtrack.

But there is yet more to it. For the women described above, the soundtrack of their action was not mere accompaniment. It did not merely follow their experience, was not merely overlaid upon it. True, the particular music may have been arbitrarily paired with the experiential moment – indeed, Diana, Maria and Lucy all describe how the music that 'brings it all back' was music that 'happened' to be playing, that was simply part of the environment or era. But the creation of that 'moment' as a heightened moment was due in part to the alchemy of respondents' perceived or sensed 'rightness' or resonance between the situation, the social relationship, the setting, the music, and themselves as emerging aesthetic agents with feelings, desires, moods such that the music *was* the mood, and the mood, the music. To the extent that music comes to penetrate experience in this way, it is informative of that experience. Music thus provides parameters – or potential parameters because it has to be meaningfully attended to – for experience constituted in real time. It serves, as was discussed in the previous chapters, as a referent for experience. This is exactly what Lucy was doing, as described in chapter 2, where she could be seen to contribute to music's 'power' over her according to the circumstances under which she consumed the music. This environmental appropriation, which is a reflexive constitution of music's affordances within a context, scene or setting, is how experience comes to be made, felt and known to self. It consists of an interlacing of experience (feeling, action) and the materials that are accessed as the referents for experience, its metaphoric and temporal parameters. It is no wonder, then, that on rehearing music that helped to structure, to inform experience, respondents describe how they are able to relive that experience; the study of human–music interaction thus reveals the subject, memory and, with it, self-identity, as being constituted on a fundamentally socio-cultural plane where the dichotomy between 'subjects' and 'objects' is, for all practical purposes, null and void.

Music may thus be seen to serve as a container for the temporal structure of past circumstances. Moreover, to the extent that, first time through, a past event was constructed and came to be meaningful with reference to music, musical structures may provide a grid or grammar for the temporal structures of emotional and embodied patterns as they were originally experienced. Music is implicated in the ways that, as Urry observes with poignant reference to Proust's famous phrase, 'our arms and legs . . . [are] full of torpid memories' (Urry 1996:49); it is a mediator of, in Proust's sense, the aesthetic, memory-encrusted unconscious (Lash and Urry 1994:43).

Finding 'the me in music' – musically composed identities

The sense of 'self' is locatable in music. Musical materials provide terms and templates for elaborating self-identity – for identity's identification. Looking more closely at this process highlights the ways in which musical materials are active ingredients in identity work, how respondents 'find themselves' in musical structures. It also highlights some of the ways that music is attended to by its recipients, how music reception and the units of meaning that listeners find within music differ dramatically from musicological and music-psychological models of music reception and their emphasis on the perception of musical structures. Consider this example from the interview with Lucy:

Q. . . . Have you ever adjusted the volume of music that's playing in your home, either to turn it down or turn it up?
Lucy: . . . I would sometimes turn it up if something was playing, if it was coming to something I really liked, a nice juicy chord, or a bit that I liked, I'd say, 'Oh turn it up' or I'd go in and listen.
Q. 'A bit that I like' – you've touched on that a couple of times earlier, that's something that's very interesting. Could you give me an example of some 'bit' of some piece of music, some chord or . . .
Lucy: Well, usually because it's just a *juicy* chord.
Q. What do you mean by 'juicy'?
Lucy: Well – a lot of notes, and, usually perhaps a lower register. I sing alto and I tend to like cello music and lower register music, you know, really punchy sound and, well, 'juicy' is the word, huge chords or just, I don't know, just a phrase. I can't think of a particular bit of music but, I think probably in the Pastoral Symphony, come to think of it, or there's lots in Vivaldi, Vivaldi has a good – and Brahms. There's certain things, that you just *wait* for that bit and you really enjoy it.

Lucy goes on to explain how these things may be highly personal: 'I don't know whether they're there for anyone else. I really don't know because they're gone in a second.' At the end of the interview, we returned to the topic of these 'juicy' musical moments, ones that feature the lower register sounds (she describes how she does not like soprano solos) and chords:

Q. . . . You said, you're an alto, and you like music that brings out the lower sounds. Why *is* that? [laughs]

Lucy: I have no idea! [laughs] Maybe because it's sort of *meatier* or something and a sort of more intense experience.

When pressed further, Lucy says that she thinks she likes the lower sonorities because they are:

Lucy: . . . part of the background. I think it's more being in the background rather than being, because the soprano tends to have the tune, even if it's not a solo soprano, whereas we [altos] provide the meat – it's the sopranos and the tenors that carry the song, if you like, and the basses and the altos that *fill out* to make it a sort of – [she stops and looks at me questioningly]

Q. A sonic whole?

Lucy: Yeah. And I think that maybe that characterizes me in life, that I don't like being in the limelight, I like to – [pause]

Q. I'm an alto too [laughs].

Lucy: [Laughs] Yes.

Q. So, not being 'in the limelight' but being?

Lucy: Being part of a group. And, you know, pressing forward and doing my bit but not – [pause]

Q. Filling in, as it were, the needed middle?

Lucy: Yeah. Seeing what needs doing and doing it but not being spotlighted and being 'out front' sort of thing.

Here Lucy makes a link between a preferred type of musical material ('juicy' chords), a concept of self-identity (the 'me in life') and a kind of social ideal ('doing my bit but not . . . being spotlighted'). She 'finds herself', so to speak, in certain musical structures that provide representations of the things she perceives and values about herself. In that sense, listening for (and turning up the volume on) the 'juicy' bits is a form of self-affirmation. Simultaneously, these bits provide images of self for self. Here, the music provides a material rendering of self-identity; a material in and with which to identify identity. Through the mutual referencing of self to music and music to self, Lucy fleshes out the meaning of each. Here then, in relation to the musical elaboration of self-identity, is a virtuous circle: music is appropriated as Lucy's ally, as an enabler for the articulation of self-identity – for its spinning out as a tale for self and other. Conversely, this tale of identity leads Lucy to value and specially attend to certain musical materials. Through this aesthetic reflexive process Lucy enhances ontological security in her self-identity by drawing upon, and drawing together within a habitat, musical artefacts. Through these artefacts she may come to 'know' herself (and thus project herself in future action – generate herself as an agent). She accomplishes this identity work through the ways she perceives herself as 'like' the material to which she refers, reflexively, to produce her self-knowledge.

Here we can follow music as it comes to be converted or transposed – in and through interpretive appropriation – into something extra-musical, something social: Lucy's registration of self-identity. Music is a 'mirror' that allows one to 'see one's self'. It is, also, however, a 'magic mirror' in so far as its specific material properties also come to configure (for example, transfigure, disfigure) the image reflected in and through its (perceived) structures. In this sense, music works as what Turner (1981) calls an 'action paradigm'. Like a cultural performance (Turner had in mind theatrical performances), then, music too may serve as a repository of value, of self-perception.

Using music in this way as a mirror for self-perception (locating within its structures the 'me in life', as Lucy puts it) is a common practice of identity work in daily life. There are some individuals, however – such as Gary, the music therapeutic client discussed in chapter 1 – who cannot and normally would not conduct this sort of identity work for themselves. They are not only removed from the aesthetic resources for the constitution and maintenance of self-identity (see Goffman 1961), they do not possess the aesthetic reflexive skills through which this work is normally accomplished. They cannot therefore produce themselves – as objects of knowledge, as concepts that can be remembered – for themselves.

Here, then, is one of the uses of music therapy: the improvisational work of a music therapist may be used to fill out and structure musical-interactive sessions. As with the session with Gary, a therapist may use music strategically to facilitate clients' self-perception and ontological self-security. In many cases one of the first aims of such therapy is to strengthen and reinforce a client's attempted musical gestures, following the 'iso' or correspondence principle (Bunt 1997) of matching the parameters of a client's music, of replaying them back to the client, to promote security (the client comes to be 'in control' of the aesthetic environment – for many clients this determination is far removed from their daily routines). Such a procedure aims to mirror a client's musical gestures so that he or she may come to perceive them as an object – as part of his or her self-expression. In this way, the therapist strategically constructs what the client is unable to build for him/herself – an aesthetic registration of self, constituted against the contrast structure provided by the music. The client's musical gestures are, through the therapist's work, bound up within the frame of the therapist's musical gestures such that they come to provide a feature or figuration of the client him/herself. The client's gestures thus become traces of his or her identity and, through the therapist's attempts to make sense, musically, of these gestures, the client comes to have, like so-called 'normal' people, a fabricated registry of self-identity.

The resultant music ratifies the client's presence (and often results in signs of pleasure from the client, such as smiling, bodily composure and physical contact). Here is a therapist describing this process as she talks us through a video tape of a session with Mandy, a severely disabled client who is also visually impaired:

I don't have any way of communicating with Mandy at all, so what she is giving me is basically nothing. She has got this – she grinds her teeth which is awful and there is *no way* I am going to reflect that back! And she has got this vocal sound she makes and she is doing this with her head all the time. So what I am trying to do in this video is I am singing a greeting song to her, which is the way I always start the session so that she knows that we have begun, and then I am following the rhythm of her head and the idea that she gets the impression that she is in control of something that when her head stops the music stops and when she starts moving her head again it starts so I am giving her some control in the hope that at some stage she will start to interact.

As David Aldridge has observed, music provides here a 'ground of being – not in verbal logic but analogous to the ground of their [clients'] own functioning. In this sense, insight is made, not in a restricted verbal intellectual sense, but achieved in composition' (1992:29). If Mandy – the music therapeutic client described above – is at one end of a continuum of musical use in regard to identity work, then Elaine, who describes her musical practices in the following quote, is at the other:

Elaine: I would say about myself that my range of musical tastes which, in talking to other people, I know are rather eclectic. It reflects something else about me, which is that I love a wide variety of experiences . . . I love food from all around the world, and will try anything, you know . . . I somehow grew up with an ability to experience diversity or something and enjoy it enormously and be stimulated by it rather than frightened by it or wanting to, you know, trying to keep things too contained . . . I could go to a party looking very hippie, you know from the old days, hippie, go out in beads and huge earrings and lots of colour, but go the next night to an opera and look like I'd just stepped off the pages of a very conservative, you know [laughs], nice young lady type book, so yes and I enjoy that. When I was in my twenties I used to puzzle over this quite a bit and think I don't know who to be. 'Which is my New York?' I would think Am I a Village person or am I a Fifth Avenue person . . . and then I came to this wonderful saying that I could be all these selves and I could choose one so I rather liked just exactly that, being able to play into any role, it's fun.

Q. Do you ever experience a difficulty in deciding on which role, or a sense of between roles? Or is that not a problem?

Elaine: No, not a problem. It's – an unconscious sense almost, of who you need to be and who you are that day and what feels right and, yes, even in a way sometimes you don't understand, you just get dressed and look in the mirror and say this – you could have worn it a week ago and it felt right, but it isn't 'working' today and so you change or put different earrings on . . .

Elaine, when asked to account for her self-identity, defines it in terms of its multi-faceted character; she is a person with many dimensions, and her musical tastes and practices demonstrate this diversity, this range of personae that make up her 'self'. Indeed, Elaine was one of the most musically explosive respondents in the study, engaging in a great deal of 'bursting into song':

I'm always singing. My kids – one thing I know this is something I always do, if somebody says something I say, 'Oh, that reminds me' because it will remind me of a song and I'll say, 'Oh there is a song about that' and then I insist on singing a few lines so they – it's kind of a little joke thing that I do. 'Oh, Mom always knows a song about that.' It can be rather loosely related, but it's just a fun thing that we do, or that I do.

And here, she describes how she musically 'dominates' her household:

Q. So if we can just go back for a moment . . . Would you be putting that kind of music on for the whole family or just you and your husband?
Elaine: Whole family.
Q. Whole family. Now do the kids or does your husband ever put music on or is this something that you do?
Elaine: Something I do.
Q. Do you think within the dynamics of the family that you tend to be the most likely person for putting the music on in communal areas?
Elaine: *Absolutely*. If it's communal, I put it on.
Q. Is that because you are most interested in doing that or is it that you are maybe more dominant in terms of taste?
Elaine: Yeah, I think my tastes are more dominant in the household, period. But my husband has very little interest in music . . . The kids wouldn't put music on because their music would be intolerable to me [laughs].
Q. OK. That's one of the things I'm getting at. OK. So there's a certain kind of negotiation process then going on here.
Elaine: And I win [laughs]. Because I think it goes without saying that as the mother, as the woman, I have the right to set the mood for dinner, even though I don't cook – my husband does all the cooking.

Here, Elaine describes how a range of music provides her with material markers of her multi-faceted 'personality', that allow her to spin the tale of 'who she is' to herself and others. And she is able to project these markers or anchors into her domestic and interpersonal environment through singing and through choosing background music. She is in command of her aesthetic environment, the environment that reminds her of and helps to hold on to the citadel of self-identity. Her environment is furnished – because she is active in this decoration work – with mnemonics of her self. Within this environment she is strong, easily able to 'find the me in life'. This dominant position with regard to the politics of aesthetic determination is taken up again in the following chapter, where music is explored as part of the furnishing of the *collective* environment.

Elaine describes a diverse array of music in relation to her self-identity and its social-cultural situation, but she does not describe any examples of lapsed or dropped music in relation to identity. For many respondents, though, identity work is achieved in and through the music to which they have *stopped* listening. Vanessa, for example, describes how she no longer listens to Brian Ferry: 'I haven't played him for years. But I was obsessed with him . . . I'm not interested at all now . . . I think that's a phase of life that's over and – I simply lost interest, I think . . .' At the end of the interview, she elaborates in more detail why she no longer listens to the music (her current favourite at the time of the interview was George Michael's 'Older'):

I think they had a certain style which you wanted to try yourself. Maybe that's why I liked Roxy Music at that particular time. The high heels, the siren look, the diva vamp – you know, that type of thing. Roxy Music conjured up all that type of thing. I think you go through, you know – now I like jazz – because of my age [fifty-two] maybe – I don't know.

Like Lucy, Vanessa was able to locate the 'me in life' musically. Unlike Lucy, that location took as its semiotic particle the complex of music and performer image. Also unlike Lucy, Vanessa can be seen to have dropped a particular musical mirror or representation of self when it no longer seemed tenable, when it no longer reflected with the terms with which she could engage in self-description. Thus, in turning to different musics and the meaningful particles that 'reflect' and register self-identity, that provide a template of self, individuals are also choosing music that produces self-images that are tenable, that seem doable, habitable. Respondents seem to access the music of 'who they are' through an elective affinity, through a feeling for what seems comfortable and what is exemplary. For example, Lucy's behavioural tendency in social situations resonates with and is reinforced by her avoidance of flashy solo arias. Elaine, by contrast, enjoys just such arias ('[In the car] I can play it as loud as I want, I can sing to it, every last note of it, you know, that I can without being worried about anybody else's response, so I love it' and, 'By the way, I mostly only like the ones where everybody dies, I don't like – you know – the ones where little shepherd girls poke around, I couldn't care less, I don't like that kind of frippery stuff . . .'). Similarly, Vanessa no longer listens to music that no longer resonates with her self-image.

In this chapter, music has been portrayed as a temporal structure, as offering semiotic particles, as a medium with attendant conventional or biographical associations – in action as a device for ordering the self as an agent, and as an object known and accountable to oneself and others. Music may be understood as providing a container for feeling and, in this sense, its specific properties contribute to the shape and quality of feeling to the extent that feeling – to be sustained, and made known to oneself and others – must be established on a public or intersubjective plane. Music is a material that actors use to elaborate, to fill out and fill in, to themselves and to others, modes of aesthetic agency and, with it, subjective stances and identities. This, then, is what *should* be meant when we speak of the 'cultural construction of subjectivity' – and this is much more than an idea that culture underwrites generic structures of feeling or aesthetic agency as is implied in so many post-structuralist writings and by musicologists trained in semiotic analysis of texts. Such structuralist perspectives remain distanced from the heart of the matter, from how individuals not only experience culture, but also how they mobilize culture for being, doing and feeling. Anything less cannot address and begin to describe or account for the mechanisms through which cultural materials get into social psychological life. Accordingly, the next chapter pushes these issues further by exploring music's role in the constitution of the body – not the overt and highly deliberate, overtly 'performed' body of dance, but rather the physiological, non-conscious and micro-behavioural body. Through this exploration a perspective is developed for thinking about embodiment as it is musically structured. This perspective is then applied, in chapter 5, to the matter of how music may be seen to be used and have effects in interaction and in public settings.

4 Music and the body

The sociology of the body

In the realm of common sense, the body is paradoxical. At once self-evident and mysterious, biologically 'given' yet modifiable, the body is characterized through contradiction. Exploring these contradictions helps to open many deeper questions concerning the relationship between bodies and the material-cultural settings of their existence. Perhaps the best place to begin is by exploring the questions of where 'body' ends and 'environment' begins. What kind of a line should be drawn, for example, between 'endogenous' and 'exogenous' bodily features?

This definitional conundrum is by no means merely academic. On the contrary, it has bearing upon the very questions that can be posed about bodily matters. In recent years it has been given new impetus through studies that focus on the reflexive relationship between body and society. Calling into question the axiomatic status of 'the' body, and its associated dualisms (mind/body, culture/nature, particular/universal, subject/object), recent perspectives within sociology, history and cultural studies have proposed a conception of the 'body' as a socialized entity, configured at – and serving also to demarcate – the interstices of nature, culture and technology (Birke 1992a; 1992b; Featherstone et al. 1991; Haraway 1985; Jaggar and Bordo 1992; Turner 1984). These perspectives offer great potential for medical science, but do not square with medical institutions and institutionalized practice as these are currently configured. They interact well with complementary medicine (Sharma 1992), however, through their focus on the body as a construction. This focus shifts away from what the body 'is' (and what can be done 'to' it), to a focus on what the body may become as it is situated within different contexts and viewed from within different terms of reference.

Thinking about the body as a construction involves much more than thinking about how, in the superficial sense, it is 'represented' (see Shilling's critique of social constructionism and body matters, 1993). At

75

its most powerful, it leads to the question of what the notion of the body-as-culturally-constructed actually means in the real time and local space of social *practice*. There is little work to date on the cultural and micro-social processes through which bodies are configured in the here and now of social life. And yet, if the body is indeed a hybrid or 'cyborg' of some kind, if its physical properties are 'made' through interchange with materials that lie outside it, then should we not be able to observe this process and to document the mechanisms of this making? To do so is to theorize the matter of how culture works at the level of embodied action and to develop theory that can be applied to practical bodily problems and procedures. In short, by moving away from discourses of the body and moving towards a focus on body–culture interaction, on tempo-ral body practices, a grounded theory of the body's cultural constitution has the capacity to move well beyond semiotic readings of bodily mean-ings. This capacity is potentially profound in so far as it is able to 'enter' the body in ways that articulate with (and even at times transform) medical and physiological perspectives.

By its very nature, though, the exploration of body–culture interac-tion cannot proceed hypothetically. Instead, the pursuit of body–culture interaction entails a slower kind of work; it is built up case by case, through empirical attention to the explicitly temporal matter of bodies in action (in real time). This project entails a grounded theory of the body as social and it depends upon intimate observations of bodies as they interact, from moment to moment, with the materials that come to 'discipline' them. Thus, just as the previous chapter featured the intersection of culture and action as it generates emotional and bio-graphical dimensions of agency and action trajectories, this chapter deals with the 'musical composition' of agency's embodied features. These features include energy, comportment, co-ordination, timing, arousal, motivation, endurance, and homoeostatic features such as breathing, heart rate and blood pressure, and the self-perception of pain and bodily pleasure. This is by no means an exhaustive list, but it serves to highlight some of the many features normally excised from sociological conceptions of agency and agency's parameters. The fol-lowing discussion seeks to illuminate some of these features as they emerge in and through reference to aesthetic and, in this case, musical materials and as they provide a map or framework against which the body is organized. It is linked to a theory of culture as something much more than a decorative overlay for bodily phenomena but as intrinsic to the constitution of the body and its physical processes, as something that can enter into and formulate bodily realities. With regard to music, such a theorization of cultural power extends well beyond the usual concern with the meanings of art objects as it conceptualizes their power at a more existential level of human being where body, consciousness and feeling intertwine.

To develop this perspective for music and embodiment, we may begin at the beginning of the human life-cycle, with the medical sub-field of neonatology (infants of thirty-seven weeks of age or less) and the recent turn, within that area, to music as a therapeutic medium (Hicks 1992). Considering music's active role in the promotion of neonatal 'state integrity' (that is, the normalization and regularization of bodily processes) helps to illuminate music's role as a device of corporeal ordering, at *all* stages of human life, as a medium that may have effects long before it is 'meaningful' in a cultural sense. Accordingly, examining music's 'force' at this early stage in the life-cycle simultaneously points to new ways of conceptualizing the links between human and non-human members of the animal kingdom (Birke 1995).

Getting into the rhythm of life

The first music we hear is inside the womb:

The sound that dominates the unborn child's world is its mother's heartbeat. Other voices and familiar sounds add harmony to the already progressive composition of the uterine symphony. From the 24th week on, the unborn child listens all the time. He or she has lots to listen to, as the pregnant abdomen and uterus are very noisy places. (Hicks 1995:31)

This 'intrauterine symphony', as it has been termed in the medical literature, consists of the mother's heartbeat, her voice as she speaks or sings, and any other sounds from the outside world, such as the voices of others. In the sonic foreground of this sound environment is what has been described within the literature as a 'rhythmic "swooshing" of the blood as it rushes through the placental vessels' (Collins and Kuck 1990:24).

One of the key indicators of health is an infant's ability to achieve homoeostasis, the regularization of physical and behavioural processes such as breathing, blood pressure, heartbeat and sleep. Increasingly, neonatologists have come to conceptualize this ability as linked to environmental factors. 'State organization', as it is called in the literature, is described as the result of 'both its own internal endogenous processes and exogenous influences from the environment' (Thoman et al. 1981). In this respect, neonatology is in the medical vanguard with its emphasis on holistic perspectives.

One of the key mechanisms for establishing homoeostasis is *entrainment*, the alignment or integration of bodily features with some recurrent features in the environment. This point is made repeatedly in the literature on neonates. For example:

Not only must the environment be conducive to physiologic homeostasis, but, according to Keefe, 'the pattern of infant state cycles must become harmoniously integrated with the salient recurrent features of the environment'. (Kaminski and Hall 1996:46)

In recent years, neonatologists have begun to pursue the matter of how to produce an environment conducive to entrainment and regularization, an environment that helps infants achieve homoeostasis. Within this set of concerns, there has been a growing emphasis on music and its potential in the neonatal unit. In particular, music is thought to facilitate state organization by encouraging entrainment.

Musical entrainment

Perhaps the most straightforward example of musical entrainment in relation to the body can be found when music is used as a basis for marching in step or otherwise synchronizing bodily movement, such as skipping rope (with lessons about 'normal' adult sexual orientation literally drummed in via the text!):

I like coffee, I like tea,
I like the boys
And the boys like me. (Children's skipping song)

Musically entrained, the body and its processes unfold in relation to musical elements (in these examples, its regular pulse); they are aligned and regularized in relation to music, they are musically organized, musically 'composed'. A more complex example can be found in dance, where the body is not only entrained rhythmically (the 1-2-3 of the waltz, for example) but also engages in stylistic manoeuvres in orientation to the music (the clenched fists in relation to some rock or pop music, the angle of the neck and chin in ballet, or the pelvis during the cha-cha-cha). This alignment, between music and body, often occurs subconsciously or unconsciously and it may entail normally imperceptible micromovements, such as how one holds one's eyebrows, cheekbones or shoulders, the tension of one's muscles. As a series of bodily gestures, then, dance and more mundane and subconscious forms of choreography are media for the autodidactic accumulation of self and gender awareness. Movement – aesthetically oriented – is, as Irigaray put it in her essay on 'The Gesture in Psychoanalysis' (1989), a means for constructing the spaces of the subject. It is the source, as Angela McRobbie put it in her pioneering essay on gender and dance, of bodily aesthetics in everyday life (1991:191).

In much the same way that bodily movements can be produced – consciously or semi-consciously – in relation to musical properties, so, too, a range of bodily processes can be entrained in relation to other temporally organized environmental media. Entrainment may involve regularizing and/or modifying physiological states (for example, oxygen levels in the blood or heart rate), behaviour (at any level of detail – for example, blinking, fidgeting, jumping or sleeping), the temporal parameters of mood and feeling (as described in chapter 3), and social role and action style, which are discussed in chapter 5. Musical entrainment and its observable character thus provide a clear example of how environmental materials and their properties may be said to afford or provide resources for particular kinds of bodies and bodily states, states that are regularized and reproduced over time. Of special interest here, in relation to the neonatal body, is the way in which music is currently being employed to mediate tensions between endogenous (bodily) and exogenous (environmental) processes within neonatal intensive care units. Examining this issue, via the neonatology literature, advances the conception of 'human–music interaction' and musical 'affordances' as developed in previous chapters and applies it to the earliest phase of human life.

Paradox of cure in the neonatal unit – the body's sonic resources

Neonatal infants are often state-disorganized. In extreme situations of bodily distress, they thrash their extremities and head, they grimace, exhibit fluctuations in heart rate, blood pressure and skin coloration, they may be intolerant to feeding, their muscles may be flaccid or rigid, they may cry, and the oxygen levels in their blood may be low. All these things are taken as symptoms of 'state instability', that is, ill health. In the face of this instability, a range of neonatal devices are deployed to regularize physiological processes and behavioural states. Within the neonatal ICU, mechanical ventilators, heart monitors and intubation (for administrating drugs and nourishment) are, often literally, life supporting.

A neonatal infant is exposed to few stimuli, apart from those that derive from medical devices. Confined to crib or incubator, unable to be touched, the neonatal infant may also not yet be able to see, and if even if she is able to see, she is not at liberty to move her head freely, to direct her gaze freely. Given these limitations, it seems reasonable to suggest that the sonic dimension of the neonatal environment is heightened.

Like temperature or lighting, the sound of a unit – with or without musical intervention – is a ubiquitous environmental feature; it is also one that the infant cannot escape. And yet, the routine sound of a neonatal intensive care unit is frequently cacophonous; it consists mainly of sounds that are the random byproduct of medical technologies (for example, the sound of respirators or the sounds of bottles clanking on the incubator top), the sounds of other infants in distress, or, perhaps worse, amplifications of the infant's own disorganized state through devices such as the heart monitor, whereby an infant's (possibly erratic) heartbeat is amplified and mirrored back as an audible beeping.

Paradoxically, then, the very environment in which neonates exist, and upon which they are dependent for life support, may also serve to inhibit an infant's autonomous capacity for, as Kaminski and Hall put it (1996, quoted above), 'harmonious integration' of body with environment in a way that can produce state regulation. Not only is the infant's auditory environment lacking 'salient recurrent features' (that is, sonic resources for embodied regularization), but the very machinery of life support may lead to the disruption of state lability, biorhythms and sleep (Kaminski and Hall 1996:46). The 'cure', in other words, brings some problems in its train.

The neonate's paradox is not unlike the situation faced by creative music therapeutic clients such as Gary, described in chapter 1, or Mandy in chapter 3, for whom the unassisted elaboration of identity and entrained (mutually co-ordinated) interaction was problematic. Gary's and Mandy's distress is related to and exacerbated by their inability to appropriate environmental-cultural materials for self-organization (identity, comportment, physiology). Neither can engage in the normal modes for co-ordinating and interacting (such as verbal communication). Moreover, because they have other disabilities (for example, Gary is visually disabled), the mundane environment presents a barrage of stressful, often apparently chaotic, events (for Gary, having his incontinence pad changed can be, according to how it is undertaken, a frightening ordeal). Music therapy sessions, on the other hand, offer a means of mitigating distress in so far as the therapist is engaged in strategic manipulations of music so as to enable them to 'compose themselves', constructively mirroring their gestures and engaging in musically 'supportive' activity. Within the sessions, their self-composition arose from their production of musical gestures that spanned time; engaging in this production they also produced themselves as actors – that is, as actors who were engaged in continuous activity – the activity of producing music. Within the realm of music therapy, then, they were able to form and hold themselves as producers of expressive forms, to engage in symbolic interaction. Thus the musical therapeutic environment allowed them to achieve something denied to them in daily life. Without this kind of musical support, as offered by the therapeutic session, Gary and Mandy are caught in a

vicious circle within which the environment and its perceived lack of
regularity impede the process of self-composition.

A similar vicious circle typifies the situation of the neonatal infant.
It is well known to clinicians and well reflected in the literature. For
example:

neonates must synchronize their behavioral states and physiologic adjustments
with an environment where there is no clear, pronounced diurnal rhythm in noise
level or in caregiving activities. This is significant because, for the neonate, one of
the primary biorhythmic elements is the distribution and flow of sleep–wake
states over a 24-hour period. In the nursery environment, continuous noise affects
neonatal biorhythms, and this affects sleep regulation and state lability. (Kaminski
and Hall 1996:46)

For a neonate, this contrast is stark. Prior to birth, the infant's environment is characterized by sonic regularity, by rhythm. Moreover, the auditory environment was probably not associated with traumatic events. As
some researchers have remarked, 'one of the most stressful changes that
occurs during the transition from intrauterine to extrauterine life is the
loss of rhythm that the foetus has become accustomed to through months
of being exposed to maternal movements, breathing, and heartbeat'
(Collins and Kuck 1990:24).

This is where music can make a difference, can be used to break out of
the vicious circle of a neonate's dependency upon technology, much as it
does for creative music therapy clients. First, auditory stimuli, which can
waft through the unit or be employed through pillow or mattress speakers, can actually 'reach' the infant where other types of entrainment
materials, such as touching, may not. Music is simply an available, practical medium in the intensive care unit for delineating a patterned and
stable or predictable environment. In addition, it can be used to mask the
unit's auditory baseline of technical equipment and other 'stressing'
noises. It is with these ends in mind that recent innovations in neonatal
care have involved musical interventions. Music is increasingly seen by
neonatal professionals as an effective means for modulating the array of
physiological states and micro-behaviours associated with instability into
an array associated with stability – stable heart rate, blood pressure,
colour, feeding, changes in posture, muscle tone, less frantic movements,
rhythmic crying, cessation of grimacing and an ability to sleep and/or
become animated and intent. For example:

Baby B, a 2,665 gm, 34-week gestational age male . . . exhibited respiratory
distress at birth . . . Fentanl [a respiratory depressant] was given every two to
four hours as needed for agitation associated with the mechanical ventilation.
Baby B's response . . . consisted of brief periods of apparent sleep, which did
not last more than 30 minutes. To provide comfort . . . we played the

'Transitions' tape for periods of one to two hours. During these periods, Baby B was able to use his pacifier for self-quieting, and he appeared to be sleeping. (Leonard 1992:47)

The introduction of music (a combination of intrauterine sound and synthesized female vocals, produced by Placenta Music Inc.) to the neonatal unit would thus appear to create, with minimal cost or effort, a modified and regularized environment. According to the medical criteria and medical observations, this musical environment helped to regularize the sleep patterns of the neonatal infant.

Such use, of which this was an instance, is increasingly common within neonatology. It is becoming more common in other realms of medicine as well; Cheryl Dileo Maranto has delineated music's use in a range of medical procedures. These include *surgery*, where music listening has been linked with, among other things, a reduction of stress hormone levels, diminished need for anaesthesia, lowered pulse and stable blood pressure rates, reduction in postoperative pain and the need for analgesic medication (1993:161). Music has also been used in conjunction with *respiratory care*, for entraining respiration, in *burn care*, and in *labour and delivery* to compress time during labour, to distract or serve as a focal point, to regulate breathing, to enhance Lamaze procedures, to enhance the 'euphoria' of birth and to decrease the length of labour. It has also been used widely in the area of pain management, to increase pain threshold and tolerance levels and to enhance relaxation. In relation to joint mobility, music can be used to profile movement. (For example, waltz music may be used to encourage 'fluid' movements and dexterity, whereas disco numbers will be used when the client needs to build up strength through more powerful and energetic movements (Bunt 1997).)

There would appear to be little doubt that music therapy holds considerable promise for clinical medicine. To be sure, it has received increasing attention in recent years, spurred on by the fact that it is highly cost effective (Maranto 1993). At its present state of development, however, music therapy still lacks a theoretical base and has a relatively undeveloped explanatory vocabulary for specifying *how* music operates – as opposed to *what* it can produce – in relation to body organization.

How does music work? Key questions

For example, how does music come to have 'effects' upon body composition? With regard to neonatology, what exactly does it mean to speak of an infant's interaction with the recurrent sonic features of his or her environment? Indeed, is it music's *regularity* that leads to self-regulation, to an infant's ability to shift her/himself to a more stable state? Or is it simply that music is a distraction or a way of masking other more noxious sounds? And if musical regularities *do* play an active role in physical entrainment, just what are the *mechanisms* through which environmental regularities come to be related to, and indeed foster, bodily regularities? Finally, what is the nature of the body–environment relationship? For example, do musical-environmental regularities simply 'cause' bodily effects? Is the realm of the corporeal, particularly at this very early and uncultured stage of life, therefore an exception to the argument that has been made in the previous three chapters against a 'stimulus' model of music's effects?

In answer to this last question, no. There is no reason why a perspective devoted to human–music interaction, to the reflexive appropriation of musical materials for the constitution and regulation of agency, does not also apply to the matter of embodied agency and its constitution, to the organization of the corporeal, at any stage of the life-cycle. True, such an application may require rethinking conventional notions of sentience and intentionality (an infant does not exercise the same type and degree of aesthetic reflexivity demonstrated, for example, by Lucy in the previous chapter), but this need not imply an infant who is affected by (but does not interact with) the materials that surround him or her. Indeed, speculation on the issue of infant–environment interaction provides a starting point for an elaboration of an area within the human sciences that is as promising as it is somewhat sketchy – the 'tacit' or non-propositional, non-discursive forms of awareness and action.

Embodied awareness and embodied security

The literature on neonatology suggests that the auditory environment of the neonatal intensive care unit does not afford entrainment. A neonate's situation is perhaps akin to that of someone attempting to skip rope who encounters an arhythmically turned rope. Without being able to locate some kind of rhythmic regularity (the pace, as discussed above, is normally set by the jumping chants, sung by the rope twirlers), entrainment is impeded. Instead, one must react to each and every fall of the rope, instant upon instant; a 'routinizable' relationship with the environment is not possible since at no level of awareness can one establish a sense of what will happen next. The environment thus produces insecurity, albeit not necessarily recognized as such consciously; it is constantly startling; it does not provide a ground against which one may, with whatever degree of consciousness, regulate self or body. Again, this is the problem discussed above in relation to Gary and Mandy. One cannot locate and employ as resources environmental patterns. These comparisons, between the phenomenological situation of the neonate and the rope skipper are, needless to say, highly speculative, but they are none the less heuristic; they are useful as a way of beginning to explore the bio-pragmatic embodied features of human being at all stages of the life course. This point requires development.

The notion of how one locates or tunes in to environmental properties and how this may have consequences for embodied agency is crucial to any understanding of how music works as an organizing device of the body, how it facilitates 'embodied awareness'. By this term ('embodied awareness') I mean a non-propositional, non-cognitive, *creaturely* orientation and expectancy towards the physical environment. All of us are bodily aware as we organize our actions and behaviour, for example, in our response to water (as something to drink or to be avoided in order to remain dry), ice underfoot, cliff faces, or sunlight versus shade. This kind of awareness is part of what we casually refer to as 'common sense', 'horse sense' and so on. Our capacity for this 'sense' is something we share – to some degree – with other species, as for example when we recognize the cat stretching out on a sunny step, the sheep who avoids a cliff edge, the cattle who avoid electric fences, the caribou who flee when they sense impending danger and so forth. Indeed, there is plenty of evidence that animals are aware of and orient to the sonic environment. Traditionally, for example, Scottish Highland milking songs and rhythmic 'charms' had their place in the cow-byre, where they were thought to increase milk yield, and there are numerous references to music's use for this purpose today. If anything, music's use in the service of animal welfare and/or agricultural productivity seems to be undergoing reappraisal among researchers. For example, a 1998 study, conducted by the National Farmers' Union and the Roslin Institute of the University of Edinburgh concluded that 'playing the radio to chickens is an easy practicable way of enriching their environment and, perhaps, of helping to reduce their fear of new noises' (Jones and Rayner 1999). (Such a practice might, however, also mask the sounds of animals in distress.)

Bodily awareness of environmental properties would appear to be a pragmatic, semi-conscious, matter. It need not involve any reflection or articulation as propositional 'knowledge', though at times it also may do so. For example, those who are able to walk – or walk on a slippery surface – need not think or talk about the physics or physiology of how walking is accomplished and yet they may produce walking as a matter of course. Beings of different kinds thus orient to and organize themselves in relation to environmental properties – for example, the waking–sleep cycle may come to be mapped on to the cycles of daylight and darkness. In this way, environmental patterns come to afford patterns of embodiment and behaviour through the ways they are responded to as entrainment devices.

Music and bodily security

We are now at the point where it is possible to begin to address the question of music's mechanisms of operation, how music may be understood to afford bodily entrainment. I suggest that the creaturely ability to locate and anticipate environmental features engenders a kind of corporeal or embodied security, by which I mean the 'fitting in' or attunement with environmental patterns, fostered by a being's embodied awareness of the materials and properties that characterize his or her environment. Embodied *insecurity*, by contrast, is what happens when one is unable to locate and appropriate such materials, when, like the jump roper, the distressed neonate, or the music therapy clients described above, one is unable to locate resources with or against which to 'gather oneself' into some kind of organized and stable state. Embodied security involves one's ability to *fit in*, or situate oneself, bodily, with an ergonomic environment.

This fitting in is fostered by embodied awareness of the patterns and textures that are to be found in an environment and the opportunities these afford for embodied security, for finding some kind of synchronous connection with an environment. Consider the example of how an infant learns to take nourishment. In order to feed, he or she must 'latch' on to, appropriate, a nipple. An infant's location of the 'right' thing to latch on to for this purpose may involve some trial and error. In light of this locating or appropriation, infants (and animals) may have a similar capacity for embodied awareness of other environmental regularities, including auditory regularities, and that they may come to latch on to these, rather as they do to the material devices of nourishment. With regard to both kinds of latching, a way (note, not necessarily *the* way) is found of synchronizing body with environment; the body and its processes must be articulated with some properties afforded by materials that lie outside it. It is in and through this approximation process that music comes to have effects upon the body, to function as an entrainment device for bodily processes and embodied conduct.

In music, pattern is engendered through regularized relationships between tensions and resolutions, sounds and silences (in Western tonal music through harmony, melody, texture, timbre), and rhythmic arrangements over time that afford expectancy. It seems likely that, for neonates, as for adult humans, latching on to aspects of an auditory environment is afforded by – among other things – perceptible sonic patterns (significant patterns for cultured humans), as found in music and in many other soundscapes – diurnal, cyclical and so forth. (Indeed, feeding is itself a rhythmic activity, one in which baby and mother are entrained.) Moreover, it must be remembered that music is a physical medium, that it consists of sound waves, vibrations that the body may feel even when it cannot hear. The aural is never distinct from the tactile as a sensuous domain.

If music affords a kind of auditory device on to which one can latch in some way or other, in relation to some or other bodily activity or process, then it is a resource for the constitution of embodied security and its properties may afford such security. Just as a feeding event may be structured to encourage or afford latching on to nipple or bottle – upon which feeding is dependent – so, too, a music therapist may structure the environment so that it affords latching on to environmental recurrences – upon which entrainment is dependent. For example, in the case of Baby B, described above, the music used was the 'Transitions' tape, from Placenta Music Inc., an actual recording of the 'intrauterine symphony' overlaid with other sounds.

As an aside, most of the music used so far with neonates has featured gentle rhythm and soothing, low-energy materials. It is interesting to speculate, however, about how 'heavy metal' or serial music would work in relation to neonatal state organization! By way of comparison, heavy metal and jazz were viewed, by the poultry farmers surveyed by Jones and Rayner, to be less effective in the henhouse than chart and easy-listening music – as the authors note, the next step in testing this issue involves allowing the birds an 'opportunity to "switch [music] on and off"' (Jones and Rayner 1999). There are, it would appear, certain cultural assumptions about what is appropriate within these settings that are at work in shaping the musical choices made.

Music has long been used for similar purposes by parents in the form of lullabies, quieting songs and the like (Unyk et al. 1992). Thinking in this way of what the auditory environment may afford for embodied awareness, and for latching, entrainment and its affiliate, embodied security, brings us somewhat closer to unpacking Raymond Williams's intriguing and oft-quoted statement:

rhythm is a way of transmitting a description of experience, in such a way that the experience is re-created in the person receiving it, not merely as an 'abstraction' or an emotion but as a physical effect on the organism – on the blood, on the breathing, on the physical patterns of the brain. We use rhythm for many ordinary purposes, but the arts . . . comprise highly developed and exceptionally powerful rhythmic means, by which the communication of experience is actually achieved . . . the dance of the body, the movements of the voice, the sounds of instruments are, like colours, forms and patterns, means of transmitting our experience in so powerful a way that the experience can literally be lived by others. This has been felt, again and again, in the actual experience of the arts, and we are now beginning to see how and why it is more than a metaphor; it is a physical experience as real as any other. (1965:40–1)

More questions

The work on neonates points to music as an organizing device, one that is implicated in state transformation. Latching on to musical properties (in so far as they are objects of embodied awareness), an infant may become entrained in relation to these properties. To be entrained in this way is to be launched upon a bodily trajectory; the infant's bodily (physiological and micro-behavioural) state comes to be patterned, rhythmically and, more broadly, bodily stylistically, in some relation to the auditory environment. This environment – including aspects of the material-cultural environment – can thus be seen as involved directly with – as a resource mobilized in and for – the formulation and translation of so-called 'endogenous' bodily states. Documenting this involvement helps dissolve the endogenous/exogenous dichotomy. No longer axiomatic, the question of where the body 'ends' and the environment 'begins' is converted from a resource – 'the' body and 'its' processes – into a topic for (situated) research on body constitution. The body – its limits, processes, capacities, thresholds – is reconceived as an emergent and flexible entity, as reflexively linked to the material-cultural environment and what that environment may afford. This shift in conceptualizing the body–environment relationship reformulates that relationship in a new key, one in which the conventional medical notion of the body – a bounded and objectivized entity characterized by endogenous properties – is reconceived as a literary trope, an artefact of discourse and its *a priori* parameters, its ways of seeing.

At the same time, it would be absurd to attempt to claim that the body is not 'real' in its displayed properties, for, as Philip Larkin once put it (1964), 'our flesh surrounds us with its own decisions'. It is, however, reasonable to suggest that, to the extent that bodily properties are reflexively constituted in relation to the body's connection to a range of other materials, the body/environment divide can be replaced by a concern with how 'bodies' are configured. This alternative (and interdisciplinary) perspective illuminates bodily states and forms of embodied agency as produced through the body's interaction with and abilities to appropriate environmental materials – materials that can be perhaps best understood as resources for the constitution of particular states over time and social space. To speak of body/environment interaction in this way is by no means to depict actors (bodies) as 'conscious' or 'deliberate' in their mobilization of environmental properties and affordances; to the contrary, as illustrated in the case of music therapy clients and neonates, bodies and agents are often caught within circumstances where they have to make do with available environmental properties and, under some circumstances and for some purposes, these properties may be useless, unconducive. Thus, the body's states are reflexively linked to the settings where the body is created, maintained and changed. Such a perspective is by no means new – it is, in fact, merely a cultural constructivist extension of the idea that bodies continually appropriate environmental materials (air, water, temperature and so forth) for a myriad of state maintenance activities, normally classified under headings such as biological and social psychological. This perspective is one that points to the active role of cultural materials in relation to state constitution and maintenance, one that seeks to develop a cultural-ecological perspective for the sociology of the body conceived as a continually renewable, temporal, configuration.

Still, there is a way to go before the 'key questions' alluded to earlier, concerning music's role in relation to the body, are addressed properly. We need more extended examples of what it means, at the level of real-time, spatially located existence, to speak of musical latching, and we need to illustrate in far greater detail what it means to describe music as an ordering device of bodily process. One way to begin to explore this process is through an investigation of body–music interactions as they occur in real time. Indeed, there have been calls for this investigative strategy from within music therapy (for example, 'future research should also consider moment-to-moment interactions with the music and the effect of this on physiological process' (Maranto 1993:167)). Only here can we begin to observe bodies as they latch on to and become entrained by musical devices.

To further these issues I now turn to an exceptional venue for pursuing music's role as an entrainment device, as a means for organizing the body: the realm of music and movement exercise. I look, in particular, at aerobics, where music is overtly employed as a device of state regularization, a means for structuring and restructuring motivation, movement, energy and the self-perception of fatigue in relation to predetermined aims and over time. My discussion draws upon an ethnography of music's role during the forty-five-minute period of an aerobic exercise class. This work was carried out by Sophie Belcher, the research assistant on the music and daily life project between 1997–8 at Exeter (Belcher and DeNora forthcoming; Belcher and DeNora 1998). Over a year, between 1997 and 1998, Belcher attended aerobic classes in South Devon (mainly

'hi/lo' but also 'step aerobics', 'toning' and 'total body workout'), conducted in-depth interviews and quick questionnaires and interviewed
production managers from leading (United Kingdom) aerobic music
firms. We began by posing the following questions: does music afford
aerobic agency and, if so, what does it take, musically, to create and
sustain that body over the course of a forty-five-minute aerobic exercise
session? Do some types of music provide better organizing devices for
aerobic order than others?

A naturally occurring experiment

One way of knowing what it takes to produce forms of organization is
through perspective by incongruity, by looking at the conditions associated with disorder, with breakdown. The value of 'troubles' and breakdowns of order within the social sciences is mostly untapped in this
regard, at least outside the areas of conversation analysis, ethnomethodology and, more recently, participatory design (as applied, for example, to
software systems).

In recent years, the study of breakdowns has been used to bring to light
many non-discursive, non-propositional and embodied practices that
computer users may not be able to describe verbally (Ehn 1988;
Winograd and Flores 1986; Bødker and Grønbaeck 1984). The study of
breakdowns has also been used to identify the ways in which organizational cultural materials come to afford work and organizational knowledge.

Transferred to the study of aerobics, a focus on breakdowns is a route,
from the so-called 'natural world', into the question of music's role as an
ordering device of embodied agency. We can compare, for example, the
music of 'good' (that is, aerobically organized) sessions with sessions of
aerobic disorder to explore music as it contributes to 'disorder' and to
'order'. In this way it is possible to illuminate the musical characteristics
that afford aerobic embodied agency, that enable the particular bodily
movements, endurance, motivation, arousal and co-ordination, and that
constrain the perception of fatigue. These features are what characterize
good or orderly aerobic execution, the situation where bodies are able to
maintain and pass through vigorous and varied movement styles over the
course of a forty-five-minute session. Aerobic disorder, by contrast, is
characterized by bodies that trip themselves up, cannot reproduce the
correct steps, get exhausted and have to stop, or are otherwise distracted
from the competent execution, ideally with gusto and with pleasure, of
the dance routine. For example, consider this example from the field
notes of one of several sessions where 'breakdown' occurred.

[T]he moves were incredibly simple yet somehow nearly all of us just couldn't get it together . . . when I scanned the room there were people totally out of synch with the routine and the music . . . about a third [of the] way into the class . . . the group was all over the place, not following the routine, out of synch, standing still and generally looking perplexed. It was also soon after this that I noticed the two women in front of me, who were regulars who usually took things very seriously, were having a conversation with one another and laughing. (Belcher n.d.)

Thus, as with neonatology and its checklist of physiological and micro-behaviours that characterize stable state organization, aerobics, too, has its checklist. Because of its high degree of rationalization (the highly gendered character of aerobics and its 'totalizing' character has been well remarked upon elsewhere (Martin 1997; Whitson 1994)), it is possible to specify versions of aerobic 'order' – bodily and situational – in some detail. This distinguishes aerobics from most of the situations and scenes that constitute daily life and, indeed, most other sports where 'in play' details (for example, how or whether a footballer achieves a goal) are not fixed in advance. By contrast, the body–temporal parameters of aerobic order are pre-scripted and deviations from that order are censured by a (typically) vigilant session leader and her or his continual calls and prompts. These pre-scripted parameters consist, within 'hi/lo' aerobics, of choreographed movements (for example, individual kicks or steps) that are in turn grouped into chunks and then into an overall sequential structure or aerobic 'grammar'. This grammar consists of basic phases, which are in turn characterized by the speed of the exercise, its degree of vigour, its style of movement and its mode of aerobic subject/body, that is the mode of embodied agency required for the 'good' execution of the phase. Thus, most forty-five-minute sessions (the equivalent of one side of a ninety-minute cassette tape) are divided into sequentially organized stages, each characterized by a specific form of movement and energy level. To the extent that each of these components is associated with a mode of embodied agency, the aerobic actor is reconfigured as an agent in real time as he or she passes through the various stages of the session. This is to say that, at different times during a session, actors are configured as different types of subject/bodies, with, for example, greater or lesser degrees of cognitive awareness, emotionality and gender identification. In the terminology of aerobics, these components are:

> *Warm-up* (slower, gentler lower impact movements, designed to get the body moving, literally warming up and heart rate slightly elevated), roughly ten minutes.
>
> *Pre-core* (music that shifts into faster higher impact movements), roughly five minutes.

Core (faster, more vigorous, involving higher impact, for example, leaping – the 'hardest' part of the session), roughly fifteen minutes.

Cool-down (slowed movements, less vigorous leading to very slow floor exercises such as sit ups at the end of the session), roughly five minutes.

Floor exercises (slow toning exercises, such as stomach crunches and sit ups), roughly ten minutes.

Comparing a good (that is, aerobically ordered) and highly typical session with a session (with the same class members) where aerobic order was subject to decay highlights many of the ways in which music is a device of aerobic ordering. Using this quasi- or natural experimental format helps to bring into relief some of the ways that music provides a device of bodily ordering in real time, as described in the following sections. First, however, it is necessary to describe the ways in which the aerobics music production companies orient to aerobics' generic grammar and try to embed particular scenarios of music use within the musical product itself.

Composing (for) the users – commercial musical profiles of music use

To be sure, music is prominent as an orientational device within any aerobic session. Produced and distributed by commercial music outlets such as Pure Energy, Music Xpress, Power Productions, Koreography Klub and Muscle Mixes, the music used in aerobic classes is oriented to highly specific circumstances, to particular segments of aerobic grammar. Perhaps not surprisingly, not unlike the Muzak corporation and other firms that produce music for ambience, aerobic music companies catalogue their stock by affect and intended use and in ways that make music's position within the aerobic grammar clear. Moreover, it is standard to involve 'fitness professionals' in the production process where they may select particular numbers and advise about where in the aerobic grammar such numbers are best placed.

For example, cassettes entitled 'Motivation', which are designed for use in the warm-up, maintain a beats-per-minute rate of 130–8, while 'Body Blitz' or 'Energy Workout', with a bpm of 140–6, are employed during the core. Cool-down numbers tend to hover at around 130 bpm and are classified under the heading 'Relaxation'.

Beyond beats per minute, aerobic music firms select and tailor the musical and stylistic features of individual numbers. One of the first things they try to do is heighten rhythmic clarity. Rhythm is typically positioned in the musical foreground, with vocals often relegated to the background. Features that might detract from this clarity (for example, complicated transitions) are deleted. The music is also entirely synthesized, which also adds to its sometimes almost surreal or hyperreal clarity (for example, no real group of musicians could produce the almost sterile sharpness of attack and release, of rapid tutti passages). These firms also try to match musical materials such as melodic patterns or formulae, genre, orchestration or particular gestural devices to particular phases and movement demands within a workout. Thirdly, most of the vocal tracks in aerobic music are sung by female voices, often pitched at or near the top of the female vocal range. A related point, the upper or higher dimensions of melody and harmony are typically positioned as the musical telos; melodies and harmonies press up and lift in ways that are homologous with the gravity resistant physical practices of aerobics.

Played at full volume throughout nearly the whole of a session, the musical features of aerobics are thus designed to provide much more than mere 'backdrop' to aerobic proceedings, and they contribute much more than the all-important grounding of beats per minute. In aerobics, music is expressly designed to be placed in the *foreground* as a device of body constitution and bodily organization, a device upon which body co-ordination and conduct may be mapped. Not only 'good to think with', music is also 'good to embody with'. This capacity of music, to afford bodily agency, draws upon certain 'exosemantic' correspondences, as Richard Middleton calls them, conventional within Western music and capitalized upon by aerobics firms:

Music is often felt to 'symbolize' awareness of time (through tempo and rhythmic structure) and space (through pitch-height relationships, and intensity and textural contrasts). We think of pitch going 'up' and 'down'; sounds being 'closer' or more 'distant'; rhythm as being 'in time', 'late', 'out of phase', and so on. Connotations relating to other senses are often attached (thus 'high' sounds are 'light', 'bright', 'clear') and so are emotions (usually related to tension/relaxation schemas); and images of movement are usually involved, too: we have already met many 'gestures', and equations of musical rhythms and body rhythms (walking, breathing, heartbeat, and so on) are commonplace. (Middleton 1990:225)

In aerobics, music defines the components of a session through its tempo changes (for example, music for warm-up, core and cool-down) and it also profiles the bodily movements associated with each of these components. This profile is achieved through the ways that musical materials – melody, rhythm, gesture, genre – are deployed. In this sense, music is a device in the foreground, a means of affording aerobic entrainment. Here, music works at what Richard Middleton refers to as the level of 'primary signification' (1990:220–32). Drawing upon Jakobson's theory of syntagmatic equivalence (1960) and Eco's (1984) notion of syntactic or grammatical signification, Middleton refers here to music's internal references and relationships, its arrangement of structural elements, to the ways in which its relationships become terms in which to map, frame and configure (in this case) the figure of the body ('as this note is to that note, as tonic is to dominant, as ascent is to descent, as accent is to weak beat (and so on), so X is to Y' (1990:223)). Music here is a medium of describing 'how' – how to move, how to think, how to include, how to begin, how to end, how to mingle.

But music also works at the level of what Middleton calls, 'secondary signification' – its connotative level – where it serves as a motivational device of bodily conduct, and where it may be said to profile a range of subject positions associated with aerobic grammar – modes of being as described in chapter 3, above, characterized by levels of arousal, emotional-stylistic orientation and bodily-gestural action such as the pace, force and style of movements and its stages of embodied agency. Thus, and this point is key, over the course of a session, the musically implied aerobic body is configured, reconfigured, composed and de-composed as it is passed through and transformed by the series of changes that constitute aerobics and its grammar. Following aerobics' musical changes and the ways in which real bodies interact with prescripted musical bodily changes, bodily changes allow us to examine the body, moment by moment, as it interacts with, and is configured in relation to, music. (This music is, moreover, expressly designed to configure the body in specific ways.) To illustrate this point, the following discussion describes music as it can be used to facilitate and/or hinder the body's passage through the components of aerobic order and its grammar, from warm-up, to core, to cool-down. The discussion draws on one typically good aerobic session and its music, which is laid out in figure 4, and makes reference to one – also typical – session as described above, where aerobic order broke down.

'Let the music move you up and down' – the warm-up

'Let's say I'm doing the warm-up,' says Sarah, the instructor whose weekly classes we studied and videotaped over the course of a year. 'You want quite catchy music because some of them [the class] are just not in the mood and if you've just got the drumming noise then you think, "Oh, what the hell's going on." But I do it to motivate people.' Later in the same interview, she elaborates this point: 'Let's say I've had a load of people who aren't really up for it and I've chosen a tape that's like OK, you find them just lolling around . . .' Sarah says here that at the beginning of a

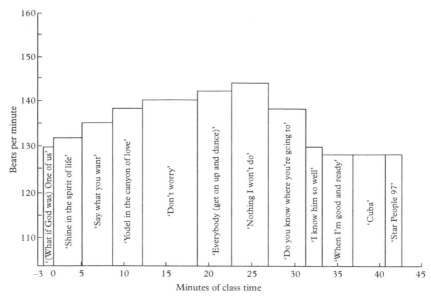

Figure 4. A 'good' aerobics session – music and beats per minute over time. −3 to 0 is 'prep-time'.

session, when the body has yet to 'get going' (that is, moving vigorously and repetitively), class members are less receptive to music that is constituted primarily by a vigorous, 'up top' beat. Coming in (literally) cold and off the street, class members are more readily aroused by catchy music that appeals to them on a variety of planes simultaneously: lyrics, melodies, rhythms, orchestration. This is one reason why Sarah makes use of several (relatively short) numbers within the warm-up phase of a session, on the principle that a variety of musical devices will provide at least one that participants will relate to, that will 'tune them in'. Akin to the function of an *antipasto* course in a Mediterranean meal, good warm-up music provides a kind of transition between two social scenes, and two different kinds of bodily energies, namely aerobic ('geared up') and everyday.

As with the start of a meal, the initiating materials of the warm-up (recall that the aerobic music catalogues refer to this music as 'motivational') are meant for what Michel Callon (1986) calls *interessement*. These pieces aim to interpose class members between aerobic and extra-aerobic realities and so lead to their enrolment into the former, to *launch* them, imaginatively and physically, upon an aerobic trajectory, along the rhythm of aerobic grammar. (For a non-theoretical but highly informative discussion of this issue from within sports science, see Gluch 1993.)

Another way of talking about this is to speak again of latching – the multi-dimensional appeal of warm-up music is designed to encourage a class member to latch on to the beginning of the aerobic trajectory, to arouse the class member aerobically, in a manner similar to the way in which the *antipasto* 'wakes up' the palate and arouses gustatory faculties.

In breakdown sessions where aerobic order was not strongly established, one of the greatest problems was class members' inability to latch on to the music, to 'get into' or locate its aerobic affordances in ways that produced musical entrainment. For example, in the 'disordered' session described above, where the regular instructor, Sarah, was ill and was replaced by a substitute, the warm-up track began in the same way that it continued, with a low-key melodic figure that repeatedly moved from the tonic of the scale (that is, 'do' of 'do, re, mi') up to the subdominant note of the scale ('fa') and then back again in a syncopated rhythm. The vocalist (female) was not introduced until a few *minutes* into the track (not the usual introduction of, say, 20–30 seconds maximum before a singer begins).

Commenting on this music in an interview (we played a number of examples that had been used in previous classes and asked for comment on each), a regular class member said she thought the example (which she did not recognize) would probably be best suited to the earlier part of the class because of its tempo ('more, sort of towards the warm-up, maybe, but not part of the main bit'). But she added that the piece was 'quite repetitive, I can imagine doing something repetitive, but because the beat "changes" [she emphasizes this word], if it wasn't something repetitive [that is, a repetitive form of movement] I'd just get lost'. She also suggested that aspects of the syncopated rhythm would have to be ignored because they would lead to confusion, because they did not profile movement clearly. This point raises an issue revisited below: class members are not passive recipients, acted upon by music, but are active sense-makers trying to use or appropriate music, agents who *try their best* to work with available materials, who are engaged in human–music interaction.

Aerobics instructors also contribute to this interaction, through their varying levels of knowledge and practical skill. Like the women discussed in the previous chapter who engage in musically reflexive practice for the projection of self, aerobics instructors, too, employ musical reflexive skills, they mobilize and deploy musical materials for specific purposes. These skills will vary from instructor to instructor. Some instructors engage minimally with the music, simply putting on a prerecorded tape and letting it play at a constant volume. Others (such as the one who led the disastrous session) hardly think about the role played by music – they just put on a tape and begin. Yet others (such as Sarah) switch tapes frequently, often employing a dual tape machine so they can blend one number into the next. They may, also like Sarah, alter the volume over the course of a session, use their voice tone and rhythm (when giving instructions) in ways that are also rhetorical (for example, 'Keep-it UP' (shouted with rising voice tone)), and give considerable thought to the links between music and choreography. (It was also not uncommon for Sarah to stop a particular track, shouting out to the class, 'Bad music!' and quickly substitute a different number when she sensed that the music was not working, not having the desired effect on the class and its movement.)

The point here is that music does not just act on the body. Its effects are the result of a lot of work oriented to fitting musical material to movement style. First, music production firms draw upon scenarios of use as they produce individual tracks and tapes. Secondly, instructors draw upon those tapes in practical circumstances and modify them through devices such as those described above. Thirdly, class members may 'do their best' to work with the musical materials they are given, ignoring some confusing aspect or focusing on something that keeps them in step or gets them going. Thus, to say that music will 'cause' things to happen, that it makes the body do things or that its objective properties will automatically entrain the body in particular ways, is to miss the collaborative dimension of how music's effectiveness is achieved, for it is always in and through the ways that it is appropriated that music provides structuring resources – devices that enable and constrain the body. Music provides environmental materials that may be *used* in ways that 'afford' different bodily capacities. But, at the same time, different types of musical materials themselves may afford the entrainment processes associated with aerobic exercise to varying degrees, as aerobic music firms are well aware. What, then, do some of these devices look like and how do they work?

Packaging and repackaging music; packaging and repackaging bodies

It is significant that breakdowns were more likely to occur when the music used was not expressly designed for aerobics sessions. For example, the music used by the substitute teacher described above (and classified as 'difficult' by class members) came from the instructor's private collection of dance tracks. As one of the class members put it, on the actual evening when the 'bad' session occurred, 'I find, like music tonight, I find very difficult because there were lots of different beats going on at once . . . and I'd be subconsciously listening to one and then I'd switch to another and I'd lose what we were doing' (conversation reconstructed from Belcher's fieldnotes). The music was not providing, this member suggests, a clear signal, one upon which the exercise moves could be mapped. As suggested earlier, what went wrong here was that the music did not afford latching; it did not make it easy to organize physical movement, to entrain and align that movement with music. The key reason for this was that the musical materials themselves did not overtly profile movement. The musical tracks provided no mnemonic rhythm for movement; they did not profile the movement of the routine. And without this rhythm, not only was co-ordination difficult; movement was laboured, uninteresting because it was not lodged in any devices of musical-aerobic arousal. (Another reason, and one that highlights how music's effects are produced through human–music interactions, was that the instructor did not use her voice to highlight music's rhythmic and stylistic affordances. She did not, for example, bellow out commands in synch with the music's rhythm or to tide over musical sections as Sarah did.)

A related feature of the problem session's music was monotony. This problem was perhaps most acute with the onset of fatigue, during the core of the session. Unlike the music normally used by Sarah, the music used here did not 'package' itself into interlinked modules; that is, it did not present a collection of diverse and interesting sonic sub-structures. Instead, the repetitiveness of the movements was *underlined* by the repetitiveness of the music, a strategy that opened the session to the perception of grinding on. Moreover, the repetition helped to construct a sense of not going anywhere. Qualitative musical features, then, such as repetition versus variation, would appear to have implications for the self-perception of bodily states. In the context of aerobics, 'sameness' did not divert, did not help take one's mind off discomfort and fatigue. Its failure to offer virtual diversions (to create a sense of varied musical terrain) resulted in the construction of 'real' fatigue.

This point has been discussed within sports medicine. Within the literature on cognitive strategies (see Okwumabua 1983), it has been suggested that less-seasoned athletes perform better when they employ 'dissociative cognitive strategies', that is, when they are able to move away from continual monitoring of their internal states (Spink and Longhurst 1986) and focus instead on a 'non-performance' related activity or topic. Dissociative strategies and their effects highlight 'energy' as at least in part a function of bodily self-perception (of fatigue and of expended effort). Cultural materials, music in this case, can serve to frame or refocus self-perception and body awareness such that fatigue and effort are minimized or fade into the background. In relation to physical exertion, then, 'the body' is a performative entity; what is not self-perceived (for example, fatigue) does not, for all practical purposes, exist.

Figure 5. 'Don't worry' (aerobics music)

Returning to the issue of musical repetition versus variation, dissocia-
tion from the repetitive and tiring movement involved in exercise can be
achieved by using music that has been 'chunked' or bunched into interrelated movements or musical units. Such units in turn package exercise
moves into temporal and (perceived) spatial components ('current to
next', 'here to there'); they have the capacity to tuck or enfold a series of
repetitive movements into a rhythmic package that translates their perceived effort. Indeed, this is one of the standard features of professionally
produced aerobic music. These components are, at the musical level,
interlinked such that one leads to the next and such that one is musically
fulfilled in the next. These structures are achieved, for example, through
cadences and closures, through the generation and resolution of harmonic suspense, through upward or cyclic melodic movement (see figure
5) and through modulation upwards to higher keys. Interlinked series of
tonal and rhythmic structures in turn may be used to seduce bodies to
keep moving, to move on up or move on into the next level, the next unit.
This is one way that they profile movement and present that movement as
being musically attainable and desirable (for example, 'this bit is interesting, let's move on to try the next bit'). Through such interlinked but
varied sections, aerobic actors are offered musical materials that afford
continual relatching and ongoing re-enlistment as musical-aerobic
agents.

    Another way of conceptualizing this re-enlistment is to think of music
as a contrast structure (Smith 1987; 1992; Woolgar 1988) against which
the figure of one's own body is configured such that the reality of each and
every movement (and the ways these subtract energy) is recontextualized
as part of a greater structure (the musical structure) that one wishes to
complete. The musical contrast structure, and the body's role within this
structure, then translates the self-perception of fatigue and converts it
into energy; the musical background 'tricks' that perception in a manner
not unlike the way in which perception of movement may be tricked when
one is on a stationary train and the train on the adjacent platform begins
to move. Against the contrast structure of the moving train, one may have
a virtual sense of moving. Similarly, bodily perception, fostered by the
contrast structure of chunked music, translates and minimizes the sense

Figure 6. 'Yodelling in the canyon of love' (aerobics music)

of 'effort expansion' in an aerobic session and magnifies the sense one has of power (for example, moving in the virtual, musical, space, one may have the sense of moving continually upward, or of taking 'giant's steps'). This musically translated sense is enabling, empowering; it has a direct effect on the bodily properties of energy, motivation and endurance.

Here, then, is how music may be understood to have power over bodies: it affords materials – structures, patterns, parameters and meanings – that bodies may appropriate or latch on to (mostly semi-consciously). Music is, in short, a material against which to shape up bodily processes, whether these are physiological states (such as exhaustion or arousal), behavioural movements (such as kicking or jumping), co-ordination in some setting (dance steps), self-perception of bodily state (pain or fatigue, pleasure), or motivational levels (being predisposed, in some embodied way, to a particular line of activity, such as, moving faster, jumping higher, slowing down and so on). Music accomplishes none of these things in its own right – it is not a 'force' like gravity or wave power. It is rather a potential 'source' of bodily powers, a resource for the generation of bodily agency. Music is, or rather can serve as, a constitutive property of bodily being.

Gearing up and staying up – musical devices

One of the most crucial stages in an aerobics workout is the pre-core or transition phase, where class members 'change gear' and begin to engage in the strenuous 'power moves' characteristic of the core of the session. It is in this pre-core stage that class members must, if they conform to the preordained aerobic order, leave behind the more workaday movements and gentler, fluid patterns of the warm-up. In the course of the ethnography, it became clear that some music was especially suited to this purpose. One of these was a number entitled, 'Yodelling in the canyon of love'. This piece, a paragon of postmodern aesthetics with its jumble of cultures and musical discourses (the piece features a *mélange* of Latin rhythm, yodelling and cow bells), makes copious use of a cha-cha-cha figure (see figure 6). Although this repeated figure passes each time in an instant, its effects were powerful. Like a hinge or switch, the figure shifted class members into a mode of moving and orienting to musical materials commensurate with the core. Its use illuminates clearly music's ability to profile movement style and to instigate movement trajectory.

In tandem with Sarah's choreography at this stage, the figure offers a kind of musical 'hop' (the cha-cha-cha figure) that in turn encourages the body, which, according to the preordained choreography, is required to hop in synchrony with it. The rhythm thus provides a model for bodily action, one that also entrains the body and encourages it to begin a 'hi-impact' routine. In this respect, the cha-cha-cha figure places on offer to class participants a type of motivational material qualitatively different from that used in the earlier warm-up music. In the latter, the *antipasto* of the session, lyrics, melodic-associative figures and musical colour are characteristic. Here, by contrast, the source of motivation is relocated at the level of a contagious rhythm and this relocation may be understood as a shift away from the more sentimental (and more cognitive), physically less demanding modality of aerobic agency afforded by typical warm-up music, where lyrics (often about romance or about the idea of movement, such as, 'Everybody get on up and dance') are most likely to be positioned in the foreground – the musical foreground and the foreground of attention. In the music of the aerobic core, focus is deliberately shifted to the *physicality* of the musical beat. This shift in focus from imagery to beat and rhythm is a deliberate design feature of aerobic music for the core. It is in turn appropriated by instructors in their attempts, at the end of the warm-up, to transform – or in Callon's (1986) terms, 'translate' – class members into fully committed exercisers, into bodies who will execute, for a gruelling ten or fifteen minutes, 'power' moves.

The 'Yodelling' track thus affords a conversion from 'warming up' to 'warmed up'. It helps to induce in class members the embodied desire to 'hop' – that is, to put, for the first time in the session, a bounce or skip in their step. In so doing they become less self-conscious, more meditatively engaged in the exercise, and as this happens, the musical materials become increasingly rhythmical, less melodic, so that for part of the number they are little more than a clear and relentless beat. If the music has done its work at this stage, class members are most fully enlisted or conscripted as aerobic agents; here the 'doing' of aerobics is all-encompassing: as the Zen expression has it, 'not a thought arises'. At this moment, within 'good' aerobics, music facilitates, in Mauss's (1979 [1934]) sense, techniques of the body (Lash and Urry 1994:45–6).

In sum, over the first half of the aerobics class the music's quality changes: specific musical devices are introduced, gradually and imperceptibly, to induce participants to 'get into the rhythm' so that they come to do what the earlier warm-up music told them to do with its lyrics ('let the music move you up and down'). Class members are aware of this at some level. As one woman put it (in an interview), '[music] can make me work harder . . . if it's just a simple strong beat then it's easier to work with . . . and if it very slowly gets faster [see again figure 4 to note tempo changes over time] I don't sort of realize it'.

Cooling off and shifting down – from 'body' to 'heart' to the 'calculus' of the crunch

'Shifting down' is an important phase in the grammar of good aerobics, as important as 'shifting up' into the core. Here, too, music affords this bodily process. At this stage, well-known ballads often make an appearance, albeit remixed by the aerobic music firms, so as to possess a rhythmic pulse that moves at twice the pace of the original melody (the result is a *slow* melody in the foreground, set against a background that moves in double time). The tempi of these ballads are not only slower than the numbers within the aerobics core; they can also be seen to afford a shifting of motivational focus yet again, from the meditatively 'bodied' mode of the core (little thinking or feeling and much moving) back to a more self-conscious, and more sentimental, mode post-core. Their elements are repositioned: familiar melodies and lyrics are brought back to the fore, and rhythm is relegated to the background. Through this, and through the use of musical and lyrical sentiment (recognizable and overtly sentimental ballads whose lyrics describe philosophical matters – 'Do you know where you're going to?' – or 'relationship' issues, such as 'I know him so well' from the musical *Chess*), bodies are, as it were, encouraged to cool off physically and to recalibrate emotionally. The aim, here, overtly stated within the prescribed order of an aerobics session, is to prime class members for the final stage of the workout where they must engage in a highly calculative mode as deliberate, rational executioners of precision-engineered exercises such as 'the crunch' (for abdominal firming) and other floor exercises such as sit ups, reverse curls, triceps dips, ski squeezes, press ups and leg raises. All of these moves are executed in conjunction with copious instructions from the class leader.

Slowing down and cooling down are, according to Sarah (and also as discussed in aerobic exercise manuals), prerequisites to doing floor exercises. Because precision is required (if injury is to be avoided), musical arousal, so crucial during the core, and especially late core, becomes, during floor exercises, a liability. Accordingly, at this stage, the music's volume is lowered, not, as one might think, for the simple reason that instructions can be *heard* (Sarah's voice projects exceptionally well, and has been heard throughout the session) but, rather, to dampen class members' motivation to move quickly and vigorously, and so to enable the mental calculation about what the body is doing (for example, 'Am I moving in precisely the right way?'). Here is how Sarah explains it:

Q. When you turn the volume down, when you are at the end and you do the stomach work, why do you do that?
   Sarah: Because you don't need it, you don't want them as motivated do you?
   Q. Right.
   Sarah: When they're doing sit ups also you need a lot of teaching points with the sit ups as well [i.e., you need them to be oriented to your verbal utterances] and you just need it for a beat not to motivate them or any way really so [i.e., just to keep in a regular rhythm, not to generate and sustain high energy].

Even Sarah's voice is modulated in this section to emphasize the 'mental' modality of cool-down. Throughout the core of the session she typically uses a loud voice, one that makes use of a good deal of long, drawn-out tones, snappy rhythms and latching-type figures to spur on class members. Here, by contrast, she speaks, rather than bellows, in an ordinary voice tone – one that sounds low-key, authoritative, even clinical. This return to cognitive consciousness is also a returning of the class member to the embodied modality (the tension levels, energy and exertion levels and motivational levels) of everyday life in modern societies (Witkin 1995:206). Many of them, for example, will be *driving* home from class.

Thus, over the course of forty-five minutes, music is used in an aerobic session to configure and reconfigure bodies and emotional-cognitive modalities as the aerobic agent is initially enlisted by the warm-up tracks (that feature emotional, romantic and fluid musical materials), launched on a trajectory of 'pure' movement during the core (where the beat occupies nearly all of the musical space) and 'cooled down' (recognitivized, resentimentalized, slowed down) into the more cognitive and less energetic mode associated with the precise forms of exercise at the end of the session.

Music as a prosthetic technology of the body

Music is an accomplice of body configuration. It is a technology of body building, a device that affords capacity, motivation, co-ordination, energy and endurance. In the case of aerobic exercise, it is possible to identify some of the specific musical materials that work, in real time, upon the body, materials that have been designed and can be appropriated for specific bodily ends. As specified in the discussion of a real-time aerobic session, these devices assume the guise of tempi, figures and gestures (rhythmic and melodic), harmonic structures, voicing, rhythmic/melodic packaging and chunking, genre. Observing them at work over forty-five minutes shows how music is much more than a mere accompaniment to aerobic movement, how it is constitutive of aerobic agency. To the extent that musical figures can be seen and documented, in real time, as configuring aerobic agency, music may be understood as having active, structuring properties on and for the body. Within an aerobic workout, music disciplines the body's performative character, configuring and transfiguring the body over the course of a session. Musical materials may, on the one hand, afford aerobic order, that is bodies that are aerobically disciplined, entrained, meditative, motivated and energetic, or, on the other hand, they may afford aerobic disorder, where bodies are undisciplined, unentrained, fatigued and unco-ordinated.

As a primary and predominant aesthetic material, music may be conceived, following Ehn's (1988:399) discussion of Weizenbaum (1976), as a 'prosthetic technology'. Prosthetic technologies are materials that extend what the body can do – for example, steam shovels, stilts, microscopes or amplification systems enhance and transform the capacities of arms, legs, eyes and voices. Through the creation and *use* of such technologies actors (bodies) are enabled and empowered, their capacities are enhanced. With such technologies, actors can do things that cannot be done independently; they are capacitated in and through their ability to appropriate what such technologies afford.

Music prosthetic technology and daily life

Neither aerobic workouts nor life in a neonatal intensive care unit are ordinary circumstances. Both are totalizing. The aim of aerobics is to inculcate a high degree of physical and emotional conformity. As in ballet or in a military parade, aerobics' parameters of experience are globally imposed. Body discipline in aerobics is stringent. In neonatal ICUs, bodily order is also globally imposed through a range of medical technologies that modify and substitute for normally autonomous bodily processes. Music's role in the ICU is to afford state organization, to provide a ground against which embodied awareness, orientation to and entrainment with the environment may occur.

Most of everyday life and its scenes and situations resemble neither aerobics classes nor intensive care units. None the less, music can be seen to function as a prosthetic device, to provide organizing properties for a range of other embodied experiences and in ways that involve varying degrees of deliberation and conscious awareness on the part of music's conscripts. One of the most interesting areas here involves music's role in the world of work. To be sure, music's role at work has changed under industrialization, and this is a crucial issue for critical sociology. (These critical issues are discussed in the next chapter.)

Music has, historically, been deeply implicated as a way of specifying not only the time it takes to conduct work processes, but also in profiling the physical manner in which tasks are executed. Examples of music's role in relation to daily tasks abound in non-Western cultures. For example, Nkeita (1988 (see also Gregory 1997:125)) describes the way in which Ghanaian grass cutters work to musical accompaniment. There, music actually enhances the speed with which the work is accomplished. In Western culture, one of the best examples of music's prosthetic capability can be found among Hebridean weavers. On the isle of Harris, music was clearly an instrument of tweed production in so far as it was used to regulate production processes (Lomax 1968; Nettl 1990:67). So-called 'waulking' songs, for example, were sung while going through the motions of hand-shrinking the cloth, a process that involves pulling and beating the cloth, moving from one end of the bolt to the other. As in aerobics, repetitive movements are inserted into a larger rhythmic structure, a structure that, potentially, can diminish the weaver's perceived effort and also helps to organize production's schedule (how long to handle the cloth for, the qualitative and quantitative dimensions of handling). There are numerous waulking songs in the Hebridean repertoire (far more than there are songs for other stages in the tweed production process, such as raising the pile of the wool). The volume of songs is related to the weavers' belief that imperfections would result if the same song were sung twice over one piece of cloth. While this belief is often regarded as mere superstition, there may also have been *practical* reasons for the custom. The songs not only governed the time it would take to deal with a whole piece of cloth but also profiled bodily motions; the music profiled the rhythm and style of movement over the length of the cloth. Altering the song for each repetition back along a length of cloth would ensure that the strength, pace and distance of the moves were varied, that hands did not simply repeat their movements in reverse along the cloth. Varying the songs thus provided a way of distributing movement over the cloth and hence ensuring an even texture in the finished product. In this way, music affords both production and skill; the worker is able to constitute herself as an embodied, productive agent and to engage in the skilled production of her work in and through reference to the music and the way in which it affords these things.

Another area of traditional work where music can be seen to provide a prosthetic technology is on the high seas. 'To the seamen of America, Britain, and northern Europe', writes Stan Hugill, 'a shanty was as much a part of the equipment as a sheath-knife and a pannikin' (1961:1). Shanties were used for a variety of specialized tasks on board a ship – hauling sails and heaving heavy weights such as the anchor. As with weaving and aerobics, these songs mapped or profiled bodily movement so as to entrain the physical process of work. ('Blow the man down', for example, is composed of alternating solo and chorus lines. During the solo line, the crew rested. They pulled or hauled as they sang the refrain, thus engaging in 'strength' moves while exhaling.) Hauling songs, such as 'Blow the man down', were set traditionally in 6/8 time, whereas heaving songs were typically in 4/4 or marching rhythms. Songs with longer verses, such as 'Shenandoah', were used for lengthy tasks. Here, too, superstitions abounded; there were traditional prohibitions against singing these songs on land. Again, there may have been practical reasons for this prohibition; perhaps, sung too frequently out of the physical context of ship work, the songs might have been altered and their affordances compromised. Perhaps, too, their motivational force would have been numbed through over-familiarity.

As an interesting aside, and in light of the aerobics songs, it is worth mentioning that many of the shanties had ribald lyrics (especially on cargo ships where the consideration of passengers or troops was not at issue – or after passengers had been landed). These works have been described by one folklorist as 'jovial, forthright, almost wholesome obscenity' (Joanna C. Colcord, quoted in Hugill 1961:33). It is interesting to speculate on the interaction between lyrics and music and the effects of this interaction on generating motivation to keep moving. To be sure, these were no more lewd than the lyrics to many aerobics numbers, whose quasi-pornographic titles are legion. Certainly, both in aerobics and on the high seas, it would seem that music's role as a prosthetic technology involves much more than rhythm and physical entrainment, much more than the synchronization of movement. To say this is to suggest that bodily agency is not purely physical or mechanical; arousal, motivation and emotional orientation are all crucial to physical agency. Thus music affords bodily agency in at least two ways. First, particular types of movement are afforded by music's 'primary significations', as Middleton terms it (discussed above), through the musical structures that profile movement and lodge it within larger structures that in turn may also afford pleasure in their completion and that help actors to locate their movements within wider schemes. An explanation for this is that this more overtly physical level applies to the neonatal infants discussed in the first part of this chapter. Secondly, music also affords subject positions, and so generates emotional stances and scenarios associated with particular physical forms – sentimentality, romance, anger, rage, calculation and so forth, as well as types of embodied actors (for example, graceful or force-ful). These two types of affordance are not distinct; to choreograph move-ment is also to organize associated forms of feeling, of subjectivity (for example, it may be more difficult to be tender with clenched fists (that is, one would need to innovate, culturally and bodily, to develop new modes of expression), or to feel angry with a slackened jaw). This is to say that music's recipients may draw links between particular musical devices and what Middleton refers to as their 'secondary significance' or recognized connotations of emotional styles or forms. They may then shape up their action and self-perception in relation to these forms, becoming, for example, sentimental at one musical moment, and roused for vigorous action at the next.

This is precisely what happens in the forty-five minutes of an aerobic workout where aerobic agency is afforded by the music, where it is configured and reconfigured over time as music specifies a series of emo-tional and physical modalities, as it changes from warm-up, to core, to cool-down. In aerobics, these changes entail shifts in motivational levels and in physical orientations, in energy levels and in consciousness. The aerobic agent – as a being in a particular state – is transformed and trans-formed again over the course of a session and can be seen to run the gamut from person-in-the-street, to aerobically enlisted and motivated to hone one's body (for example, desiring to be 'feminine', constructed as thin), to non-conscious, powerful moving being, to sentimental and reim-bued with consciousness, to cognitively engaged in precision toning moves. Aerobics is by no means the only social province where actors engage in constant gear changes of emotional and embodied agency. On the contrary, this ability to shift and respond to semiotic cues is part and parcel of socialization into any institution, where one takes on organiza-tionally sponsored feeling and action modes. This aspect is perhaps espe-cially clear in the military. Consider the following statements, from a veteran of the Second World War (DeNora n.d.):

I remember boarding a ship in New York – they had a band while we walked up the gangplank. It was both sad and inspiring.

Band music is wonderful to march to – it puts a bounce in your walk and makes it sparkle, especially in a parade. Marching to music is so different; it's almost auto-matic. The music almost carries you on air and the beat keeps perfect step.

I was thinking about the first night I heard taps, very touchy. I cried and so did many more . . . you think they could be playing them for *you*.

Although the degree of musical-corporeal discipline demanded by aerobics and by the military is not typical of the bulk of daily life and its experiences, the molten and fragmentary character of embodied and emotional agency as it is configured and reconfigured within these enclaves as different states of being (throughout the aerobic grammar, as illustrated in these quotes describing different modes of military agency) is by no means atypical of the way in which agency is configured across social time and space in many less formal settings. Music's role just happens to be made more overt in aerobics and in some aspects of the military where its use is deliberate and in the foreground. But the aesthetic flexibility involved in both these settings can be found in many of the settings of modern life as individuals pass through varied relations and circumstances in institutions, organizations and encounters. Indeed, the aesthetic configuration of subjects is what gives the scenes and occasions of daily life their specificity, their particular forms of order, composed and sustained by acting subjects, whether these be weavers, sailors, soldiers, those taking part in aerobics, or other sorts of social actors.

In chapter 3, the ways in which individuals configure themselves as subjects who act and feel things in relation to music, how music is a resource for producing and recalling emotional states, were considered. In this chapter, music's link to the body, its role as a prosthetic device of bodily order, has been considered. It should be clear at this stage that these two matters are interlinked. On the one hand, music is a prosthetic technology of the body because it provides a resource for configuring motivation and entrainment, enabling the body to do what, without music, it could not do. On the other hand, the bodily movements that music profiles may lead actors to identify, work-up and modulate emotional and motivational states. For example, marching music may put listeners in mind of bodily states, and in mind of the movements profiled by that music, even when they remain seated. It may, in other words, rouse them because of the movement it implies and, more fundamentally, because it is doing movement in a similar manner, because the materiality of how notes are attacked and released, sustained and projected partakes of similar physical movements and gestures. In music therapy, for example, a therapist may structure group music-making so as to quiet the group and encourage them to listen to and pay attention to each other, deliberately playing with tempo, slowing down and speeding up a drum beat or instigating imitative games to get clients to focus on the movements and musical expressions of others.

Music's role as a resource for configuring emotional and embodied agency is not one that can be predetermined (because it is a resource that must be appropriated by music consumers). Music is not an objective 'force' or a 'stimulus', but it is real in its effects and its specific properties provide mechanisms for achieving those effects. Music not only affects how people feel emotionally; it also affects the physical body by providing a ground for self-perception of the body, and by providing entrainment devices and prosthetic technologies for the body. How, then, are these structuring properties of music appropriated within institutions, organizations and situations so as to have organizing effects on social and embodied action? And how does music work at the interactive level where institutions, organizations and occasions are sustained and reproduced over time? These issues are explored in the following chapter.

5   Music as a device of social ordering

'Pools of order', writes John Law, 'are illusory, but even such illusions are the exception. They do not last for long. They are pretty limited. And they are the product, the outcome, or the effect, of a lot of work – work that may occasionally be more or less successfully hidden behind an appearance of ordered simplicity' (1994:5). Law is writing about a research laboratory at a time of stress, but his observations perfectly introduce the concept of social order as an achievement, an effect of temporal action, and as his description of scientific work makes clear, such action draws upon (and is in turn shaped by) media and materials of all kinds – objects, discourses and technologies.

In daily life, as we have seen, music is one of these materials. This chapter considers music's role as a device of collective ordering, how music may be employed, albeit at times unwittingly, as a means of organizing potentially disparate individuals such that their actions may appear to be intersubjective, mutually oriented, co-ordinated, entrained and aligned. This social calm and the conductivity for social navigation that it facilitates is akin to Law's notion of order's 'pools'. This notion captures the temporal and achieved dimension of ordering. It gives sociological conceptions of order a tilt towards the ethnomethodological focus on order as an effect of work. At the same time, it creates an important space for culture as a medium of and for this work.

Adding music to the catalogue of cultural materials or devices of ordering contributes a whole new dimension to the focus of human–non-human interaction. It dispenses with the notion that society is merely 'people doing things'. It brings into relief the expressive and aesthetic dimension of ordering activity, a topic too often ignored in favour of cognitive and discursive 'skill' (Lash and Urry 1994; Mestrovic 1999). It highlights agency as consisting of feeling, as a corporeal and stylistic entity, and as something that may possess ceremonial features (Strong 1979). This vision of action has been taken up recently within social movement theory (Eyerman and Jamieson 1998; Melucci 1996a; Hetherington 1998; Tota 1999), where questions of aesthetic being and non-propositional paradigms for action have been broached. These issues are discussed below.

Such an approach orbits around action-as-practice. It is less concerned with depicting actors as 'knowing', that is deliberate or instrumentally rational subjects, and more concerned with exploring the matter of how forms of social life are established and renewed, albeit at the often sub-conscious levels of practice, habit, passion and routine. In so far as cultural forms are, within this perspective, seen to get into or inform social action and social relations, the production or creation of culture is politicized (Hobsbawm and Ranger 1983; Fyfe and Law 1992; Zolberg 1996). Aesthetic materials may provide paradigms and templates for the construction of non-aesthetic matters, styles of productive activity in the paid workplace, politics and statecraft, for example.

Chapter 2 made the point that sociologists have been reluctant to consider the aesthetic dimensions of social organization and that aesthetic materials can be understood to afford modes of action, feeling and embodiment. Chapters 3 and 4 developed this argument by showing how music is a device of emotional, biographical and corporeal regulation. It was necessary to begin with these topics in order to theorize agency in a way that brings to the fore feeling, body and energy. Accordingly, in this chapter, the aim is to advance that perspective by considering music's role as a resource for social ordering at the collective and collaborative levels. Focus is on materially and aesthetically configured spaces that are created – by actors themselves or for those actors by other actors (such as retailers, social planners or employers) – prior to and as part of action's scenes. Concern with this topic leads to the matter of music's role in the production and structuring of agency in real time. It articulates with a panoply of 'postmodern' issues – interactional or micro-politics, the construction of subjectivity, intersubjectivity, co-subjectivity, the virtual and the tacit. Such matters emphasize the rich domain of the precognitive, embodied, emotional and sensual bases of social action and order as it is produced by reflexive aesthetic ordering activity. These issues are broached by considering actors themselves as they may be seen to mobilize musical materials in an attempt to define the parameters of social scenarios, to provide cues for crafting agency in real-time social settings. Examining this issue helps to show how music is a device of social occasioning, how it can be used to regulate and structure social encounters, and how it lends aesthetic texture to those encounters. Music provides, in other words, a resource for establishing the prospective parameters of agency's aesthetic dimension.

One of the clearest illustrations of this issue lies in individuals' attempts, within the domestic sphere and among friendship groups, to create musical 'pre-texts' for action. To this end, it is worth returning to the in-depth interview data discussed in chapter 3, to consider how the women interviewed described their efforts to set the social scene with music. Through the prism of this data, it is possible to see music being used and working as a device for clarifying social order, for structuring subjectivity (desire and the temporal parameters of emotion and the emotive dimension of interaction) and for establishing a basis for collaborative action. In particular, we can see music as it is used as a resource or template against which styles and temporal patterns of feeling, moving and being come to be organized and produced in real time. Chapter 3 considered music's role as a part of routine identity work, and how it provides a means for the regulation of feeling, mood, concentration and energy level. So, too, music operates on an interactive plane, and so, too, music can be used to regulate the parameters of collaborative and collective aesthetic agency. At both individual and collective levels, these parameters encompass feeling, mood, energy, comportment and styles of awareness (for example, cognitive and propositional, embodied and tacit).

Musical prescription? Music and intimate culture

Daily, all around the world, individuals attempt to 'orchestrate' social activity. As discussed below, at times this work resembles the activities of marketing professionals who seek to structure conduct in public and commercial settings such as terminals, restaurants and shops. It is aimed at the creation of scenic specificity, at rendering places and spaces hospitable to some types of action, inhospitable to others. Through these forms of musical 'work' (and certainly many other forms of work), actors produce the aesthetic textures of social occasions, situations and action styles. The audio-environment is thus part of what actors refer to in their reflexive monitoring of situations; it is one of the things that actors may consider to determine what is, should or could be going on. To address this issue I begin with music's role as an active ingredient in close relationships and intimate settings. Such relationships exhibit collaborative action at the face-to-face level and in an emotionally heightened form where two actors are mutually engaged in producing an intimate mode of communicative, embodied, expressive action.

For example, Melinda is a twenty-year-old American student, completing a description of music as it had featured in her life on the day before the interview. In the following extract, she describes how the end of the day involved going to her 'new person's' house (she had been 'going out' with him for roughly a week), and how they had chosen music to listen to in his room:

Melinda: I think, last night, it was really funny, it was like 'mood setting' in a way. 'Cause he had Enya on, and as people call that 'chick music' [that is, 'women's' music that young men may choose to play when entertaining women because they think it is what women prefer] . . . and he was trying to produce a relaxed atmosphere and I think in a way it does promote physical, or just intimacy in general because it's just like certain music's more calming and, I remember . . . I think Stigma or Hyper came on and we were like, 'No no no, we don't want that!' and we tried to get this piece, like I had him play the *First Night* soundtrack, which I love, and there's like, a love song I, there, that's so beautiful, but everything else is like, 'bu bu de bah' [she sings here a triplet followed by a whole note the interval of a fifth higher than the triplet figure] and I'm like, 'No, no, this is not good' but I do, I think it was just very, it's very calming, very intimacy . . .

Q. So it's part of what creates an intimate atmosphere?

Melinda: Yeah, definitely. I think it's . . . setting is very important, and music is a very big part of that.

Q. Now, do you choose the music, also for those settings, or does he tend to choose them?

Melinda: I think he originally chose them but then I said, um, we heard Enya and then I was like, 'All right, let's change it' and he was like, whatever I wanted, he was just like 'Sure', so we both picked out some stuff. He's got a fifteen million CD changer. I'm like 'I didn't know they existed!'

Melinda's account of how she and her 'new person' negotiated the musical backdrop of their time together highlights not only her understanding of what is musically appropriate to the occasion, but also her apparent equality, perhaps even leading role, in articulating the aesthetic parameters of the occasion, that is, for specifying that occasion's scenic specificity. Certainly, her friend, who was also her host (they were in his room, listening to his CD collection, on his machine), was concerned with pleasing Melinda musically ('he was like, whatever I wanted, he was just like "Sure"'). Melinda persuades him, for example, to change the music when it seems 'wrong'. She refers to Enya as 'chick music' because she perceives it as a generic form of seduction music within the university scene. She rejects Stigma and Hyper, previously cued up ('we were like, "No no no, we don't want that!"') in favour of a 'love song' from the *First Night* soundtrack ('I had him play the *First Night* soundtrack, which I love'). She also then rejects a louder and energetic number ('and I'm like, 'No, no, this is not good') that was characterized, as she illustrates by bursting into song in the interview, by a 'fanfare' figure (not relaxed, calming or beautiful, but public, militaristic, energized).

Given that Melinda and her friend are students, the material-cultural settings of their domestic lives are somewhat constrained. Confined to one room with only basic furnishings, some candles, posters and the like, music is one of the few available materials for altering and specifying the scenes in which their encounters occur. It is a way of establishing a sense of setting the stage, as it were, of the encounter, structuring the parameters of the happening. 'Setting', as Melinda puts it, 'is very important and music is a very big part of that.'

What, then, are Melinda and her partner doing with music? How is music an active ingredient here in the ongoing configuration of their encounter and, within it, themselves as social agents? The answers to these questions involve reference to music's material and symbolic properties, its parameters as they are invoked and selected during musical production, performance and distribution.

Melinda's preferred music here gives prominence to conventional representations of love, relationships and romance, through lyrics and through melodic conventions (for example, soft and sensual – colour, texture and slow tempi). Moreover, the music she describes as 'good' occasionally alludes to romantic and exotic locations and cultures, again, through lyrics (for example, Enya's 'Caribbean blue', 'The Celts', 'China roses', 'Storms in Africa') and through musical conventions such as 'Celtic' melodies. Melinda also prefers music that is characterized by only mild dynamic shifts and where rhythmic pulse is not a prominent feature. Finally, Melinda prefers music that features female voices and performers who cultivate a 'feminine' image or who occupy, within the context of the lyrics or Broadway show story-lines, 'feminine' roles. Indeed, Enya's big hair, lace and velvet aptly exemplify these stereotypically feminine, romantic values. In short, Melinda and her partner were engaging in the aesthetic reflexive activity of configuring, via their musical choices, the prospective structure of their encounter: a time for relaxing, being sensual, slowing down, being romantic and celebrating things 'feminine' – softness, slowness, quiet, decoration. In this respect we can see, expanded on to the local, real-time interactive plane, music's role as a device for configuring aesthetic agency. Music provides, in other words, an exemplar for styles of being; it may be perceived as representing, or making accessible to awareness various parameters of emotional and embodied conduct and, in this way, it enables the possibility of (at least apparently) intersubjective, entrained physical conduct as an ongoing accomplishment.

Although this discussion has focused on individual cultural practice, Melinda's musical preferences are by no means unique; on the contrary, they are typical of what other writers have observed in relation to gender and musical taste (Peterson and Simkus 1992; Bryson 1996; Frith and McRobbie 1990 [1978]). Less obvious, perhaps, is that the stylistic trappings of intimacy preferred by Melinda conform to what previous studies of gender and sexual conduct have revealed: that women value the temporal structures and embodied practices commensurate with slowing down.

Perhaps this is because leisurely pace, whether as a feature of music, speech or action, affords equivocation, interruption, languor, redirection, digression and so is commensurate with narratives of intimate conduct that feature the liminal and the non-purposive, that 'get down off the beanstalk' as McClary has put it in reference to the upward mobility often used to signify sexuality in Western cultures (McClary 1991:112–31). Given that young women often find it difficult to verbalize tastes and dispositions to their partners (from lack of experience and general diffidence (Holland et al. 1994)), the salience of non-verbal, aesthetic means for pre-scripting scenes, for instigating scenarios and associated desires and conduct forms, is heightened. 'Setting is very important', as Melinda says, perhaps because getting the music right is a way of trying to make the action right, not merely in the embodied and technical sense, but as a way of prospectively calling out forms of agency that are comfortable and preferable, that feel right in emotional and embodied terms.

Intimate conduct is often bodily conduct. It is therefore worth bearing in mind issues raised in chapter 4, particularly those that relate to the configuration and reconfiguration of embodied energy, tempo and consciousness style, as discussed in relation to the body and the transformations it undergoes over forty-five minutes of aerobic exercise. There, the body could be seen to be organized musically, and aligned with a preconfigured aerobic grammar or sequential order of how the body is meant to be during an aerobic session. In an aerobic session, slower and more sentimental ballad forms were used to cool-down participants, to bring them back from the mind-less and more physically encompassing forms of movement that they had engaged in during the core of the exercise, to bring them back into a more conscious and reflective mode of attention. In relation to the real-time intimate encounter, so, too, slower, less rhythmically and harmonically forward-moving, more textural and tonally ambiguous musical materials may be preferred by women because they afford a less mechanical and more sentimental mode of bodily conduct; they also work, in a manner akin to the warm-up music of aerobics in its celebration of the 'feminine', to maintain the intimate encounter as an aesthetic encounter, as involving more than bodily processes and techniques. Moreover, as with aerobics, slower and more sentimental music may be commensurate with low-impact forms of movement.

Observations such as these may be (too) quickly taken to imply essentialist conceptions of 'female desire'. But essentialist perspectives on 'women and music' preclude consideration of the aesthetic-pragmatic dimension of women's musical practice, for example, women's attempts to renegotiate stereotypical representations of intimacy (representations that have been made and initiated perhaps mostly by men), and to inter-ject nuance or alternative practice into the proceedings. Essentialist read-ings also preclude the ways in which desire is culturally constituted in and through reference to scripts, representations and a variety of cultural materials, one of which is music (DeNora 1997). The desire for a back-drop of slow or romantic music is thus not necessarily linked to 'female-ness' *per se*, but rather to a perceived need for relaxation and/or a desire to sentimentalize interaction, to hold it as an object upon which to reflect (and change). Slow, relaxing music, then, may be deployed so as to slow action and to open its course to the possibility of negotiation. The follow-ing excerpt, concerning a situation where the male rather than female participant makes recourse to 'romance' music as a backdrop for intimate interaction, shows how, for men too, music may be used as a means for slowing intimate interaction, for conferring a degree of sentimentality on to it and thus for reconfiguring intimate possibilities by raising its level of consciousness, its degree of sentimentality:

Q. Another question I ask everybody, some people say yes, some people say no, in a romantic context do you ever use music for, kind of, intimate situations or how do you ever, or does anyone ever, put on music as a complement to seduction or intimacy?

Becky: Yeah, I do, 'cause I tend to, although the last boyfriend I had I didn't actually put the music on, he did, he was in my house so he sort of took the initia-tive to put the music on and, I think he actively took my CD player upstairs so he quite sort of . . . [pause]

Q. . . . Do you remember what he chose? . . .

Becky: I think it was, I think it was – I've got the love albums; I've got the com-plete [set]. I think it was [volume] two or three and he chose that. Which took me by surprise, I must admit at the time I thought 'Oh, cheeky so-and-so' [laughs]. Taking my CD player . . . [from the living room to the bedroom]. There is a funny story behind it but please don't laugh. Afterwards I found out, well it sort of devel-oped into just a friendship because there wasn't, there was no spark there and it turned out that he was actually homosexual and he didn't know how to come out and he was trying to convince himself he still liked women and in the end I sort of helped him through it and he now lives in Manchester with his boyfriend [laughs]. He was very effeminate and I was always a little bit suspicious but didn't sort of let on so that might have something to do with why he chose the music . . . At the time it wasn't, I can tell you, it was shell-shock with that one, and I'm getting the standing jokes like 'That's what you do to men is it? Put them right off women' [laughs].

Q. And if you're in a position to chose music for an intimate situation what might you chose?

Becky: I tend to go for more relaxing CDs. I go more towards that because I em – I mean since I've been separated, or divorced now, for five years – and I tend to go more towards that because it's been a long time, I've only had three relation-ships since then, I must say this last one, which was last year, was so brief I'm always very nervous when I meet somebody new so I tend to try and sort of relax a bit with them. I might have even known them for several months but they still feel [inaudible] [laughs].

Q. Now, how have they responded to this relaxing music, do they like it? It doesn't bother them, they don't say 'Turn that off' or anything?

Becky: No, nobody, they haven't said anything, they're probably amused, sort of humour her, leave it on [laughs], keep the woman happy [laughs].

Of the fifty-two women interviewed for the music and daily life study, not one indicated fast-paced or high-volume music as something they associated with intimacy (for example, heavy metal, dance music or aerobics music), but many reported enjoying and employing in intimate situations 'romantic', 'relaxing' or 'smoochy' music – the terms are theirs – and some bemoaned the fact that the music they 'would' like to hear as a prelude or accompaniment to intimacy was disdained by their partners. As suggested above, these preferences are perhaps best viewed as non-discursive strategies, ones that open up intimate encounters, slow them and configure them as sentimental (that is, conscious) occasions. Such practical work then facilitates a negotiation of the situation and its happenings. Music is thus a device of sexual-political negotiation or, put less combatively, a device for configuring the intimate environment. But women's musical preferences – at least those espoused by the women interviewed here – also tap into gender-stereotypical scripts of intimate conduct, ones within which feminine desire is, in bodily terms, not urgent, and, in behavioural terms, laced with romance, a quasi-sacred occasion.

For example, Jennifer's partner likes 'Gangster Rap', which she disdains ('The things that I listen to are more feminine, more like Girl music. That's what I call his music – Boy music'). She goes on to speculate that he does not actually 'like' this music but feels obliged, within his 'boy' peer group, to espouse a taste for it. None the less, at times of physical intimacy they listen to the music of her choice:

Jennifer: I like things that are, kind of, maybe a little mystical.

Q. Is there any special reason for that? I can imagine some.

Jennifer: I guess because when I'm alone with my fiancée it's kind of a magical, mystical type thing, we're both very into non-traditional religion.

She goes on to describe the music in more detail as 'classical music with nature sounds . . . a Tchaikovsky CD with nature sounds [thunder storms, rain, birds] put into the music . . . a CD with like ocean sounds, it's really nice . . .'.

Conversely, as Nancy describes, a musical backdrop for intimacy is not always welcomed by both partners:

Q. If you were going to have people around, I'm just going to jump ahead a bit, for a meal or a drink or something, would you put music on for that?

Nancy: Yeah, I think for a meal, at Christmas we had a Christmas meal and we had the Christmas tape on in the background, that sort of thing.

Q. Do you ever use any other kind of music to set the mood in any circumstances?

Nancy: Um – I try quite often with my boyfriend [laughs] but he never . . . [breaks off]

Q. Can you tell me about that?

Nancy: Yeah, we'll watch telly before we go to bed, which is what we like to do to relax, and then we turn it off and as I said, I don't really like silence that much anyway so I say, 'Oh, can we have a CD on?' and every single time it'll be 'No, why do you want a CD on?' [laughs]. So he's not very big on having the mood set with music, which if it's at my house I might put a tape on to relax to.

Q. He's the one with the CD [player] though?

Nancy: Yes.

Q. What kind of a CD would you be wanting to listen to at that stage of the day?

Nancy: Ah, it would have to be something quite relaxing and quiet, I think.

Q. Could you give me some examples of what from his collection you would choose?

Nancy: Probably, he hasn't got much, he's got the Beatles, which I like, so probably something like that would suit me. And the sort of thing I think would be a compilation of female singers.

Q. Can you, I'm going to press, can you be as specific as possible, what kind of music and what kind of female singers?

Nancy: I guess any sort, really. You know it could be sort of background music, not the sort you have to really listen to.

Q. How would you describe what is the mood that it evokes if you are putting them on?

Nancy: Relaxation, I think, is the main one. Also because I don't like silence too much I feel relaxed because there is a noise in the background. I think it's quite relaxing to have all sorts of love songs, something like that.

Q. Actually, one of the questions I ask everybody is, do you ever like to have music on in the background as a prelude to, you know, 'romance'?

Nancy: Yes, well I try to [laughs].

Q. If it's not for going to sleep but is background for intimacy, why do you think he doesn't want it and you want it?

Nancy: I don't know – I can't really think. I have thought about it, I sort of lie there thinking 'Why can't we have the CD on?' I think maybe males see music or hear music differently to us, maybe a romantic soundtrack to them would be too soppy and a bit too stereotypical, I think.

Nancy, a twenty-year-old English university student, would like to decorate the auditory spaces in which relaxing and being intimate with her partner occurs. But she perceives her partner as non-co-operative in this regard. She goes on to describe how, if she puts her tapes on in other less intimate circumstances, such as while driving, 'He'll have a little snigger when I'm in the car [laughs]. So I think he probably finds them quite amusing. So we probably are quite different, actually.' When I go on to ask her if she thinks this is because her musical choices connote the 'romantic' and that perhaps he doesn't care for overtly romantic configurations of intimacy and couples, she says (echoing McRobbie's (1991) discussion of the downplaying of 'romance' in young women's culture): 'It may be – I think men tend to avoid sort of typical romantic situations. They don't really like [them]. I guess they get a lot of stick for being too romantic now and it's a bit naff to be over the top and romantic.'

It would be misleading to jump to conclusions about female sexuality on the basis of this (non-representative, exploratory) data. Indeed, within the sample of women discussed here, not all described using music as a device for intimate occasioning. None the less, the responses of the women in my sample give rise to some fruitful speculation concerning why music may be woven into the fabric of an intimate encounter. For instance, respondents who did not use music in intimate circumstances were typically involved in a longer-term relationship and/or in a relationship where they seemed to have less need to prestructure or to negotiate the parameters of intimacy, where less uncertainty existed and where the need for relaxation was not felt as pressing. Ulrika, for example, a twenty-year-old university student – originally from Sweden – said that there was 'no time' before intimate encounters for setting the scene with music, 'it all happens too fast' with her boyfriend. She was clearly not complaining about pace but was rather trying to underline how her relationship was characteristically passionate; she meant they felt no need for musical enhancement in their physical relationship. Indeed, love songs and sentimental pop tunes were not part of her repertoire of musical tastes and practices (she tended to listen to high-energy dance music and, frequently, to go out to clubs with the express purpose of dancing). And for fifty-something Elaine, playing music as a backdrop for intimacy would be like 'a signal to the household' and so is avoided, though she recalls using music for such encounters in her youth.

In short, when music was used as a backdrop for intimacy, it was because it contributed to intimate interaction – for example, it served as an aid to relaxation, a signal about style, a motivator, an occasioning device. Music was a resource one could turn to as one engaged in the collaborative production of an intimate scene, rather as it was in other types of circumstances, such as when one wanted to get psyched up for a particular task, as described in chapter 3. Perhaps, for this reason, it is not surprising that the use of slow music, new age music, nature sounds, 'spiritual' music, sentimental and romantic ballads and the like, as used for intimacy, is more common among the young, among those who are still getting to know each other, the nervous and the uncertain, and those who wish to reconfigure otherwise pregiven, stereotypical or routine intimate practices. These musical materials seem, for the respondents, to afford sentimentalizing, slowing down and deconstructing teleological grammars of intimate conduct. They also reflect a conventional and gendered division of musical taste, a difference between what men versus women may feel is appropriate for them to espouse and play in social situations, or between what men and women come to associate with familiarity and musical security. In our ethnography of karaoke, for example, when women performed they usually chose love songs, lyrical songs that dealt with the topic of relationships. When men sang, they opted for a wider range of musical material – hard rock, rap, Elvis hits, famous Sinatra classics such as 'My way'. They rarely performed romantic numbers. Investigating the actual musical practices of intimate encounters thus echoes Walser's observations about music's role as a resource for gender display (1993:114–17, 'No girls allowed'), and provides ethnographic data in line with Frith and McRobbie's semiotic reading of music's erotic affordances in their pioneering essay on rock and sexuality:

Cock rock performers are aggressive, dominating, and boastful, and they constantly seek to remind to audience of their prowess, their control. Their stance is obvious in live shows; male bodies on display, plunging shirts and tight trousers, a visual emphasis on chest hair and genitals . . . mikes and guitars are phallic symbols; the music is loud, rhythmically insistent, built around techniques of arousal and climax; the lyrics are assertive and arrogant, though the exact words are less significant than the vocal styles involved, the shouting and screaming. (Frith and McRobbie 1990 [1978]:374)

Frith and McRobbie were clear at the time that they were not suggesting that the rhythmic 'insistence' of rock was equated with 'natural' sexuality; rather they were attempting to observe – rather as one might observe the properties of conversation – how rock's 'thrusting' musical character 'can be heard as a sexual insistence' (1990 [1978]:383) and, as such, can be contrasted with musical materials that configure hesitation, feeling as opposed to action. For example, Kate Bush's 'Wuthering heights' has the following characteristics:

Both her vocal and her piano lines are disrupted, swooping, unsteady; the song does not have a regular melodic or rhythmic structure, even in the chorus, with its unsettling stress – the words that are emphasized are 'nervous', 'desperate', 'nobody else'. . . . The music contradicts the enjoyment that the lyrics assert. Kate Bush's aesthetic intentions are denied by the musical conventions she uses. (Frith and McRobbie 1990 [1978]:386)

Frith and McRobbie were concerned with how music could be used to represent sexuality, with how its structures could come to inform and engender desire. This project is akin to Susan McClary's, as discussed in chapter 2 – we can see, for example, musical structures mapped on to gendered action such that musical conventions and materials may come to connote gendered meanings. Frith and McRobbie's concerns are adjacent to but different from the project outlined here, which is concerned with how actors mobilize musical materials and conventions as resources for constituting agency and its locations. A focus on how music is mobilized in the course of action is linked to the ethnographic realm and to the question of what actors actually *do* with music, how music is implicated in what they do and how it may structure what can be done.

Richard Dyer (1990) was also concerned with this question, which he addressed, in autobiographical mode, in his 1979 essay 'In Defense of Disco', where he compares the 'disembodied' eroticism of pop songs with the 'thrusting' eroticism of rock and the 'whole body' eroticism of disco. Dyer's essay is valuable today because it offers an account of how, for a particular individual, music may afford configurations of desire and erotic agency. As in the case study of aerobics discussed in chapter 4, music can be understood as an accomplice for bodily entrainment; it can heighten or suppress cognitive forms of awareness and the tendency to be emotional or sentimental; it can interest the body such that it is drawn into a temporal trajectory (a rhythm, a pulse, a corporeal grammar and style of movement); it can enlist the body to forget about itself; it can serve as a non-verbal accomplice for certain forms of action. This is why the question of who puts what on the record player as a backdrop for intimacy is of necessity a question of intimate politics.

Increasingly, music distribution companies have tapped this market for what they refer to as 'romantic compilation albums'. A 1994 issue of *Cue* magazine devoted a feature to these albums and describes the growing market as follows:

[It is] the idea that for a few quid you can kit yourself out with a completely legal mood-manipulator which, together with soft lights and optional bearskin rug, will work hard on your behalf before, during and after making the beast with two backs. Ambience to go. (*Cue* 1994:68)

The albums are produced in consultation with focus groups and are advertised on national television. They are aimed expressly at the so-called 'light purchaser', the individuals with little knowledge about music who buy no more than three music CDs a year. According to Nick Moran, of Dino Records (who lead the market with a five-volume 'That lovin' feeling' series): 'We do try to steer clear of clichés, but this very stylised image of love and happiness is what is expected to go with the songs

... It's very aspirational, especially among women – so research has told us ...' (*Cue* 1994:69).

This point was born out by the interview data. Many of the interviewees themselves described how, although their (male) partners were mostly interested in music and had particular tastes, that they could take charge of music when they wished:

He wouldn't know what to put on.

He's really not that bothered about what I put on.

He's not as keen on music anyway as me so he generally will go along with what I say ... he's probably the most dominant in our relationship, but when it comes to music, I think I probably would win.

I think my tastes are more dominant in the household, period. But my husband has very little interest in music.

Accounts such as these are difficult to evaluate; they may be occasioned expressly for the in-depth interview and its conventional style of rapport between two women. They may, in other words, be part of the doing – the performance – of confidentiality, part of how speaker and hearer collude in producing cultural scripts and images, in this case, for example, of 'female power' (on this point, see Frith and Kitzinger 1998). Interviewees may, in other words, slip into what C.W. Mills once referred to as 'vocabularies of motive' (Mills 1940). The interview procedure was designed to address this problem by repeatedly leading respondents back to the practical level of real-life examples of who-did-what-when-how, the 'nitty-gritty' level of mundane action that has the capacity to undermine accounts and the various identity claims, posturings and role play that often occur within an interview. Sticking close to the level of respondents' musical practices helped to reveal how respondents used music rather than their depictions of relations between themselves and others. If, in fact, women are more likely to resort to aesthetic means for configuring intimate occasions, there is an important lesson there for theories of gender and power in close relationships, one that could be further illuminated through more ethnographic research on couple culture and its production over the course of a relationship.

Music and collective occasions

Jennifer: We had a party a couple of weeks ago. It was supposed to be like a wine and cheese party but it was desserts and mixed drinks! We had candles in here and it was weird because we played Billy Joel and we played a lot of [dance music] at the end of the evening because everybody was going from my party, out to go dancing. We played a lot of pretty things in other languages.

Particularly at the start of the evening – for music was here used to outline a temporal structure of conduct style over the duration of an evening – Jennifer and her housemates were trying, she explains, to create a relaxed yet refined environment, one in which participants dressed up, consumed desserts and mixed drinks (as opposed to the more usual beer and snack food), and conversed quietly or danced (slowly) to the strains of 'pretty' music with lyrics 'in other languages', signalling travel and things European (often synonymous with high culture in the United States). Here, music was part and parcel of Jennifer and her friends' orientation to (what they perceived as) prestigious forms of symbolic capital, forms residing on the perimeter of their usual leisure practices. This form of what Mauss has called 'prestigious imitation' (Lash and Urry 1994:45; Mauss 1979:101) delimited the parameters of conduct in ways that were commensurate with their values of glamour, relaxed pace, sophistication and romance. Thus, through the ways it is perceived to be related to a network of other objects, meanings and modes of agency, music can be seen as providing an ongoing tracking device for participants, a cue or template for the formulation of energy levels and conduct styles that can be examined when and/or if uncertainty about appropriate agency arises, when/if one needs to get a handle on how to 'be' within a setting. In this sense, music is a template or model for the formulation of emotional, social and embodied agency over the course of real-time interaction. Just as it may be difficult, for example, to reconcile 'pretty things in other languages' with beer, or candles with sweatshirts, jeans and trainers, so too it is difficult to engage in some of the earthier modes of intimacy against the background entailments of, say, Celine Dion's 'Our love will go on', the *Titanic* themesong. The point is not that music delineates modes of subjectivity and embodied action *per se*, but that actors perceive it as implying (or as associated with) modes of agency; they also feel it to be analogous or homologous to modes of being:

I would have the music on before they [houseguests] come because I like to create an atmosphere. And because – it would depend to some extent on what [the occasion is]. If it were a very elegant little cocktail party then I would probably be going to put on some kind of classical or something like that, although I might make it a little more – what I would think of as informal classical like classical guitar, for example. When it's around the holidays I always put on music that's related to the holidays but not singing music, I like instrumental music for that, harps, or whatever. If we're doing a Friday night dinner, kind of informal with friends, I might put on folk music or light jazz, something like that . . . If I want things to be very lively and a little boisterous, you know, then I am going to play loud or fast-paced music obviously if I want people to dance but just, you know, if you have twenty people there and you don't want quiet for the conversation which the lower music lends itself to, then I might put on something that would be more, you know, something a little hipper [laughs] . . . I think people, they need to know what's happening to them, we all respond to the emotional tone of music so I think music can be very, very soothing and quiet or it can sort of jazz things up or it can put a cast of utter pall over, you know. Have you ever been to a party where they want people to dance but they put the wrong music on and you just can't move with it? (Elaine, age fifty-five, United States)

Music is thus part of the cultural material through which 'scenes' are constructed, scenes that afford different kinds of agency, different sorts of pleasure and ways of being. It is important to underline, as described in chapter 4, that this process and the use of music as a device of scene construction may elide rational consciousness. Without being aware of how they are responding to and interpreting music, actors may latch on to and fall in with musical structures. This falling in with may entail realignment of bodily comportment as discussed in chapter 4 (for example, the tapping of a foot or a shift in physical energy or motivation), a realignment of emotional state (chapter 3) or a realignment of social conduct, as addressed in this chapter. As is discussed in chapter 6, human action is assembled at least in part by a practical appropriation of models and resources for action's configuration. We see this perhaps most clearly in examinations of situated discourse, for example in how actors may draw upon conventional narratives, registers and manners of speaking to generate a voice and point of view locally, to 'get through' the activity of face-to-face communication (Frazer and Cameron 1989). This need not imply the absence of a subject but, rather, that subjects, if they are to realize themselves as speakers, must find the words and so cast about for available and appropriate linguistic techniques. So, too, subjects may find available auditory structures with which to configure themselves, not only as speaking and acting subjects, but as subjects whose speech and action possess an emotional and corporeal dimension – as aesthetic agents. Within social spaces, then, prominent music may allude to modes of aesthetic agency – feeling, being, moving, acting – and so may place near-to-hand certain aesthetic styles that can be used as referents for configuring agency in real time, for the bodily technique of producing oneself as an agent in the full sense of that word (that is, beyond the discursive and cognitive dimensions normally understood within the social sciences).

Music works in this way through two interrelated avenues. First, it may be perceived as carrying connotations or, as discussed in chapter 4, 'secondary significations'. Secondly, it may profile and place on offer ways of moving, being and feeling through the ways its materials are configured into a range of sonic parameters such as pace, rhythm, the vertical and horizontal 'distances' between tones, the musical envelope of particular tones and tone groups – 'attack and release' as it is termed in music analysis, timbre or volume. For example, when the music 'hops' and 'skips', so too bodies may feel motivated to move, as it were, like the music. In these cases, music is doing something more than re-presenting or simulating bodily patterns and bringing them to mind; it is providing a ground or medium within which to be a body, a medium against which the body comes to be organized in terms of its own physical and temporal organization (for example, as it springs from the ground in a way that is entrained to the musical pulse). So, aligned with and entrained by the physical patterns music profiles, bodies not only *feel* empowered, they may *be* empowered in the sense of gaining a capacity. These capacities are sometimes visible, as, for example, when we can observe the body gestures of people listening to music via headphones or orchestral conductors' movements; this visibility is heightened when musical materials shift, for example, from slow to fast, from genre to genre, where contiguous but contradictory forms of musical agency rub up against each other.

This tendency to fall in with the music was something that arose repeatedly in all aspects of the music in the daily life study. As a phenomenon, it highlights the capacity, perhaps even the tendency, on the part of human beings, to adopt and adapt, not necessarily consciously, to resources within an environment. At the same time, actors' non-discursive, corporeal, emotional, falling in with music does not imply that music works like a stimulus. Actors may have awareness of what music entails and yet also be aware that those entailments feel wrong; they may wish to override music's perceived implications, to resist or reappropriate music's force (for example, when the ballad 'Stand by your man' is reappropriated as an ironic commentary on patriarchal relations). Melinda, quoted earlier in this chapter, made this clear when she said, about a follow-on track on a CD her boyfriend had chosen, 'we were like, "No no no, we don't want that!"' In short, music's capacity to serve as a device of social ordering can be seen in the fact that it can serve as the source of social discomfort:

Becky: . . . A lot of the people [at a party] were working together [so] they didn't like slow music, I got the impression they felt quite uneasy because they felt they had to touch their workmates [laughs] and it didn't go down very well . . . One chap that I worked quite closely with came over and asked me to actually dance and I felt *very* conscious, I personally felt conscious that I was dancing to a slow dance and his wife was only over there and it was all very uncomfortable, really.

In this example, tension arose between, on the one hand, the general social value of being polite at a special function for people who were colleagues rather than friends (for example, to refuse an invitation to dance might be read as a snub or as not contributing to the social 'work' of geniality and festivity) and, on the other, wishing to avoid what were perceived as the music's entailments (intimacy and romance and, more specifically, a range of minute bodily actions associated with these things). Thus when actors 'dislike' particular music, it may be because they sense that the resources from which their agency is generated are subject to threat (in this case, preserving certain bodily habits that constitute collegiality versus intimacy). When they speak of music as 'inappropriate', then, this 'troubles talk' brings into relief respondents' understanding of what music entails for the constitution of agency and social scene. This is by no means the same thing as suggesting that music *causes* respondents to behave in certain ways.

On the contrary, as discussed in chapter 2, music's force is made manifest through appropriation and reception. Within these constraints, however, it is perfectly reasonable to speak of music as a material of social organization, because styles of movement, emotional and social roles come to be associated with it and may issue from it. In the presence of music, actors may take pleasure in falling in with music or displeasure in trying to avoid what they perceive the music to imply in a behavioural sense. Music may indeed be conceptualized as a prospective device of agency, a way of cueing or tuning in to the ongoing formation of order, or, more accurately, 'pools' of order, locally achieved. It is in this sense, then, that music may be pre-scriptive (Akrich 1991) of social order(s). Whether or not it is actually *used* as a referent for producing order in real time, though, is always open to question. There is thus little point in producing an abstract taxonomy of what music will do; certain patterns may emerge over time within particular settings or relationships and these may be specified with degrees of precision, though they are always in process. A stimulus–response model of how music works is simply inaccurate because it elides the meaningful and interpretive acts of music recipients as they draw upon music's affordances as part of mundane musical practice.

The point is that although music's meanings and effects are constructed and dependent upon how they are appropriated, patterns of appropriation – associated with particular styles within particular settings – emerge and accrue over time. For example, actors often have a sense of 'what goes with what how' – the candles, the mixed drinks and the 'pretty things in other languages', the 'informal' dinner on Friday night with friends and the folk music, the 'beautiful . . . calming' music of the *First Night* soundtrack and a 'relaxed' intimate encounter. The analysis of representations as propounded by mass-distributed culture forms (for example, what music is used to signal intimacy and romance in films) is thus an important component to the study of how specific actors appropriate aesthetic materials as ordering devices because it illuminates many of the available resources for action and experience. Analysis of popular forms and media representations is not, however, a substitute for the analysis of cultural practice and everyday life. To conflate the two is to return to the problems faced by scholars such as Adorno when the bases for their claims about the level of experience and what music causes are exposed to critical examination. The individual experience of culture is a topic that cannot be encompassed by the homology concept as it is traditionally conceived. Nor can it be addressed by the idea that music inculcates, instigates or nurtures particular mind-sets. The level of musical practice, of appropriation – of what music may offer as a resource for the practical matter of world building – is a matter in its own right and it may be best to work upwards from it to so-called 'larger' questions about music and social structure.

Music as a touchstone of social relations

This last point can be seen perhaps most clearly when we consider how music is used not only to reinforce but also to undermine particular relations between friends and intimates. Here, for example, Lesley describes how a shift in music listening habits and tastes at home was associated with the deterioration of her relationship with her partner.

Lesley: In the '80s I sort of got distanced from music. My [children] were little and my husband didn't really like a lot of music going on – he wasn't particularly keen on the radio being on all the time, probably – I suppose the bands I didn't identify with at the time were Dire Straits – those sort of bands. I liked some of the things they did but I think it was more excitable and so my ex-husband liked them and didn't mind them being put on, whereas some of the other music I'd put on he thought would upset the [children] and of course then they got to identify with some of the things I liked with being morose, like the Leonard Cohen. So it tended to be more popular jiggly music . . . Normally if I listened to Leonard Cohen I wanted to be in my own space listening and of course so normally I would have been in a bit of a strange mood in comparison to how I would be, and I suppose he picked upon that and maybe the [children] did as well . . . When we first got married we used to listen to the radio a lot, and within nine months I was listening to Radio 4 rather than Radio 1 because he just didn't like Radio 1 at all. When the boys were young, babies, occasionally I'd put something on raucous or heavy metal or something and his attitude was that he definitely didn't want it on because it was too noisy. But I think the [children] picked up on that as well because if I put anything on that was a bit loud – [here she gestures that they would act up] . . . during the '80s I didn't really bother with music because I thought it would cause friction – be upsetting or whatever – so I stopped . . . The late '80s I started listening to Beehive and the Thompson Twins, which of course my husband didn't identify with at all . . .

Lesley describes how she began to make a deliberate musical move away from her relationship, replacing the 'popular jiggly' music that she perceived as within the bounds of the relationship – for example, Dire Straits – and also the more, as she perceived it, 'intellectual' mode of Radio 4, with music that her husband disliked and viewed with disapproval. Lesley goes on to describe how, near the end of her relationship with her ex-husband, she would sometimes, when she was angry, play a Soft Cell song entitled, 'Say hello, wave goodbye' (from an album called *Erotic Cabaret*). She would play the track at high volume so that it would be audible from any room in the house. As she puts it, 'It was a hint really', but admits that she is not sure her husband understood ('He didn't say anything').

Lesley used music to convey a message (perhaps about her evolving aesthetic and stylistic stance) that she had not yet formulated in words – she was formulating a sense of how she was 'different' from her partner, thinking through musical practice about leaving that partner. Via music, Lesley may also have been undermining the aesthetic basis of their relationship, preparing the aesthetic ground for her departure, creating an aesthetic trajectory for the agency of her departure. The first step in this process was to move away from the music that had hitherto been located in the centre of their relationship (albeit a weak centre – music was never particularly important to them as a couple). The second step was to turn, instead, to the sort of music her husband had always frowned upon, 'raucous or heavy metal or something', as she puts it, or else something conducive to introspection (and alienation), such as Leonard Cohen or Susanne Vega, to the sort of music that did not signify, from her partner's point of view, 'happy families'. In a sense, Lesley presaged her leap from a social relationship – her marriage – by trying it out 'virtually' in the aesthetic sphere. Changes in musical practice provided, in other words, a practice genre for the 'real' or social and economic move that was to follow – leaving home.

Within an intimate relationship, even minute aesthetic turnings may cause distress, albeit without any accompanying recognition of why things seem uneasy (one may say, 'I can't put my finger on it but I sense something is wrong'). Non-negotiated aesthetic changes may cut off access to the aesthetic resources from which relationships and modes of being are generated and sustained. In this regard, denying access to aesthetic resources within micro- or idiocultural settings can illuminate the social dynamics of artistic censorship in wider collectivities, the suppression of seditious songs, of instrumental music in Cromwell's time, of the Welsh harp or of local variants of medieval plainsong. The materials that had hitherto provided the tacit reference points for collective identity work, for entrainment and for the shaping up of embodied aesthetic agency, are removed. With this removal, actors are deprived of a resource for the renewal of a social form and the modes of arousal, motivation and readiness for action that go with these forms. Is it any wonder, then, that actors may go to extraordinary lengths to preserve their access to aesthetic materials – the cryptic portraits of Bonny Prince Charlie, the 'cried down sangs' (that is, proscribed songs) of the Jacobite rebellion that reappeared in encoded form, for example Bonnie Prince Charlie reappears as 'our guideman' or as a blackbird or a 'bonnie moorhen':

> My bonnie moorhen has feathers enew
> She's a' fine colours, but nane o' them blue;
> She's red and she's white and she's green and she's grey.
> My bonnie moorhen, come hither away.
> Come up by Glenduich and down by Glendee
> And round by Kinclaven and hither to me;
> For Ronald and Donald are out on the fen,
> To break the wing o' my bonnie moorhen. (STR 1981 [1960])

Echoing Victor Turner's discussion of paradigms (1981), Ron Eyerman and Andrew Jamieson have recently begun to specify this particular type of action in relation to music and social movements:

> To the categories of action discussed by sociologists we wish to add the concept of exemplary action. As represented or articulated in the cognitive praxis of social movements, exemplary action can be thought of as a specification of the symbolic action discussed by Melucci and others. The exemplary action of cognitive praxis is symbolic in several senses; but it is also 'more' than merely symbolic. As real cultural representations – art, literature, songs – it is artefactual and material, as well. What we are attempting to capture with the term is the exemplary use of music and art in social movements, the various ways in which songs and singers can serve a function akin to the exemplary works that Thomas Kuhn characterized as being central to scientific revolutions: the paradigm-constituting entities that serve to realign scientific thinking and that represent ideal examples of fundamentally innovative scientific work [Kuhn 1970]. The difference between culture and science, however, is that the exemplary action of music and art is lived as well as thought: it is cognitive, but it also draws on more emotive aspects of human consciousness. (1998:23)

In the examples discussed so far in this chapter, actors can be seen to have used music so as to call out or call ahead manners of conduct, value, style and mutual orientation. Music, in this sense, whether or not it actually works as such, is a prescriptive device, a cue for social agency. Within music's structures, its perceived connotations, its sensual parameters (dynamics, sound envelopes, harmonies, textures, colours and so on), actors may 'find' or gather themselves as agents with particular capacities for social action. These specific examples thus help us to see how, to varying degrees, actors are engaged in tacit aesthetic activities that produce their action, in laying down potential aesthetic grounding for future conduct. Aesthetic materials here may be seen as akin to what

Robert Witkin once referred to as 'holding forms' (Witkin 1974). They provide motifs that precede, and serve as a reference point for, lines of conduct over time. In this way their function is similar to that of memory artefacts, as discussed by Urry (1996) and Radley (1990), described in chapter 3. Such motifs are seen by actors to somehow encapsulate and provide a container for what might otherwise pass as a momentary impulse to act, or a momentary identification of some kind. Holding forms thus provide a touchstone to which actors may return as they engage in expressive activity. They are resources against which future agency takes shape.

Seen in this light, the study of how music is used in daily life helps to illuminate the practical activity of casting ahead and furnishing the social space with material-cultural resources for feeling, being and doing. This is part of how the habitat for social life – its support system – is produced and sustained. And aesthetic reflexive action, that is the reference to aesthetic materials as a means for generating agency, is a crucial aspect of structuration. It is a keystone for the project of knowing what to say, how to move, how to feel. In short, music is a resource for producing social life.

Critical then is the issue, as was discussed at the end of chapter 1, of how the production of an agency-sustaining habitat is itself controlled – for example, constructed, maintained, deconstructed. Within social settings, particular musical materials may place on offer some aesthetic resources for the production of agency while they make others inaccessible (for example, the loud rock and the beer versus the 'pretty things in other languages' and the 'mixed drinks and desserts'). And if music is a device of social ordering, if – in and through its manner of appropriation – it is a resource against which holding forms, templates and parameters of action and experience are forged, if it can be seen to have effects upon bodies, hearts and minds, *then* the matter of music in the social space is, as discussed above, an aesthetic-political matter. This is why matters of taste have, throughout history and across cultures, often been contentious. What, then, of situations – so common in late-modern societies – where the circumstances of music's deployment are beyond actors' control?

Music for strangers

For the most part, the unit of analysis in this book has been the individual and the small social group. With the exception of aerobics, moreover, this focus so far has been directed at individuals' own – albeit at times contested – music practices, with the ways they mobilize music – primarily mechanically reproduced, mass-distributed music – as a backdrop or soundtrack for their private lives. It was necessary to begin at the level of individual practice because it is there that music's links to identity and subjectivity can be seen most clearly. But the project of exploring how music works as an organizing device of human social life would be incomplete without moving beyond this level to consider music's organizing role in more impersonal and socially diffuse circumstances in public settings. Indeed, music's link to the regulation of self and the configuration of subjectivity and agency is of concern to a range of economically and politically interested actors – manufacturers concerned with 'worker satisfaction', motivation and 'fatigue', marketeers interested in 'purchase behaviour', political parties and their desire to win over voters, nations and regimes concerned with fostering belief in their legitimacy, churches, cults and sects seeking to inspire and reinforce 'devotion', and municipalities who wish to suppress hooligan forms of behaviour and crime. All of these actor groups are collectivities who at times have exploited music's powers in their attempts to structure motivation, energy and desire. The burgeoning of the background music industry (Lanza 1994) further attests to the way in which music is increasingly considered as a 'solution' to the 'problem' of social control and management.

Empirical studies, primarily within psychology (North and Hargreaves 1997a; 1997b) and market research (Alpert and Alpert 1989; 1990; Eroglu and Machleit 1993; Kellaris and Kent 1992), have suggested that music can be used to structure conduct in public – feeling, comportment, behaviour, energy, conduct style and identity formation. These studies suggest that music is a device for focusing conduct, drawing conduct into channels associated with a range of organizationally sponsored aims. There is an impressive body of data so far. On-site experiments suggest that background music can influence the time it takes to eat a meal (Milliman 1986; Roballey et al. 1985), drink a soft drink (McElrea and Standing 1992), the average length of stay in a shop (Milliman 1982; Smith and Curnow 1966), the choice of one brand or style over another (North and Hargreaves 1997b) and the amount of money spent (Areni and Kim 1993). In short, in the commercial sector, where results are assessed by profit margins, considerable investment has been devoted to finding out just what music can make people do.

Most sociologists have been slow to appreciate the significance of these findings. In part, this reluctance is linked to the behaviourist discourses in which most studies of 'what music causes' are couched. Those sociologists who have considered the world of marketing, however, have observed that there is much more at stake than the question of how to 'manipulate' consumers. Indeed, what appears to be behaviourism when viewed from a distance is far more complex upon closer scrutiny, involving questions of meaning, appropriation and interpretive work, as described in chapter 2. Moreover, applications in marketing provide access to 'the question that philosophers have posed as the cornerstone of their most complex theoretical edifices: the relationship between subject and object' (Hennion and Meadel 1989:191). To interrogate this relationship is to delve into the sociologically profound matter of how a species of organizationally sponsored agency – mood, energy, desire, action – is informed by and shaped up with reference to organizational-aesthetic materials. How and to what extent, then, is music, as one of the more subtle of these materials, a building material for the production of consumption?

Music in public places – the case of the retail sector

One of the most appropriate settings for investigating music's 'public' powers is the retail sector, where, in recent years, the nature of consumption has undergone development and change. As it is characterized, the shift consists of a move from a utilitarian acquisition of needed objects (such as, when shoes wear out or when a forthcoming social engagement demands 'appropriate' dress) into a key component – particularly for the young, but increasingly the middle-aged as well – of identity construction. Indeed, identity construction and maintenance has become a leisure pursuit in its own right, through the various activities of self-care and cultivation such as body shaping, grooming procedures, therapy and the appropriation of 'style', where a good part of the pleasure associated with these pursuits is linked to the playing out of fantasy life (Bocock 1993; Holbrook and Hirschman 1982; Zepp 1986; Friedberg 1993; Bowlby 1985; Williams 1982). In short, the role of expressive action has expanded in late modern culture. At the level of practice, identity is now construed as put together in and through a range of identifications with aesthetic materials and representations, perhaps most clearly visible in the consumer realm where shopping is now about much more than status distinction (Campbell 1987; Baudrillard 1988; Featherstone et al. 1991; Bocock 1993). It is perhaps best encapsulated by Baudrillard's, 'I shop, therefore I am', but also exemplified in the ways individuals interact with self-help literature (Lichterman 1992), museums (Macdonald 1998; Zolberg 1996) and new social movements (Hetherington 1998; Rojek 1995).

At the level of social theory, the Enlightenment tradition upheld by Max Weber's (1970) belief that the realm of feeling and the romantic were perilous to proper citizenship (which also deeply concerned the critical theorists such as Adorno) has been counterposed, in recent years, to a Durkheimian emphasis on the cultural and aesthetic bases of the subject

who is conceptualized as standing well inside the frame of cultural structures and is interpolated by them (Hetherington 1998:41–59). To delve
into this matter in relation to the retail sector is to speak about the matter
of how identities are constructed from within the technologically
configured 'landscapes of power' (Zukin 1992), which in turn merges
with the more general concern with the interface between material
culture, social action and subjectivity as discussed in chapter 2.

Interest in the interaction between environment and emotional action
is by no means new with regard to consumption; as Anne Friedberg has
observed, nineteenth-century commentators viewed the large department stores as 'machines' for producing consumption, a metaphor that
lives on in the discourse of 1990s shopping mall planners and their preoccupation with 'generators, flow and pull' (Friedberg 1993:112). With
regard to music, it was not uncommon in the department stores of the
early twentieth century for live music to be performed (for example, the
pipe organ at the Philadelphia store, John Wannamakers). However, it
was not until the advent of mechanically reproduced 'muzak' that in-store
sound was converted from overt 'entertainment' to more subliminal
'ambience'. Studying music's in-store presence thus raises the question of
how retail spaces may make designs upon the shopping subject, and how
consumer agency is produced locally, in-store. Moreover, consideration
of retail environments' dependence upon and attempts to advance emotionally flexible, pliable consumer-subjects (as described below) draws
together the otherwise incongruous disciplines of critical social theory
and marketing research. It is in this context, then, that we need to
conceptualize in-store music; it is deployed as a device of social ordering,
an aesthetic means through which consumer agency may be articulated,
changed and sustained. In this sense, the sociology of consumption
cannot afford to ignore the soundtrack of consumer purchasing.

Music is a ubiquitous feature of shopping. Wafting discreetly from con-
cealed speakers or blaring from a prominent VDU, it is as integral to the
artificial environment of the retail sector as climate control, lighting and
interior design. Yet music's presence has passed virtually unnoticed
within the social sciences, where attention has been devoted to the field of
vision in-store, to the mobilization of desire via 'displayed' objects. This
'visualist' conception of in-store subjectivity and its construction (Buck-
Morss 1977; Friedberg 1993) implicitly conceives of shopping as involving the gaze and the mobilization of the gaze.

Perhaps this is because the ears of sociologists, like those of the general
public, are, as Adorno once observed (1976:51), passive. The eye, by contrast, attends selectively – it can close, rivet, avert itself – and so, Adorno
suggests, it is linked more closely to consciousness. By anatomical design,

the ear is 'always open', less, as Richard Middleton puts it, 'subjectively organized than the eye' (1990:94). Moreover, sound objects are fleeting, mercurial; without musical training, it is difficult to 'point' to them or 'see' them, it is more difficult to be aware of and remember sound objects, as they are configured and reconfigured within an instant. Our conceptual vocabulary for music's effects and the mechanisms through which these effects are produced is undeveloped. For these reasons music's powers remain invisible and often fall into a residual category of analysis. (For example, one of the international chain stores we studied handled in-store music under the rubric of 'Visuals' (that is, store design).)

The sound of consumption

The ethnomusicologist Jonathan Sterne (1997) has developed this line of thinking in his study of a U.S. mega-mall, the Mall of America. Sterne conceives of music as a sonic 'framing' device, one that helps mall management to define and differentiate and link together mall spaces through manipulations of the auditory environment. Following the notion that daily life poses a heterogeny of opportunities for existence, Sterne speaks of music as, 'one of the energy flows (such as electricity or air) which continually produce . . . social space' (1997:29). This idea is promising, but it does not go far enough to illuminate the actual mechanisms and moments through and within which such 'flows' are appropriated and get into action. If, moreover, we adhere to the concept of agency, in the sense that has been used so far in this book – as a capacity for emotional, embodied and cognitive being, the shaping up of action in relation to aesthetic parameters – we can apply that concept to the study of the retail sector by investigating the matter of how that sector engages in the activity of helping to sponsor or structure the materials with which agency is constructed in-store.

To be sure, the music of the retail space is organizationally sponsored; it is one of a range of devices by which forms of affective agency can be understood to be placed on offer to shoppers who not only try on or try out goods, but who use the retail space to try on or try out new subject positions, identities and stances. Key, then, is that the shop can be seen to provide a 'natural laboratory', one within which actors may be followed as they are acted upon by aesthetic materials, that is, as those materials are deployed with particular organizational designs on the structure of its object – the structure of the consuming subject. We can also track actors as they enter, move around in and exit the aesthetic field of the retail scene, and we can observe, throughout that time, actors' interactions with the material environments of those scenes. In short, the retail environment is a place where subjectivity and action may be examined as they are constituted in real time and in a sonic setting the parameters of which lie for the most part outside of actors' control. The retail outlet is a useful enclave, then, for considering the matter of how music may function as an organizing device and the related issues of so-called 'people management' and 'social control'. Here, music serves as part of a collection of cultural resources that can be used to create scenic specificity, and to place on offer modes of being. Deliberately and *de facto*, retail outlets seek to foster particular in-store cultures and images of implied clientele.

Clothes have always been carriers of meaning (Davis 1985; Lurie 1992; Mukerji 1994) and key resources for identity work, but their role as resources for identity work varies across age lines (Vincent 1995). Whereas the older women typically make fewer excursions to the shops and have in mind aims and objectives when they do and do not enjoy being distracted, younger women are more likely to view shopping as a leisure-time pursuit, more likely to visit a shop with no specific purchase in mind. The clothing purchases of older women are more likely to be linked to specific needs (professional and social) or to their household budgets. For these women, identity will be further removed, than for younger women, from how they look and its significance. It will be linked to matters such as professional standing, children, social roles and obligations. By contrast, younger women purchase things that help them expand and alter their self-perceived identities and images. Entities far more complex than clothes are being tried on in the changing rooms, where a dress becomes something that 'fits' or may be 'grown into' in a symbolic as well as a physical sense. Young women purchase things they believe to be 'cool' (this word was used repeatedly by shoppers observed in our study) or somehow expressive of how they feel or of images to which they aspire. In our own fieldwork, we viewed, time and time again, young people trying things on as an end in itself, as part of the formation of group culture, and as part of the project of identity work.

These are the kinds of shoppers most likely to make 'impulse purchases', unplanned, on-the-spot spending. Market researchers describe many of these impulse buys as 'experiential purchases', that is, purchases accompanied by emotional reactions such as 'sudden desire to purchase, feeling of helplessness, feeling good, purchasing in response to moods and feeling guilty' (Piron 1993:341). Key to the concept of the 'experiential purchase' is that the arena where desire is formulated as desire 'for' something is the in-store environment. The *emotional* dimension of shopping and the unplanned purchase is thus of major interest to market researchers, who suggest that up to 60 per cent of all purchase decisions are not premeditated but arise as a result of in-store browsing (Yelanjian 1991). If this is so, it helps to highlight the extent to which at least some forms of action are locally organized and so illuminates the notion that subjectivity may be constructed in and through reference to cultural materials as these are encountered during a course of action.

Bearing in mind the significance of the browser, then, the project of configuring consumers and enrolling them into certain emotional states commensurate with displayed goods – seducing consumers – is therefore of paramount importance to retailers. As the 'food of love', music is perhaps the medium *par excellence* for igniting such passions and for structuring in-store subjectivity. In conjunction with window displays, décor, assistants dressed in employee-discounted merchandise and, indeed, the merchandise itself, music is a means of delineating retail territory, a way of projecting imaginary shoppers on to the aesthetically configured space of the shop floor.

Case study: music on an English high street

From January to September 1998, Sophie Belcher and I conducted participant observation and interviews in and around the high street shops in a small city in England. The study considered a total of eleven shops – eight national or international 'chain' shops and three 'independents'. In the discussion that follows (and in accordance with the wishes of outlet managers) these shops are referred to by pseudonyms.

> Canyon: Global chain with U.S. headquarters, specializing in casual wear and cotton goods for men, women and children (T-shirts, shorts, jeans, jackets, small selection of casual skirts and dresses).
>
> Mistral: U.K. company, branches throughout United Kingdom and Europe; clothes for women and children. Dresses, skirts, jackets and trousers in natural materials (silk, linen, cotton, wool), rich colours and floral prints – exotic or ethnic in style.
>
> Elysium: U.K. chain, trendy clothes aimed at affluent young women. Hip-hugger trousers, coats with feather collars, luminous and neon-coloured dresses, shrink-fit T-shirts and sweaters, club wear.
>
> Axiom: U.K. chain, suits, dresses, career clothes in synthetic fabrics, evening wear, shoes. Separate 'Petites' section and men's section.
>
> Linea: U.K. chain, suits, dresses, career clothes, jeans, underwear, bathing suits; men's, children's and furniture sections. Large mail-order department.

Meadow River: Global chain. Floral pattern dresses, skirts, straw hats, some tailored items, furnishings and home décor.

Babe: U.K. chain. Trendy mini-dresses, basque tops, hip-hugger trousers, crochet tops, lower price range.

Directions: U.K. chain. Lower-priced sports wear for young women. Trendy.

Persuasion: Independently owned shop for women. Club wear, quasi-designer labels. 'Funky' type clothing.

Euphoria: Independently owned, trendy menswear, mainly for men in their twenties. Disco clothes; street wear.

Naked: Regional chain selling clubby trainers, platforms, sandals, boots, Doc Martens for men and women.

At the most basic, musical materials serve as 'welcome mats' and 'keep out' notices, depending upon how they are received. Some shops, such as Mistral, may be more lenient about disciplining retail space with musical devices ('The music is a bit of everything for the clientele because they are not one specific age group' (interview with manager)), yet at the same time attempt to construct themselves as a 'style-conscious' store with music in the foreground. Others use music merely to present a bland but recognizable retail identity, such as Canyon, where the music is barely audible and where a policy of playing music in changing rooms was cancelled because, according to the branch manger, 'Clients found it invasive.' Still other shops use a narrower range of overtly prominent music to fine tune their image, broadcast their market niche and heighten their exclusivity. At Babe, for example, music is used to 'encapsulate the corporate identity of young, modern, female and let the customers know that they are in tune with what's going on in the music industry' (interview with manager).

At the locally based independent shops, music's role as a way of specifying store identity – and hence target consumers – is more overt. In these stores, catering to particular market niches and to local clientele in a highly personal manner, the managers expounded upon the importance of sound to the retail environment. For example, Janice, owner and manager of Persuasion, told us, 'Music is essential to the shop image. It creates an environment. When you have come from the hustle . . . it marks a distinct space.' She described the commercial music that plays in most shops as boring, counterposing her own music as, 'more alternative, like my shop . . .'. But she was not in favour of high volume levels for her small shop space. She told us how she aims for subtlety: 'You want it to be mellow, have rhythm . . . not be obtrusive . . .'. The manager of Euphoria, whose target clientele are 'predominantly lads', told us, 'You have to know what will work, and at Euphoria you don't want anything too "soulful" – certainly no classical, but not even jazz' (the shop sticks to drum-and-bass and club numbers). At Naked, the manager described how music 'gives the store an image'. For the young, club-oriented clientele, 'cheesy pop tunes, jazz and classical would be a no-no'. (The shop plays a steady diet of drum-and-bass.)

How and where are store music policies made?

According to the type of store, we found that shop workers had different degrees of autonomy in developing music policy. At the large national and international chain stores, local or branch variation was minimized, in favour of homogeneity. The manager of Canyon told us that they had the idea that in any branch within the same time zone, one should be able to hear the same music at the same instant. Canyon's head office in the United States chooses the music for the United Kingdom, United States and Canada. Supplied by the Muzak corporation, it is changed roughly every two months. The cassette decks are designed to play tapes on auto-reverse, so that store employees cannot play tapes of their own choosing, and company music policy is thus technologically enforced. The staff, we were told by the manager, get bored hearing the same tape over extended periods of time and 'can't wait for a new tape to arrive'. As one staff member put it, 'I hardly ever listen to it. Somehow I switch off, sometimes there are parts that obviously are much more pleasing so you can notice that, but very often I, I suppose when you work in there you have to switch off somehow [i.e., ignore the music].' At Babe, tapes come down from head office every two weeks, two at a time. They have four tapes per deck and every two weeks half of these are changed. At Linea they get a tape each month from head office. At Mistral, tapes come from head office, two per month, but they also keep a backlog of old tapes that they feel they can use since they are not oriented to current chart numbers.

Other stores encourage a form of partial autonomy, in collaboration with record shops from whom CDs are borrowed or purchased. For example, Directions receives a memo every month from its regional head office listing a range of music options. The manager then chooses from this list and borrows tapes from MVC. They usually borrow two a week, one that is 'quite funky/clubby' and one that is 'more mellow'.

While Directions has to work within management-specified parameters, at Naked and Elysium staff enjoy greater autonomy, purchasing, at their own discretion, music from HMV. Both have a monthly budget for music and the manager decides what should be played, though all staff can make suggestions about what should be purchased and played. This, the manager told us, is because the staff are culturally very like the shop's target consumers, they function like 'lead-users' for the product lines. Finally, at the local independent shops, staff have the greatest degree of autonomy; they do not need to work within budgetary or policy constraints. At Euphoria, for example, staff decide what will be played, though when the boss is in, he does the choosing. Staff also bring in music from home. At Euphoria, the manager told us that he chooses music on the basis of what he knows of his customers, that you get to know them and know what they like. At Persuasion, Janice chooses music on the basis of what is going on in the club scene (her partner is a local DJ). She chooses it and changes it every two weeks.

These local and quasi-local music marketing practices are characteristic of newer and more flexible patterns of employment. They also reduce costs by drawing upon skills that are allowed to go unrecognized. Instead of supporting an entire marketing department for music production and policy, retailers can delegate the responsibilities to local staff. These staff, because they are chosen in part for their similarity to target consumers, perform the tasks otherwise allocated to a brand manager, simply by drawing upon their own tastes and preferences in choosing instore music. They are, in effect, prototypical target customers. They also, occasionally, spend their own money on music for the shop. Similarly at HMV and MVC, the local record shops where clothing retailers go to buy or borrow their music, the 'advisory service' that record shop staff provide is unacknowledged (and not remunerated). For example, Dave, from HMV, told us how he tries to be 'reactive not proactive' when giving advice about what music might work in a retail space, and Peter, at MVC, said he wishes he could offer more advice because, in his opinion, many of the shops get their music wrong.

Creating scene, creating agency – music as ambience

In all the stores we studied, music was employed as a resource for creating and heightening scenic specificity, for imparting a sense of occasion and, therefore, for placing modes of agency on offer. For retailers, these affective dimensions of agency are critical because 'point-of-purchase' or 'impulse' sales are typically transactions that involve consumers' emotions, for example, 'purchasing in response to moods' (Piron 1990; 1993; Rook 1987; Rook and Hoch 1985). For this reason, retailers are concerned, as noted above, to structure the aesthetic environment and, through this, the emotional conduct of consumers. This structuring of agency – in particular, emotional agency – applies to shop staff as well as shoppers. Indeed, in the marketing literature, concern with manipulating the moods of *employees* is common. With regard to staff, the idea is that music helps them to do 'emotional work' (Hochschild 1983), enter into a mode of agency conducive to the emotional features of their job – that is, acting like a lead-user (of shop goods) and generally fitting in, in terms of appearance and temperament, with the shop's ambience. With regard to shoppers, the idea is that music helps to enrol them into an appropriate, or institutionally sponsored, mode of agency, that is, a mode of agency that is oriented to purchase behaviour. Certainly during the ethnographic phase of our research we noted numerous examples of staff behaving as if they were co-shoppers, 'confessing' to consumers their own shopping difficulties and dilemmas in a cosy, gossipy manner ('I'm tempted to spend all my salary on clothes here,' for example (overheard in the changing room of Mistral)).

Each shop is engaged in structuring agency through its attempts to create a sense of occasion and a type of scenic specificity. The use of musical means for these purposes is perhaps most visible through music's use in helping to instil temporal specificity to the in-store environment. All the stores we studied, even those with globally organized music policies, such as Canyon, tailored their music to fit temporal trends, and to construct and reinforce temporal realities, whether daily, weekly or seasonal. These constructions were aimed at both staff and shoppers. For example, morning in all the stores is when as one manager put it, 'laid-back' music is played, typically at lower volume levels. In Euphoria, relaxing music is standard for morning. In Naked, Rick described how a typical day begins with 'quite a slow tempo in the morning which rises throughout the day and begins to slow again near the end of the day. That's for staff as well . . .' At Directions the manager described how more 'clubby, up-tempo' music is used at lunchtime and 'always on Saturday' (their busiest day). In fact, all the stores provide louder, more up-beat music for Saturdays – the time when shoppers are oriented to 'The Weekend' and going out. Even at Canyon, where the music is changed roughly every two months, different tapes are used on Saturday: 'more up-tempo music when . . . people [young women] are shopping for outfits for that evening' (quote from interview with manager). At Mistral they begin the day with 'more ambient' tunes, 'more gentle, as loud music would be off-putting'. As the day wears on, from around 11.30 to 12.30, music 'gets more soulful', with cuts from the Brand New Heavies and Ella Fitzgerald, for example. And at Elysium, the music for Saturdays is, as the manager puts it, 'brighter, funkier' though not strictly more up-tempo. This is because, as it was explained to us, there are more young people on a Saturday and the music helps to get everyone in high spirits.

Some of the stores also use music to mark seasonal changes and events. For example, Babe used the soundtrack to the 1997 *Romeo and Juliet* for their Valentine's Day promotions, and in December Linea and Canyon used Christmas music. Directions, on the other hand, whose choice of music from the local MVC is made from within regional office stipulated parameters, were given a Christmas option but rejected it because, 'shoppers were sick of Christmas music . . . to entice them [to] stay we played club and party music, so [it was] seasonal without being Christmassy' (interview with manager). Elysium, by contrast, did use Christmas music and made a point of using special, more 'light-hearted, up-tempo' music during the summer. At the time of Princess Diana's death, Elysium played music that the manager felt, 'matched the mood of the nation', including Diana Ross tapes. (At the time of Diana's funeral, Mistral frequently played the reworked version of 'Candle in the wind'.)

That music is a resource for the temporal construction of occasion is reflected in company music policies, most clearly visible perhaps when those policies are articulated and broadcast downwards in terms of options to local branches where a degree of autonomy is available. For example, at Directions, the instructions sent down from regional headquarters describe how different options are linked to different musical 'effects'. The 3 December memo reads:

Chosen tapes for December:
(1) 'The No. 1 Xmas Album'
I'm afraid there's no escaping Bing Crosby's White Xmas, but this tape is a new release and includes more recent Xmas hits. This tape will be particularly effective on Sundays & late nights.

(2) 'Best Party in the World Ever'
This tape is excellent and includes new mixes of old and new hits. Customers have reacted very well to this. Suitable for every day . . .

It goes on to suggest the following as 'other suitable tapes if you borrow or buy as an individual, which can be played' and describes both when the music will be most effective and also the type of mood it will foster:

(1) 'Best Club Anthems (2) Ever' – Clubby, released last week.
(2) 'Funky Divas' – Very girl power, released today. Varied and upbeat.
(3) 'Wham! The Best Of' – making a huge impact and is predicted to be top 3 for Xmas. Suitable for during the week.

Music is a flexible but powerful interpretative resource

Compared to the other aesthetic materials in-store, music is easily controlled. With the flick of a switch, it can be added, removed, adjusted, altered. Not surprisingly, therefore, music is one of the most frequently altered aspects of in-store environments and, because of its flexibility, it is an ideal medium for temporal definition. Through its ongoing variation, music provides an aesthetic contrast structure, against which more stationary materials can be contextualized and recontextualized. For example, music may lead consumers to attend selectively to some kinds of goods more than others. In Mistral, for example, at the time of Christmas and seasonal parties or summer balls, party and dancing music is played to reinforce the goods displayed at the front of the shop, the party dresses. The slower and more dreamlike numbers are not featured and the 'day wear' is moved to the back of the shop.

What music *does* when it acts as a clarifying material is to serve as an index for a whole style or gestalt of in-store conduct. According to how it is perceived, music may serve as a referent for the formulation of such diverse matters as how to move, how to imagine one's self-identity, how to browse (and thus, perhaps, what to purchase), how to mould one's appearance, and how to think, feel and act. Music is 'there' if and when it is needed for these non-cognitive purposes; if it is not needed it can and is often ignored as, for example, when a shopper becomes engrossed in a particular item. (Music may not, however, be ignored by all – style and volume levels may intervene, as discussed above.) Moreover, particular kinds of music – their perceived genre, their actual materials such as tempo or orchestration, their perceived secondary significations – may carry social and behavioural entailments. These entailments may be active in the public sphere just as they are in the realm of private life within intimate encounters and social gatherings as discussed at the start of this chapter.

In this regard, the wine outlet has received particular attention from environmental psychologists. Recent studies have suggested that music may be particularly effective under conditions of uncertainty, when customers have less knowledge about a product, and are unsure how to discriminate between different options or where the actual choice between different products is not greatly important. For example, when 'classical' (Mozart, Vivaldi, Mendelssohn) music was alternated with 'pop' in a wine outlet, customers exposed to the classical selections bought more expensive items (Areni and Kim 1993). Most of the customers who visited a wine outlet studied by Areni and Kim confessed to having little experience of wine. Given that inexperience, and customers' associated 'vague expectations and intentions' (1993:338), Areni and Kim suggest that 'background music may have operated independently of the expected purchase experience'. By this they mean that:

consumers, consciously or unconsciously, sought external cues as to appropriate behaviour. The classical music may have communicated a sophisticated, upper class, atmosphere, suggesting that only expensive merchandise should be considered. Customers may even have felt pressure to conform to the setting implied by the music by purchasing expensive wine. A second possibility is that the background music communicated to shoppers the price and quality of the merchandise in the store . . . a high prestige, high price image . . . (1993:338)

Following from this work, Adrian North and David Hargreaves have suggested that music can be used to structure product choice (1997b). Using an Asda wine department, they arranged a display featuring two wines, one German, one French, both at the same – relatively inexpensive – price. When background music featured French accordion music, French wines sales rose significantly over German, and when German 'Bierkeller' music was played, the opposite occurred, leading the authors to conclude that music is a referent to which consumers may turn to clarify choice (albeit unconsciously – few admitted, when questioned upon exiting the area, to having 'noticed' the music). Product choice, in other words, is 'fitted' to the aesthetic atmosphere in-store, that is to what MacInnis and Park (1991:162) have described as, 'consumers' subjective perceptions of the music's relevance or appropriateness'.

These studies are exciting from the sociological perspective because they emphasize the importance of 'the symbolic meaning underlying each purchase experience' (Areni and Kim 1993:338). They emphasize shopping as a form of social action, meaningfully oriented in its course and characterized by a range of interpretive activity. (Incidentally, they show, too, how carefully constructed, reflexively administered experimental methods – long snubbed by cultural sociologists – can be used with benefit by sociologists.) This environmental psychological work also underlines consumption as *aesthetic* activity and illuminates the importance, particularly in relation to browsing activity, of the local aesthetic environment as a ground against which purchase behaviour is configured; as discussed above, the point-of-purchase sale is increasingly significant within the retail trade. And the rise of point-of-purchase activity in turn points to the increasing tendency of consumers to visit shops as if they were galleries whose displays are also repositories of identity, modes of aesthetic being. Consumers may enter shops, in other words, simply to 'try on' ideas, goods, as opportunities arise. Given this characteristic form of consumer uncertainty – one goes to a shop to see what the experience will bring, rather as one might go to a park, film or gallery – the salience of in-store aesthetics is heightened. The shop thus provides an ideal case in point for the study of organizational aesthetics. Consumers may also orient to in-store aesthetics as a routine part of their efforts to place or recognize a shop's style and the possibilities for agency that it offers or implies.

What does music do within organizational settings?

It has been suggested above that music can be usefully conceived of as a device of scenic placement. It provides contextual cues (Gumperz 1977; DeNora 1986b) that can be used to shape up the meaning of character and situation. It works, within the scenes of 'real life' as it works in the cinema, bestowing meaning upon the actions and settings that transpire within its sonic frame (Brown 1994; Mundy 1999; Flinn 1992). As the manager of Persuasion put it during an interview, 'When you're trying something on, you picture yourself in a place where they are playing this kind of music.' In similar vein, the manager of Directions opined, 'The music is to get people into the mood of the style of the clothes and the store image.' In retail settings, then, music can serve as a cultural material, a resource to which customers and staff can turn when, with varying levels of discursive awareness, they articulate and execute forms of agency, perhaps particularly under conditions of uncertainty. For example, customers may attend to the shop environment – music and décor – so as to form an overall impression of the setting and the goods purveyed, and also of themselves. Thus music's secondary significations have an impact on the cognitive and interpretive dimension of consumer agency.

But the fact that music is, by definition, a temporal medium, and that it is capable of fluctuating from moment to moment, song to song, and tape to tape, means that music is also an ideal medium for corporeal and social forms of entrainment. Music adds rhythm and pace to settings, temporal qualities with which consumers may, perhaps mostly without conscious awareness, interact, to which they may adapt in (non-cognitive) embodied and emotional ways. Here, through its links to bodily conduct, music's relationship to the 'motional' and emotional aspects of agency are often visible.

One of the most obvious topics in this regard is the connection between musical tempo and movement style. At Babe, fast-paced music is used to create activity and also to reinforce activity, to match fast flow. There, and in other stores, the staff we spoke with believed that fast music encouraged fast shopping. At sale time, when it is host to greater numbers of customers and more goods crammed into the shopping space, Mistral uses faster-paced, snappier music, the kind that may serve as inspiration and template for snappy bodily movements and – implicitly – snap decisions. In this regard, consumption behaviour can be understood – at least sometimes – as a kind of dance.

At other times, when business is slow, shops may attempt to hold customers in the store, to encourage them to look at things slowly, and to seduce them, ultimately, into handling the goods, trying them on and making a purchase. As the manager of Elysium put it, 'Slow music creates a slower mood among staff and shoppers.' There are a number of experimental studies of commercial or catering environments that have also reported correlations between 'slow' music and 'slower' patterns of behaviour (Milliman 1986; Roballey et al. 1985).

Beyond the link between music and bodily pace, however, are yet more intriguing issues concerning what one could think of as mundane choreography. These issues concern the interrelationship between musical rhythm, motional and emotional form. In a discussion of parallels between musical structures and choreographic structures perceived in dance performances, the music psychologists Carol Krumhansl and Diana Lynn Schenck have suggested that dance may express the 'basic "kinetic feel" or "energy shape" of the music' (1997:65). At the more workaday level of mundane movement, we observed in our ethnography of the retail scene a similar phenomenon that we came to term 'brief body encounters with music'. These were moments – sometimes of only a second's duration – where shoppers could be seen to 'fall in' with the music's style and rhythm and where music was visibly profiling consumers' comportment, where it had an impact on the mundane choreography of in-store movement. Some of the 'brief encounters' we witnessed consisted of snapping the fingers or nodding the head (to jazz), waving the hands, palms outwards (to show tunes), slowing movement, making it more fluid and putting the body in balletic postures and subtly raising the chin and head (to slow-paced, languorous music). All the managers we interviewed told us that they commonly observed customers engaging bodily with the music. In Euphoria, the manager told us it was common to see the young male customers 'singing and dancing in front of the mirrors'. In Babe, young women frequently danced, especially in the changing rooms when they were trying on outfits. In Directions, 'People dance around the store, especially when they are trying on stuff', the manager told us. The manager of one of the local record shops was also quick to speak of how he saw people 'singing and dancing all the time'. He described how he saw a variety of imitative behaviour, for example, when he plays a Tom Jones CD he sees male customers putting 'a swagger in their walk'. (Conversely, he told us about 'a certain country and western artist who, when played, empties the store, because it's so depressing. So we don't play him.')

Dancing, toe-tapping, moving about in front of the mirrors, even singing, were all common occurrences in our study. Indeed, the matter of 'mundane choreography', or micro-stylistic changes in comportment and its relationship with social and cultural settings, is an area ripe for development within the field of sociology of everyday life. For how the body is entrained – the motional character of the body in music – may provide a basis for the formulation of emotional matters, energy levels and action styles; in other words, how one moves may provide, through gesture, as discussed in chapter 4, media for the autodidactic process of self-constitution in real time. Dance and/or mundane choreography are, in Scruton's (1995) sense (and also discussed by Frith 1996:265–7), providing a means of grasping the (perceived) aesthetic character of music. 'We should not study listening,' Scruton argues, 'which has so much in common with reading and looking, but dancing, which places music in the very centre of our bodily lives' (quoted in Frith 1996:266). How one moves one's body – and the connotations that one ascribes to those movements ('funky' or 'graceful') – is a resource that, once generated, can be used in turn to clarify or constitute the connotations of the merchandise displayed and its 'desirability' – cool versus uncool, sexy versus cheap, for example.

This bodily 'falling in with' music was evident in our 'consumer shadowing expeditions' (we shadowed a volunteer shopper such that both shopper and shadower wore clip-on microphones: the shopper was asked simply to 'think out loud' and the shadower commented on the volunteer's activities. Tapes could be synchronized because they shared the same in-store soundtrack (see DeNora and Belcher 2000)). We found that, irrespective of what the volunteers said (and irrespective of what we said about the volunteers we were observing!), how they spoke turned out to be as important as what they said in so far as it seemed to correlate, noticeably, with the in-store aesthetic environment. For example, on a shopping expedition with a volunteer that included a spacious shop, decorated with fresh flowers, furniture and laid-back music from George Michael, both volunteer and shadower, who were some distance from each other, commented on how 'nice' the shop was, the volunteer commented that the shop was 'quite relaxing' and, on both tapes, voices audibly slowed, became less clipped and lowered in pitch.

Here, then, we can begin to get at possible connections between musical style and bodily conduct on the one hand, and bodily conduct, browsing and purchase activity on the other. According to the manager of Euphoria, 'Music helps [customers] buy.' What he means by this is that customers purchase products that have stylistic affinities with the background music and with the kind of corporeality that comes to be associated with that music – for example, 'If drum-and-bass music is playing, they will buy street wear, if "clubby clubby" music is playing, they are more likely to purchase tight tops.' Similarly, at Naked, the manager told us that the music may not increase the market *niche* that his store occupies locally (it is a specialist shoe store featuring 'club wear' style shoes and there are only so many members of the local population interested in this kind of shoes) but that it may 'enhance' his market *share* because the type of customers who come to him like the music and return to his store for the music (they are more intensely loyal to his store's culture, and making a purchase in his store is a cultural act in its own right – that is, the store has a high semiotic profile). Conversely, the music provides a mechanism for sharpening his client image by repelling customers whose personal style would be less 'cool'.

In all of these circumstances, the retail outlet produces potential sources of identification for the consumer, who may visit such a location as a kind of identity repository, as a storehouse of possible ways of being and possible stances. By making a purchase, the consumer is exporting a way of being from the shop and importing it into her or his personal repertory of modes of being, where it becomes a resource for the production of self-identity. In this sense, the shop, like the art gallery and the temple, is not only a distributor of fashion and trend, not only a promoter of commodities, but an instrument of social stability, of a particular version of order and its associated modes of consciousness and aesthetic agency. The retail outlet provides cultural resources that in turn structure agency; it is a setting in which the public – goods, images and ambiences – is transposed on to and serves to construct the private realm of subjectivity, value and expressive action. In this sense, music is employed to tune the spirit, to remind the faithful of its value commitments and to align agency with organizational images of model actors. It has the potential to operate at the connotative level and can put its recipients 'in mind' of other social situations, scenes and relations. This is precisely why there have been so many controversies about liturgical music over time. For example, when J.S. Bach was reprimanded in 1730 for including 'new and hitherto unknown' hymns in the liturgical service, 'such an arbitrary procedure is not to be tolerated', wrote the members of the Consistory of the Elector and Prince of Saxony to Bach's boss, Dr Salomon Deyling, the Superintendent of the Thomas-Schule in Leipzig (David and Mendel 1966:118–19). Thus, just as Janice, owner of Persuasion, put it in reference to music's role as a medium that fosters the mental and emotional tuning in a context where one might be wearing the garb one is trying on ('When you're trying something on you imagine yourself in a place where they're playing this kind of music'), so, too, in situations ostensibly devoted to worship it is possible that music helps actors to picture their relation to God and to religious values. In both cases, sacred and profane, music helps to order consciousness, imagination and memory.

The sounds of silence

During the music and daily life study we visited a number of U.S. and U.K. cities and towns to record the 'sound of shopping'. At the end of one of these field trips, we visited a traditional 'ladies' outfitters', whose clientele, with the decline of transgenerational merchandising, has dwindled to (primarily) elderly women. Wending our way through racks of A-line skirts, flower-patterned frocks and good woollen cardigans, we commented on the incongruous silence, strange to us after the relentless soundtracks of 'young people's shops'. Our very footsteps were annulled by thick pile carpeting. In the course of the study we came to realize that, to shoppers two or three generations older than ourselves, the very idea of background music is abhorrent as the following excerpts from exit interviews make clear:

I don't like it when it's jumping because I've got a hearing aid, you see, so it's pretty awful . . . [Besides] I've got other things on my mind, you know. I'm not thinking about music. I'm thinking where am I going to get this skirt I'm looking for.

I call that pollution . . . I don't like any music in shops or in lifts or anywhere.

Reflecting on this matter in the context of the cross-generational interviews with women about music in their lives, and also on 128 exit interviews conducted outside the shops we studied during our ethnography, we concluded that, for older women, local passages in and through music (as, for example, when one encounters music in a social setting) are less significant as a resource for the constitution of self and social setting. This is not to say that music itself was less significant as a cultural medium of agency's constitution, but that the older women with whom we spoke were more likely to conceive of music as something that one stops and listens to with intent. To be sure, the mobilization of electronic music equipment is a cultural practice associated with youth and middle age, but, as the discussion in chapter 3 began to illustrate, the older women who were interviewed for the music in daily life study were less likely to engage in the music-reflexive practices of managing mood through music programming. Music was not something they 'used' to get them into, or get them adjusted to, appropriate or desired emotions, nor was it something they used to structure social scenes and settings within which they acted in concert with others. Indeed, most of them were less reflexive about the production of their agency, and less self-conscious about their self-identity. While it would be misleading to speak of them as more 'secure', they seemed to be less preoccupied with self-monitoring, with observing themselves as feeling, being subjects. They were, perhaps, therefore more impervious to music's deployment as a part of the furniture of public space. They were not so overtly objects of knowledge to themselves, less likely to speak of what they might 'need' to hear and less likely to be 'influenced' by music (apart from music with special biographical significance). They were also most likely to do nothing but *listen* when they put music on the stereo, whether or not they had musical training. These age-linked uses of music in private life and in the retail clothing sector therefore should be explored in relation to the history of consciousness. Are they in line with what some have suggested is an historical transformation of the relations of production and self-production of social agency? To be sure, the social world is more variegated, more complex and contradictory than at any time in the past. Given the discussion above of music's heightened salience under conditions of uncertainty, might this suggest, *pace* recent thinking within social and cultural theory, that agency's configuration has taken on, under late modernity, an increasingly 'other directed' dimension? In what way may the study of music in daily life address these issues?

'Sounds', John Cage once said, 'when allowed to be themselves do not require that those who hear them do so unfeelingly. The opposite is what is meant by response ability' (Cage 1961:10). The point here is that, increasingly, within organizational sectors sounds are not allowed to be themselves or to arise spontaneously (as, for example, when someone bursts into song). Instead they are planned and programmed with the aim of affording organizationally specific ends. In many of the spaces inhabited by younger people – shops, clubs – music is oriented to an agency constituted in real-time and in relation to locally provided audio-aesthetic materials. This form of agency is formulated in relation to mood, ambience and image. In keeping with more recent modes of 'flexible' production, this agency is one that is constituted in relation to the aesthetic materials at hand, here and now; it is adaptive, receptive to being moulded by a range of sensory stimuli. It is not only an aesthetically reflexive mode of agency; it is also aesthetically responsive.

Some commentators have suggested that this new emotional flexibility and the aesthetic reflexivity to which it is linked is liberating (Lash and Urry 1994:3, 31). Others, such as Donald M. Lowe (1995), view the consuming subject in its post-commodity phase as having rescinded autonomy. Today, Lowe argues, retailers no longer cater to pre-existing 'lifestyle' groups but actually instigate the image of such groups by fabricating and placing on offer images of agency that are achievable in and through participation in retail scenes, in and through the purchase of significant items (*pace* the present Archbishop of Canterbury's thesis that malls are becoming sites where the sacred is constructed and worshipped). In a similar critical vein, Stjepan Mestrovic (1999) has suggested that emotional flexibility is a sign of an advanced 'other directedness' (cf. Riesman 1950), an increasingly characteristic tendency, in late modernity, to experience emotion vicariously and according to the parameters of feeling that are placed on offer within specific situations (the classic example here is surely the new brand of 'talk shows').

In a recently translated essay on the 'sociology of music', Adorno observes that, '[w]hat should be close at hand, the "consciousness of suffering", becomes unbelievably alien. The most alien thing of all, however, the process that hammers the machinery into men's consciousness and has ceased to contain that which is human, invades them body and soul and appears to be the nearest and dearest thing of all' (1999:14). Like Adorno, Mestrovic is concerned with the proliferation of a particular kind of emotionality proffered by and in the interests of administration:

What appears to be postmodern disorder or the circulation of random fictions, as depicted by Jean Baudrillard, turns out to have a hidden order of its own, and to be highly automatized, rehearsed, and planned. (1999:2)

There is little doubt that the retail organizations we studied were overtly, deliberately oriented to the deployment of symbols within the social spaces of their shops; there and in many other public social spaces – transport terminals, dentists' chairs, clubs, pubs, restaurants, fitness studies. Indeed, film, television, video and virtual reality as representative 'visual' media all make ample use of music to enhance and sometimes substitute for more overt depiction.

Whether or not one agrees with Mestrovic's neo-Orwellian diagnosis of late modernity, it is easy to see music's role in relation to the processes of administration he describes; indeed, music's role in relation to the 'dialectic of enlightenment' was the subject of Adorno's life work. As an ephemeral and subtle medium, one that can be changed in an instant, music's role is key here in helping to instantiate scenarios of desire, styles of (momentary) agency, and in fostering a new and 'postmodern' form of communitas – a co-subjectivity where two or more individuals may come to exhibit similar modes of feeling and acting, constituted in relation to extra-personal parameters, such as those provided by musical materials. Such co-subjectivity differs in important ways from the more traditional (and modern) notion of 'inter-subjectivity', which presumes interpersonal dialogue and the collaborative production of meaning and cognition. Inter-subjectivity – even if understood in the ethnomethodological sense where it is only apparent and 'for all practical purposes'(Garfinkel 1967) – involves a collaborative version of reflexivity. By contrast, co-subjectivity is the result of isolated *individually* reflexive alignments to an environment and its materials. There is no doubt that *in situ* studies of music in relation to the constitution of subjectivity and agency are crucial to understandings of 'post-emotional' society, and it is all the more strange, therefore, that music has scarcely featured so far in these literatures. For surely it is easy to discern the nucleus of Disneyland in Wagner and the legacy of both in the *Gesamtkunstwerk* of the modern shopping mall?

6   Music's social powers

Music has organizational properties. It may serve as a resource in daily life, and it may be understood to have social 'powers' in relation to human social being. The previous chapters have moved from music's connection to what are generally thought of as the innermost recesses of the self – emotion, memory, self-identity – through music's interrelationship with the body, to music's role as an active ingredient within the settings of interaction. Music is but one type of cultural material; volumes could also be written about the role of many other types of aesthetic materials – visual, even olfactory – in relation to human agency. And music's 'powers' vacillate; within some contexts and for some people, music is a neutral medium.

At other times, music's powers may be profound. In a footnote to his famous study of *encephalitis lethargica* survivors, Oliver Sacks speaks of music's liberating 'power' in relation to Parkinsonism sufferers:

This was shown beautifully, and discussed with great insight, by Edith T., a former music teacher. She said that she had become 'graceless' with the onset of Parkinsonism, that her movements had become 'wooden, mechanical – like a robot or doll', that she had lost her former 'naturalness' and 'musicalness' of movement, that – in a word – she had been 'unmusicked'. Fortunately, she added, the disease was 'accompanied' by its own cure. I raised an eyebrow: 'Music,' she said, 'as I am unmusicked, I must be remusicked.' Often she said, she would find herself 'frozen', utterly motionless, deprived of the power, the impulse, the *thought*, of any motion; she felt at such times 'like a still photo, a frozen frame' – a mere optical flat, without substance or life. In this state, this statelessness, this timeless irreality, she would remain, motionless-helpless, *until music came*: 'Songs, tunes I know from years ago, catchy tunes, rhythmic tunes, the sort I loved to dance to.' (1990:60n, emphasis in original)

Upon hearing or imagining music, Edith T. explained to Sacks, her 'inner music' – the capacity to move and to act – was returned. 'It was like', she said, 'suddenly remembering myself, my own living tune' (1990:60n).

Sacks refers to Kant's conception of music as 'the quickening art', a means for arousing a person's liveliness. For Edith T., as Sacks puts it, music aroused, 'her living-and-moving identity and will, which is otherwise dormant for so much of the time' (1990:61n). He goes on to say, 'this is what I mean when I speak of these patients as "asleep," and why I speak of their arousals as physiological and existential "awakenings," whether these be through the spirit of music or living people, or through chemical rectification of deficiencies in the "go" parts of the brain' (1990:61n).

This link between music and 'awakening' is not metaphorical, it is fiduciary, in the sense that music provides a basis of reckoning, an animating force or flow of energy, feeling, desire and aesthetic sensibility that is action's matrix. The study of music and its powers within social life thus opens a window on to agency as a human creation, to its 'here and now' as existential being. This vista abounds with life; it has vibrancy, a busy or tapestried quality.

In his introduction to his phenomenology of everyday experience, Alberto Melucci eloquently defends the importance of this realm:

Each and every day we make ritual gestures, we move to the rhythm of external and personal cadences, we cultivate our memories, we plan for the future. And everyone else does likewise. Daily experiences are only fragments in the life of an individual, far removed from the collective events more visible to us, and distant from the great changes sweeping through our culture. Yet almost everything that is important for social life unfolds within this minute web of times, spaces, gestures, and relations. It is through this web that our sense of what we are doing is created, and in it lie dormant those energies that unleash sensational events. (1996b:1)

The playing out of social change, politics, social movements, relations of production is experienced and renewed from within this 'web', as Melucci calls it; it is from within the matrix of 'times, spaces, gestures and relations' that these 'larger' things are realized. Put differently, the theatre of social life is performed on the stage of the quotidian; it is on the platform of the mundane and the sensual that social dramas are rendered. In a chapter devoted to the body, Melucci observes, as he puts it, the 'earthly consistency' of emotions, 'fed as they are by moods and sounds, by odours and vibrations. Fear and joy, tenderness and sorrow are not merely ideas but tears and laughter, warmth and trembling' (1996b:72).

In this book I have sought to illuminate but a few of the ways in which music features in this life-web. My aim has been to delve into the matter of how music is constitutive of agency, how it is a medium with a capacity for imparting shape and texture to being, feeling and doing. I have tried to show how music works in this regard through specific circumstances and for particular individuals. Moving between so-called 'normal' and 'disabled' individuals, across settings and life stages, I have tried to show that music is not about life but is rather implicated in the formulation of life; it is something that gets into action, something that is a formative, albeit often unrecognized, resource of social agency. In this final chapter I want to dwell upon the matter of how music works, how its powers come to be harnessed for and converted into action, and how this process can help to illuminate our understanding of social agency.

'Sleepers awake' – music as a resource for human being

In 1731 J.S. Bach wrote the famous cantata, 'Wachet auf, ruft uns die Stimme' (BWV 140) for the twenty-seventh Sunday after Trinity. The opening of this work exhorts those who have been sleeping to 'wake up' and quickly join the procession of the Trinitarian King. Underpinned by dotted – agitated? – rhythms, the sopranos sing the three-syllable message ('Wachet auf') on three sustained notes of the E flat major triad, and this tonally centred, authoritative 'call' is underpinned by a busy counterpoint of the altos, tenors and basses and a 'rushing', forward-moving obbligato in the treble instrumental accompaniment. (The opening is illustrated in figure 7.)

The metaphor of using music to call 'sleepers' to action is apposite. For agency is perhaps the opposite of social 'sleep'. To possess agency, to be an agent, is to possess a kind of grace; it is certainly not merely the exertion of free will or interest. It is, rather, the ability to possess some capacity for social action and its modes of feeling. Judith Butler makes this point clearly in her conceptualization of gender as an outcome of recurrent cultural performance, as the result of how actors mobilize cultural forms and discourses such as language. As she puts it, we need not 'assume the existence of a choosing and constituting agent prior to language . . . there is also a more radical use of the doctrine of constitution that takes the social agent as an *object* rather than the subject of constitutive acts' (1990:270–1, emphasis in original). To be an agent, in the fullest sense, is thus to be imbued – albeit fleetingly – with forms of *aesthesia*. Feeling and sensitivity – the aesthetic dimension of social being – are action's animators; they give action and actors a life spark and a particular energy shape that burns, like a comet or a firecracker, for a time and along a trajectory or path. Following the etymological sense of the word, to be aestheticized is to be capacitated, to be able to perceive or to use one's senses, to be awake as opposed to anaestheticized, dormant or inert. It is also to be awake in a particular manner, to possess a particular calibration of consciousness, an embodied orientation and mode of energy, a particular mixture of feeling. It is in this sense, then, that aesthetic materials such as music afford perception, action, feeling, corporeality. They are vitalizing, part of the process through which the capacity to articulate and experience feeling is achieved and located on a social plane, how it is made real in relation to self and other(s).

Figure 7. Johann Sebastian Bach, Cantata BWV 140, 'Wachet auf, ruft uns die Stimme'

What, then, does it mean to speak of entering into or identifying with music such that one may become aestheticized? If music is a 'quickening art', then how does it work? And how does an understanding of music's mechanisms of operation help to advance sociological conceptions of agency? To address these questions properly requires consideration of how our very concept of social order and its basis is historically specific.

Non-rational orderings

Just as it is customary within sociology to distinguish between 'traditional' and 'modern' societies (Beck et al. 1994), conventional distinctions are also made between 'traditional' and 'modern' musical practice (see, for example, Nettl 1990:1–3; Bebey 1975; Crozier 1997:124). In the latter form, characterized by a commercial and professional mode of music production, and also a pop–serious music aesthetic divide, the activity of music consumption or use is depicted as a relatively private affair, and the predominant category of analysis devoted to this topic is the idea of taste, value and the affiliation of musical predilection with social standing. By contrast, musical use within 'traditional' societies is portrayed as deeply embedded in temporal and ritual custom and in communal practice. The implication is that musical experience is impoverished in modern cultures; this assumption often derives from a tendency to romanticize 'exotic' and 'folk' cultures, to imply, *pace* Weber, that aesthetic and affective bases of action have declined in relation to bureaucratic and rational modes of ordering. Sociological discourse itself is biased against the perception of the aesthetic dimension in modern life. Instead, the sources of orderly conduct are depicted as residing in rules, knowledge, skills and sanctions. This aspect of sociological discourse separates individual from society, subject from object, and culture from agency. It achieves this separation through its use of concepts such as 'interest', 'rationality' and 'free will'.

The notion of 'disenchantment' so pervasive in Weber and Adorno (Greisman 1976), and which usually trails this discourse, orbits around the idea that the aesthetic and sensuous bases of human subjectivity and human activity have been eroded by the tide of rational administration and rational, calculative modes of consciousness. This notion may, however, be an artefact of 'modernistic' sociological discourse, a part of the discourse's tropes rather than an accurate description of social and aesthetic practice. Indeed, as was discussed in chapter 5, the notion of disenchantment has been subject to revision in recent years (Campbell 1987; Hetherington 1998). In its stead, culture's role in modern societies has been made more central in relation to the structuring of social action. The study of musical practice in modern societies – what one might refer to as an 'ethnomethodological ethnomusicology', if it were not so clumsy to enunciate – has the potential to enhance significantly this neo-Durkheimian strand of thinking about culture and agency. Contrary to received notions about music's waning role within modern cultures:

in advanced industrial societies music is all around us, a major element in our
culture, in contrast to the situation in pre-electronic times when it was a much less
pervasive medium, and a much smaller part of most people's experience. It is this
contrast, though, that may serve to arouse our sociological curiosity: instead of
just taking music for granted, we might begin to ask why it has come to occupy
such a prominent place in our world. (Martin 1995:1)

A sociology of music concerned with the ground level of musical practice (Weber's (1958 [1921])) was not), quickly leads to the idea that it is
probably more reasonable to propose that music's relation to forms of
social order within Western cultures is not inactive, but, rather, usually
unnoticed by social scientists. This is not to say that there are no cross-
cultural and historical differences in music's social position, its functions
and uses; there are many. But the central difference between so-called
'modern' and 'traditional' music cultures, probably does not reside in
music's disembeddedness from social practice, its disjuncture from social
'function' and its reinstatement as an object of 'listening only', from the
processes of putting together subjects and situations. By contrast, the
major differences between music in modern versus traditional cultures
can be seen to lie in the *relations* of music's production – how and where
music is created, how musical forms undergo change, how music is performed and the quality of the performer–consumer relationship (for
example, modes of attention, spatial relationship, who may count as a
musician and how evaluation takes place and how music is distributed –
such as many to many, one to one, one to many, many to one). Key, here,
is the issue of how music distribution is controlled and, in modern societies, consolidated, as with the large record production firms and the burgeoning empires of music distribution. Key, too, are the social relations of
how music is deployed within settings and the degree to which soundtracks for settings are negotiated.

There are many informal ways in which music is employed as an ordering device in social life within modern societies. This book has only
scratched the surface of this topic. At the level of individual experience,
these practices may not be overtly regulated at the communal, collective
level (apart from criticism, professional or lay), though they are typically
oriented to imagined communities and imagined (and often aspirational)
scenarios – peer groups, idealized situations, conventional images and
associations. A given individual may turn to a wide gamut of recorded
music for any task and at any hour of the day and, if using a Walkman,
may listen to music nearly anywhere. At the same time, musical practice is
by no means individuated; regularities of musical use abound, as for
example when retail outlets draw upon conventional notions of musical
energy levels at different times of the day or week, or when transport sta-

tions employ Vivaldi, Mozart and Delius to soothe irate travellers and to disperse potential hooligans. A thorough examination of these practices would have the potential to illuminate the (typically overlooked) aesthetic structures of social action, structures that undergo constant revision and renegotiation at the level of action. Seen in this light, the recent theorization of aesthetic reflexivity only serves to reveal matters that are – in more traditional cultures – more explicitly recognized as central to aesthetic ordering and its practice. How, then, might we account for the invisibility, within daily life, of music's powers to produce order?

Ever since Beethoven uttered the notorious phrase, 'I will not play for such swine' (in response to some aristocratic listeners who talked through one of his performances), Western music has been encumbered with the paraphernalia of 'high art'; 'good' music has become, and been designed as, an object upon which to reflect, an object for rapt contemplation. This ideology has also been projected backward on music that was originally designed to be heard within social contexts: Telemann's *Tafelmusik* is perhaps the most famous example, but even Mozart was often heard amidst cries from the sausage sellers. The august music patron Baron van Swieten was described by one of Mozart's nineteenth-century biographers as exerting:

all his influence in the cause of music, even for so subordinate an end as to enforce silence and attention during musical performances. Whenever a whispered conversation arose among the audience, his excellence would rise from his seat in the first row, draw himself up to his full majestic height, measure the offenders with a long, serious look and then very slowly resume his seat. (Jahn 1882,II:385)

Within the modern institution of 'serious' listening, to listen 'correctly' is to be 'transported', to abandon, albeit temporarily, the realm of material and temporal being, to allow oneself to be taken over by music's textual time. In this sense, 'serious' music may have been the earliest and most elaborated form of virtual reality. The abstraction of music from the flux of daily existence, and its excision of the body – both in terms of bodily rhythms in compositions and in terms of the motionlessness stipulated as appropriate listening conduct – have served to obliterate the none the less vital tradition of other music and its role in social life outside the concert hall, its role as it is woven into the tapestry of social life through the informal singing of songs, the pop concert, the car radio, the jukebox, ambient music, organizational music, amateur music production, singing, whistling and humming, and the playing of records, tapes and CDs. It is in all of these locations – from gilded concert hall to mega-mall, from bus terminal to bedroom – that music makes available ways of feeling, being, moving and thinking, that it animates us, that it keeps us 'awake'.

Reprise – what does music do?

Auden once said of poetry that it 'makes nothing happen', but rather that it survives as, 'a way of happening, a mouth' (1940). Music, too, is a way of happening, it issues as an audible channel, a series of audible articulated signals. In this sense, music is not 'about' anything but is rather a material that happens over time and in particular ways. Music is a medium, *par excellence*, of showing us how happening may occur; its forms and gestures stand, in Eyerman and Jamieson's (1998) sense, as exemplars. One against many, all together, fugal, homophonic, softly, loudly, gentle or abrupt, legato, staccato, relaxed, tense, juxtapositions, variations, monotony – music is a medium that shows us ways of happening and, in common with dance, drama and cinema, music moves through time; indeed, it creates its own time and its own history, cyclical, linear, recursive. Music is also a physical medium, one that in and through its production shows us actors as they are engaged in forms of embodied production – the alarmingly extended cheeks of Dizzy Gillespie, the 'throaty' voice of Louis Armstrong, the apparent ease of Joan Baez's upper range, the oarsmen-like approach of a tutti string section. Just how these things are perceived, what they are taken to mean and what they may afford cannot be specified through musical analysis, traditionally conceived. These matters are, as was argued in chapter 2, best pursued through ethnographic investigation.

In the earlier chapters of this book, examples were provided where music was seen to work as a model – for conception, for a range of bodily and situational activities, and for feeling, whether as emotional work or as a way of heightening particular modes of feeling. We have also seen how the appropriation of music as a model often occurs at the semi-conscious, non-rational level of human existence even as and when its appropriation may be understood as aesthetically reflexive action. Music may serve, for example, as a model of self, a resource for articulating and stabilizing self-identity ('the me in music', as Lucy put it). One can find one's self in music's ways of happening, draw parallels between it and one's self such that one may say to self and others, 'as this music happens, so do I'. One can also recall one's self on rehearing music (for instance, 'as this music happened, so did I') and music is a key resource for the production of autobiography and the narrative thread of self. We have also seen how music may serve as a model of where one is, is going, or where one 'ought' to be emotionally ('it gets you in the mood'), such that an individual may say to him or herself something on the order of, 'as this music is, so I should or wish to be'. Music is one of the resources to which actors turn when they engage in the aesthetic reflexive practice of configuring self and/or others as emotional and aesthetic agents, across a variety of scenes, from quasi-public (a 'buzzy' barbecue or a 'sophisticated' cocktail party) to intensely private (an intimate encounter). In public, music may be most effective at times when individuals experience social and aesthetic uncertainty, such as that described in chapter 5, where music may proffer cues and models for 'appropriate' agency within a setting. There, too, we saw music as providing a way of modelling future action and interaction, 'setting the scene', so to speak, by exemplifying action styles and ways of happening. Music's capacity for exemplification arises from its primary and secondary significations; actors may refer to music's sensuous properties as well as to the connotations they perceive within its structures. As a model, music serves as a resource for the generation and elaboration of ways of happening in many other realms. In this capacity it also serves as a means of melding present to future in so far as it may be applied in ways that permit cultural innovation in non-musical realms. As music is seen to be organized, so too can people and institutions be organized. In this sense, music may serve as a resource for utopian imaginations, for alternate worlds and institutions, and it may be used strategically to presage new worlds. As Pelle Ehn describes this role of 'sensuous knowledge' in the workplace (Ehn 1988:449), so, too, music provides a fund of materials that serve as paradigms, metaphors, analogues, hints and reminders of activity, practice and social procedure.

But music's powers extend beyond its capacity to serve as a paradigm. Its temporal dimension, the fact that it is a non-verbal, non-depictive medium, and that it is a physical presence whose vibrations can be felt, all enhance its ability to work at non-cognitive or subconscious levels. Indeed, to speak of music merely as a kind of exemplar is to remain committed to a cognitivist conception of agency, one that is organized around the notions of mental skill and interpretive practice. Such a conception stops short of the more profound levels on which music also operates, the levels on which we do not turn to music as a resource but are rather caught up in it, find ourselves in the middle of it, are awakened by it. Victor Turner, whose work offers one of the most extensive theorizations of culture-as-performance, has himself emphasized this point, suggesting that the notion of the cultural paradigm, 'goes beyond the cognitive and even the moral to the existential domain' (1981:149).

In the discussion of music and aerobic exercise this point is perhaps most strikingly illustrated. There, when music is used successfully to configure the aerobic embodied subject over forty-five minutes, we can actually see music as it configures, reconfigures and transfigures subjects, their modes of consciousness and their embodied capacities. There, music works as a prosthetic technology of the body, heightening and extending bodily capacities. There, too, different types of music enable different relocations and levels of awareness, heightening and suppressing bodily energies and capacities, modes of attention and feeling. In the examples where actors used music to facilitate concentration, to vent unpleasant emotions, to manage and modulate emotional states, and to relive past emotional states, we can see music getting into action in ways that elide conscious reflection. In the retail realm, where music is used to instigate modes of orienting to goods, actors also enter into musical moods and rhythms. In these examples, music is much more than a model, much more than an object upon which to reflect and from which to get ideas or take inspiration. Rather, music can be seen to place in the foreground of perception an ongoing, physical and material 'way of happening' into which actors may slip, fall, acquiesce. This passing over into music, this musical mediation of action, is often observable, often known to self as a feeling or energy state. It is also a local phenomenon, something that occurs in the here and now of action's flux, as actors interact with music's presence in an environment or social space. This aspect of music illuminates the body as an entity configured in relation to its material-cultural environment. It speaks directly to medical and physiological concerns.

Musical power and its mechanisms

There is little evidence in favour of a behaviourist conception of music's powers in respect to agency, though, as discussed in chapter 2, it is perhaps to be expected that certain, to some degree predictable, associations between music and action have come to be established and maintained to varying degrees. Arguments such as those advanced by Aristotle or the Parents' Music Resource Centre, that certain melodies are 'conducive to virtue' or destructive of well-being are non-explanatory; they do not offer any account for the mechanisms through which music comes to produce its alleged effects. On its own, music has no more power to make things happen than does kindling to produce combustion. In both cases, certain catalytic processes need to occur. Theorizing the catalyst that conjoins music and human being is, however, no easy task.

One entry to this topic can be found via the concepts of embodied awareness and latching, as described in chapter 4. These terms were used in relation to non-cognitive, non-conscious, embodied engagement with music that is the first step to becoming a musically enlisted, musically animated agent. Latching, which is a kind of musical version of Callon's *interessement* (1986), is always a local process; it occurs in relation to music as it is encountered in the here and now of social life. The simplest example of such latching involves movement to music, whether toe tapping or finger snapping, or more complex movement styles that merge into what we would normally refer to as dance. In these examples, the body actually engages in movements that are organized in relation to, and in some way homologous with, music's properties, its ways of happening, such as tempo, rhythm or gestural devices, and so becomes entrained with the music. Certainly, no music will reliably move all listeners. But for particular listeners and perhaps types of listeners, certain musical figures, devices, genres, forms or works may serve as triggers or latches that draw music's recipients into the process of entrainment and hence into particular modes of agency. 'Juicy chords', cha-cha-cha rhythms, slow 'smoochy' vocals, biographically significant pieces, formal developments – features such as these were able to move particular actors in or on to particular states or trains of feeling, moving and acting. These features will be significant for actors; they will stand out in some way.

Tuning in to music also involves a kind of identification, a recognition, at a sympathetic and embodied level of the various shapes and textures of 'happening', of, as discussed above, the body in music (in Barthes's terminology, the 'grain of voice' (1977)) and of the ways in which music handles itself. Perhaps music has the capacity to be socially powerful as a resource for agency because, as a way of happening that moves through time, it allows us, should we latch on to it, to engage in a kind of visceral communion with its perceived properties. We can imagine and 'feel', for example, the close-knit texture of dissonant polyphony, or the 'wide-open spaces' of fifths and fourths, or the 'depressed' character of the minor triad. Perhaps the clearest and most dramatic example of this process can be found in medical-based music therapy, where music is employed as a template for bio-feedback, where one may, in and through identification with particular musical properties, alter physiological and emotional states and bodily awareness. Under such circumstances, music can be said to reformulate parameters of embodied experience, to alter pulse or breathing, for example, to diminish awareness of pain. One's pulse 'becomes' – is modified in relation to – that of the music; one's pain 'replaced' by the state of music. Examples such as these, where music is employed deliberately so as to reformulate embodied agency, show music's formative powers in relation to agency across the flux of social existence. Music's recipients may not become the music *per se*, but they become music filtered through themselves and it is this that should be meant by the concept of music's powers to mediate and to inform.

In all of these examples, articulations are made, within the web of daily existence, between musical procedures and social and social psychological ones; in all of these examples, music serves as a medium in, through and against which feeling, perception, attention, consciousness, action and embodied processes are produced. At times, actors may engage in this appropriation process with deliberation, knowing how certain music works on them from past experience. But at other times, music may take actors unaware. The matter of how music is distributed is thus inextricable from concerns about social control, from the matter of how a citizenry or a workforce is constituted, and from the issue of how desire may be manufactured.

Politics of music in the public space

In his pioneering history of background music, Joseph Lanza quotes Howard Martin, a researcher at the forefront of background music design, who, rather alarmingly, compares music to a drug (and so echoes Jimi Hendrix's view that 'music is . . . a safe kind of fix'):

He is among a new generation of thinkers interested in advancing the background music philosophy further: 'People will start to look at music the way they used to look at dope. They will see music for its specific psychological effects. Music has the power to change moods and attitudes. Using music with these applications makes more sense now with the time crunch everyone's in.' (1994:231)

Lanza goes on to report on recent trends in Japanese office music providers who have now expanded the concept of muzak to the total office environment – 'Sense Business' or 'New Office' – dedicated to creating 'the good human environment of sound, vision, and aroma' (1994:231), reviews the dis-utopian objections to such a vision but concludes that:

A world without elevator music would be much grimmer than its detractors (and those who take it for granted) could ever realize. This is because most of us, in our hearts, want a world tailored by Walt Disney's 'imagineers', an ergonomical 'Main Street U.S.A', where the buildings never make you feel too small, where the act of paying admission is tantamount to a screen-test – and where the music never stops. (1994:233)

In this passage, Lanza glosses over a key issue, one that lies at the heart of why music is, more than ever, a topic for sociology. If music is a medium for the construction of social reality, then control over the distribution of the musical resources in and through which we are configured as agents is increasingly politicized and the movements, such as Pipedown in the United Kingdom, against piped background music, have been spawned in reaction to what is perceived as the commercial dominance of the public sonic sphere.

At issue here is the matter of consciousness itself and how actors come to connect with the musical resources which are agency's building materials and how this process transpires across a variety of social scenes and settings. There is a significant difference between employing music that one makes oneself (performing or composing) for this purpose and employing music that just happens to occupy a social setting; that difference consists of the degree to which one may negotiate the aesthetic parameters of action. As was described above, there are times when the ability to control one's aesthetic environment is crucial to individuals – in intimate settings, at times of stress, to afford concentration, to vent aggression, to avoid painful music. To the extent that music can be seen to get into or inform subjectivity and action, then, the issue of aesthetic control and its relation to the constitution of agency is serious, particularly as organizations and marketeers are becoming increasingly sophisticated in their deployment of music. Further explorations of music as it is used and deployed in daily life in relation to agency's configuration will only serve to highlight what Adorno, and the Greek philosophers, regarded as a fundamental matter in relation to the polis, the citizen and the configuration of consciousness; namely, that music is much more than a decorative art; that it is a powerful medium of social order. Conceived in this way, and documented through empirical research, music's presence is clearly political, in every sense that the political can be conceived.

Bibliography

Adorno, T.W. 1967. *Prisms* (trans. S. and S. Weber). London: Neville Spearman.
  1973. *Philosophy of Modern Music* (trans. W. Blomster). New York: Seabury.
  1976. *Introduction to the Sociology of Music* (trans. E.B. Ashby). New York: Seabury.
  1991. 'On the Fetish Character in Music and the Regression of Listening', in T.W. Adorno, *The Culture Industry* (J. Bernstein, ed.), pp. 26–52. London: Routledge.
  1999. *Sound Figures*. Stanford: Stanford University Press.
AEI Music. n.d. *Business Music Services*. Orpington, Kent: AEI Rediffusion Music Ltd.
Akrich, Madeleine. 1991. 'The De-scription of Technical Objects', in W. E. Bijker and J. Law (eds.), *Shaping Technology/Building Society: Studies in Sociotechnical Change*, pp. 205–44. Cambridge, MA: MIT Press.
Akrich, Madeleine and Bruno Latour. 1991. 'A Summary of a Convenient Vocabulary for the Semiotics of Human and Nonhuman Assemblies', in W.E. Bijker and J. Law (eds.), *Shaping Technology/Building Society: Studies in Sociotechnical Change*, pp. 259–64. Cambridge, MA: MIT Press.
Aldridge, David. 1992. *Music Therapy Research and Practice in Medicine: From Out of the Silence*. London: Jessica Kingsley Publishers.
Allanbrook, Wye Jamison. 1983. *Rhythmic Gesture in Mozart: Le Nozze di Figaro and Don Giovanni*. Chicago: University of Chicago Press.
Alpert, J.I. and M.I. Alpert. 1989. 'Background Music as an Influence in Consumer Mood and Advertising Responses', *Advances in Consumer Research* 16:485–91.
  1990. 'Music Influences on Mood and Purchase Intentions', *Psychology and Marketing* 7:109–33.
Anderson, Robert and Wesley Sharrock. 1993. 'Can Organizations Afford Knowledge?' *Computer Supported Cooperative Work* 1:143–61.
Areni, C.S. and D. Kim. 1993. 'The Influence of Background Music on Shopping Behaviour: Classical versus Top-forty Music in a Wine Store', *Advances in Consumer Research* 20:336–40.
Atkinson, Paul. 1990. *The Ethnographic Imagination*. London: Routledge.
Attali, Jacques. 1985. *Noise: A Political Economy of Sound*. Minneapolis: University of Minnesota Press.
Auden, W.H. 1940. 'In Memory of W.B. Yeats', in *The Collected Poetry of W.H. Auden*. New York: Random House.

Auerbach, Erich. 1953. *Mimesis: The Representation of Reality in Western Literature.* Princeton: Princeton University Press [1957 Anchor Book edition].

Barnes, Barry. 1982. 'On the Extension of Concepts and the Growth of Knowledge', *Sociological Review* 30:23–44.

1995. *The Elements of Social Theory.* London: University of London Press.

Barnes, Barry and Steven Shapin (eds.). 1979. *Natural Order: Historical Studies of Scientific Culture.* London and Beverly Hills: Sage.

Barthes, Roland. 1977. 'The Grain of the Voice', reprinted in S. Frith and A. Goodwin (eds.), *On Record: Pop, Rock and the Written Word,* pp. 293–300. London: Routledge

Barzun, Jacques. 1980. 'The Meaning of Meaning in Music: Berlioz Once More', *The Musical Quarterly* 66:1–20.

Baudrillard, J. 1988. 'Consumer Society', in M. Poster (ed.), *Jean Baudrillard: Selected Writings.* Stanford: Stanford University Press.

Bebey, F. 1975. *African Music: A People's Art.* Westport, CT: Lawrence Hill.

Beck, Ulrich, Anthony Giddens and Scott Lash. 1994. *Reflexive Modernization.* Cambridge: Polity.

Becker, Howard, S. 1982. *Art Worlds.* Berkeley, Los Angeles and London: University of California Press.

1989a. 'Ethnomusicology and Sociology: A Letter to Charles Seeger', *Ethnomusicology* 33:275–85.

1989b. *Doing Things Together.* Chicago: University of Chicago Press.

Belcher, Sophie. 1997. *The Metropolis and Aesthetic Life: An Ethnography of London's Design Elite.* MA Dissertation, Department of Sociology, University of Exeter.

n.d. Fieldnotes on Music Therapy, *ESRC Project on 'Human–Music Interaction'.* Department of Sociology, University of Exeter.

Belcher, Sophie and Tia DeNora. 1998. 'Good Music Produces Hard Bodies', *Fitness Direct* 7 and 8.

Forthcoming. 'Good Music, Powerful Bodies, Strong Constructivism: The Musical Composition of Embodied Agency during 45 Minutes of Aerobic Exercise', *Body & Society.*

Berger, Bennett. 1995. *An Essay on Culture.* Berkeley, Los Angeles and London: University of California Press.

Bertaux, Daniel (ed.). 1986. *Biography and Society: The Life History Approach in the Social Sciences.* London: Sage.

Birke, Lynda. 1992a. 'In Pursuit of Difference: Scientific Studies of Men and Women', in G. Kirkup and L. Smith Keller (eds.), *Inventing Women: Science, Technology and Gender,* pp. 81–102. Cambridge: Polity.

1992b. 'Transforming Biology', in H. Crowley and S. Himmelweit (eds.), *Knowing Women: Feminism and Knowledge,* pp. 66–77. Cambridge: Polity.

1995. *Feminism, Science and Animals: The Naming of the Shrew.* Milton Keynes: Open University Press.

Blomster, W.V. 1977. 'Adorno and his Critics: Adorno's Musico-sociological Thought in the Decade Following his Death', *Musicology at the University of Colorado*: 200–17.

Bocock, Robert. 1993. *Consumption.* London: Routledge.

Bødker, Susanne and Kaj Grønbaeck. 1984. 'Cooperative Prototyping: Users and

Designers in Mutual Activity', *International Journal of Man-Machine Studies* 34:453–78.

Born, Georgina. 1995. *Rationalizing Culture: IRCAM, Boulex, and the Institutionalization of the Musical Avant-Garde*. Berkeley, Los Angeles and London: University of California Press.

Bourdieu, Pierre. 1984. *Distinction: A Social Critique of the Judgement of Taste*. Cambridge, MA: Harvard University Press.

Bowlby, Rachel. 1985. *Just Looking: Consumer Culture in Dreiser, Gissing and Zola*. New York: Methuen.

Bowler, Anne. 1994. 'Methodological Dilemmas in the Sociology of Art', in D. Crane (ed.), *The Sociology of Culture*, pp. 247–66. Oxford: Blackwell.

Brown, Royal, S. 1994. *Overtones and Undertones: Reading Film Music*. Berkeley, Los Angeles and London: University of California Press.

Bryson, Bethany. 1996. '"Anything But Heavy Metal": Symbolic Exclusion and Musical Dislikes', *American Sociological Review* 61:884–99.

Buck-Morss, Susan. 1977. *The Origin of Negative Dialectics*. New York: The Free Press.

Bunt, Leslie. 1997. 'Clinical and Therapuetic Uses of Music', in D.J. Hargreaves and A.C. North (eds.), *The Social Psychology of Music*, pp. 249–67. Oxford: Oxford University Press.

Butler, Judith. 1990. 'Performative Acts and Gender Constitution: An Essay in Phenomenology and Feminist Theory', in Sue-Ellen Case (ed.), *Performing Feminisms: Feminist Critical Theory and Theatre*, pp. 270–82. Baltimore and London: The Johns Hopkins University Press.

Cage, John. 1961. *Silence*. Middletown, CT: Wesleyan University Press.

Callon, Michel. 1986. 'Some Elements of a Sociology of Translation: Domestication of the Scallops and the Fishermen of St Brieuc Bay', in J. Law (ed.), *Power, Action and Belief: A New Sociology of Knowledge*, pp. 196–233. London: Routledge.

Campbell, Colin. 1987. *The Romantic Ethic and the Spirit of Modern Consumerism*. Oxford: Blackwell.

Candy Rock. n.d. 'Music and Systems for Businesses', in *Total Sound Solutions Ltd* brochure. Sheffield: Candy Rock Recording Ltd.

Clarke, Adele. 1990. 'The Sociology of Science and Symbolic Interactionism', in H.S. Becker and M. McColl (eds.), *Symbolic Interaction and Cultural Theory*. Chicago: University of Chicago Press.

Cockburn, Cynthia. 1983. *Brothers: Male Dominance and Technological Change*. London: Pluto Press.

Cohen, Sarah. 1993. 'Ethnography and Popular Music Studies', *Popular Music* 12(2):123–38.

Collins, S. and K. Kuck. 1990. 'Music Therapy in the Neonatal Intensive Care Unit', *Neonatal Network* 9(6):23–6.

Coser, Lewis (ed.). 1978. Special issue, 'The Production of Culture', *Social Research* 45(2).

Crafts, Susan, Daniel Cavicchi and Charles Keil. 1993. *My Music*. Hanover, NH and London: Wesleyan University Press.

Crozier, W. Ray. 1997. 'Music and Social Influence', in D.J. Hargreaves and A.C.

North (eds.), *The Social Psychology of Music*, pp. 67–83. Oxford: Oxford University Press.

Cue [Magazine]. 1994. 'The Fast Food of Love', February: 68–71.

David, Hans T. and Arthur Mendel (eds.). 1966. *The Bach Reader: A Life of Johann Sebastian Bach in Letters and Documents* (revised with a supplement). London: J.M. Dent and Sons Ltd.

Davis, Fred. 1985. *Fashion*. New York: The Free Press.

De Las Heras, V. 1997. 'What Does Music Collecting Add to our Knowledge of the Functions and Uses of Music?' Unpublished MSc. dissertation, Department of Psychology, Keele University.

DeNora, Tia. 1986a. 'Structure, Chaos and Emancipation: Adorno's Philosophy of Modern Music and the Post-war Avant-garde', in R. Monk (ed.), *Structures of Knowing*, pp. 293–322. New York: University Press of America.

1986b. 'How is Extra-musical Meaning Possible? Music as a Place and Space for Work', *Sociological Theory* 4:84–94.

1995a. 'The Musical Composition of Reality? Music, Action and Reflexivity', *Sociological Review* 43:295–315.

1995b. *Beethoven and the Construction of Genius: Musical Politics in Vienna 1792–1803*. Berkeley, Los Angeles and London: University of California Press.

1995c. 'Deconstructing Periodization: Sociological Methods and Historical Ethnography in 18th Century Vienna', *Beethoven Forum* 4:1–18.

1997. 'Music and Erotic Agency – Sonic Resources and Social-sexual Action', *Body & Society* 3(2):43–65.

n.d. 'Interview with a World War II Veteran'. University of Exeter.

DeNora, Tia and Sophie Belcher. 2000. 'When you're Trying Something on you Picture Yourself in a Place where they're Playing this Kind of Music – Musically Sponsored Agency in the British Clothing Retail Sector', *Sociological Review* (February).

Denzin, Norman. 1989. *Interpretive Biography*. London and Los Angeles: Sage.

DiMaggio, Paul. 1982. 'Cultural Entrepreneurship in Nineteenth-century Boston: The Creation of an Organizational Base for High Culture in America', Parts 1 and 2, *Media, Culture and Society* 4:35–50; 303–22.

DiMaggio, Paul, Michael Useem and Paula Brown. 1978. *Audience Studies in the Performing Arts and Museums: A Critical Review*. Washington, DC: National Endowment for the Arts.

DiMaggio, Paul and Michael Useem. 1979. 'Cultural Democracy in a Period of Cultural Expansion: The Social Composition of Arts Audiences in the United States', *Social Problems* 26:180–97.

Dorn, Ed. 1978. *Hello La Jolla*. Berkeley: Wingbow Press.

Dyer, Richard. 1990 [1979]. 'In Defense of Disco', reprinted in S. Frith and A. Goodwin (eds.), *On Record: Rock, Pop and the Written Word*, pp. 410–18. London: Routledge.

Eco, Umberto. 1984. *Semiotics and the Philosophy of Language*. London: Macmillan.

Ehn, Pelle. 1988. *Work-oriented Design of Computer Artifacts*. Stockholm: Arbetslivscentrum.

Eroglu, S. and K. Machleit. 1993. 'An Empirical Study of Retail Crowding: Antecedents and Consequences', *Journal of Retailing* 66:201–21.

Eyerman, Ron and Andrew Jamieson. 1998. *Music and Social Movements: Mobilizing Tradition in the 20th Century*. Cambridge: Cambridge University Press.

Featherstone, Mike, Mike Hepworth and Bryan S. Turner (eds.). 1991. *The Body: Social Process and Cultural Theory*. London: Sage.

Flinn, Caryl. 1992. S*trains of Utopia: Gender, Nostalgia, and Hollywood Film Music*. Princeton: Princeton University Press.

Ford, Charles. 1991. *Cosi? Sexual Politics in Mozart's Operas*. Manchester: Manchester University Press.

Frazer, Elizabeth and Deborah Cameron. 1989. 'On Knowing What to Say', in R. Grillo (ed.), *Social Anthropology and the Politics of Language*, pp. 25–40. London: Routledge.

Friedberg, Anne. 1993. *Window Shopping: Cinema and the Postmodern*. Berkeley, Los Angeles and London: University of California Press.

Frith, Hannah and Celia Kitzinger. 1998. '"Emotion Work" as a Participant Resource: A Feminist Analysis of Young Women's Talk-in-interaction', *Sociology* 32(2):299–320.

Frith, Simon. 1978. *The Sociology of Rock*. London: Constable.

1981. *Sound Effects: Youth, Leisure, and the Politics of Rock 'n' Roll*. New York: Pantheon.

1987. 'Towards an Aesthetic of Popular Music', in Richard Leppert and Susan McClary (eds.), *Music and Society: The Politics of Composition, Performance and Reception*, pp. 133–50. Cambridge: Cambridge University Press.

1990a. 'What is Good Music?', in J. Shepherd (ed.), *Alternative Musicologies/Les Musicologies alternatives*. Special issue of the *Canadian University Music Review/Revue de musique des universités canadiennes*, 10(2):92–102. Toronto: Toronto University Press.

1990b [1985]. 'Afterthoughts', reprinted in S. Frith and A. Goodwin (eds.), *On Record: Pop, Rock and the Written Word*, pp. 419–24. London: Routledge.

1996. *Performing Rites: Evaluating Popular Music*. Oxford: Oxford University Press.

Frith, Simon and Angela McRobbie. 1990 [1978]. 'Rock and Sexuality', reprinted in S. Frith and A. Goodwin (eds.), *On Record: Pop, Rock and the Written Word*, pp. 371–89. London: Routledge.

Fyfe, Gordon and John Law. 1992. *Picturing Power*. Oxford: Blackwell.

Garfinkel, Harold. 1967. *Studies in Ethnomethodology*. Cambridge: Polity.

Gibson, J.J. 1966. *The Senses Considered as Perceptual Systems*. Boston: Houghton Mifflin.

Giddens, Anthony. 1990. *The Consequences of Modernity*. Cambridge: Polity.

1991. *Modernity and Self-identity: Self and Society in the Late Modern Age*. Cambridge: Polity.

Gilmore, Samuel. 1987. 'Coordination and Convention: The Organization of the Concert Art World', *Symbolic Interaction* 10:209–27.

Gluch, Paul. 1993. 'The Use of Music in Preparing for Sport Performance', *Contemporary Thought* (2):33–53.

Goffman, Erving. 1961. *Asylums: Essays on the Social Situation of Mental Patients and Other Inmates*. New York: Anchor Books.

Gregory, Andrew H. 1997. 'The Roles of Music in Society: the Ethnomusicological Perspective', in D.J. Hargreaves and A.C. North (eds.), *The Social Psychology of Music*, pp. 123–38. Oxford: Oxford University Press.

Greisman, Harvey. 1976. 'Disenchantment of the World: Romanticism, Aesthetics and Sociological Theory', *British Journal of Sociology* 27:425–507.

1986. 'The Paradigm that Failed', in R. Monk (ed.), *Structures of Knowing*, pp. 273–91. New York: University Press of America.

Grint, Keith and Steve Woolgar. 1997. *The Machine at Work*. Cambridge: Polity.

Gumperz, John. 1977. 'Sociocultural Knowledge in Conversational Inference', Peter Cole and Jerry L. Morgan (eds.), *Linguistics and Anthropology*. Washington, DC: Georgetown University Press.

Hall, Stuart. 1980. 'Recent Developments in Theories of Language and Ideology: A Critical Note', in Stuart Hall, Dorothy Hobson, Andrew Lowe and Paul Willis (eds.), *Culture, Media, Language: Working Papers in Cultural Studies 1972–79*, pp. 157–62. London: Hutchinson.

1986. 'On Postmodernism and Articulation: An Interview with Stuart Hall', *Journal of Communication Inquiry* 10(2):45–60.

Haraway, Donna. 1985. 'A Manifesto for Cyborgs: Science, Technology and Socialist Feminism in the 1980s', *Socialist Review* 80:65 107.

1991. 'Situated Knowledges: The Science Question in Feminism and the Privilege of Partial Perspective', in her *Simians, Cyborgs and Women*, pp. 183–201. London: Free Association Books.

Harré, Rom. 1998. *The Singular Self*. London: Sage.

Harris, Catherine and Clemens Sandresky. 1985. 'Love and Death in Classical Music: Methodological Problems in Analyzing Human Meanings in Music', *Symbolic Interaction* 8:291–310.

Held, David. 1984. *Introduction to Critical Theory: Horkheimer to Habermas*. London: Hutchinson.

Hennion, Antoine. 1993. *La passion musicale*. Paris: Metaille.

1995. 'The History of Art – Lessons in Mediation', *Reseaux: The French Journal of Communication* 3(2):233–62.

1997. 'Baroque and Rock: Music, Mediators and Musical Taste', *Poetics* 24:415–35.

Hennion, Antoine and Emilie Gomart. 1999. 'A Sociology of Attachment: Music, Amateurs, Drug Users', in John Law and John Hassard (eds.), *Actor Network Theory and After*, pp. 220–47. Oxford: Blackwell.

Hennion, Antoine and Line Grenier. 1998. 'Sociology of Art: New Stakes in a Post-critical Time', in Stella Quah (ed.), *Sociology: Advances and Challenges in the 1990s*. London: Sage Publications.

Hennion, Antoine and Cecile Meadel. 1989. 'Artisans of Desire', *Sociological Theory* 7(2):191–209.

Hetherington, Kevin. 1998. *Expressions of Identity: Space, Performance, Politics*. London: Sage.

Hicks, F.M. 1992. 'The Power of Music', *Nursing Times*, 88:72–4.

1995. 'The Role of Music Therapy in the Care of the Newborn', *Nursing Times*, 91:31–3.

Hobsbawm, Eric and Terrence Ranger. 1983. *The Invention of Tradition*. Cambridge: Cambridge University Press.

Hochschild, Arlie. 1979. 'Emotion Work, Feeling Rules and Social Structure', *American Journal of Sociology* 85:551–75.
    1983. *The Managed Heart*. Berkeley, Los Angeles and London: University of California Press.
Holland, Janet, Carolyn Ramazanoglu, Sue Sharpe and Rachel Thompson. 1994. 'Power and Desire: The Embodiment of Female Sexuality', *Feminist Review* 46:21–38.
Holbrook, M.B. and E. Hirschman. 1982. 'The Experiential Aspects of Consumption: Consumer Fantasies, Feelings and Fun', *Journal of Consumer Research* 9:132–40.
Hugill, Stan. 1961. *Shanties from the Seven Seas*. London: Routledge and Kegan Paul.
Irigary, Luce. 1989. 'The Gesture in Psychoanalysis', in T. Brennan (ed.), *Between Feminism and Psychoanalysis*. London: Routledge.
Jaggar, Alison M. and Susan R. Bordo. 1992. *Gender/Body/Knowledge: Feminist Reconstructions of Being and Knowing*. New Brunswick, NJ: Rutgers University Press.
Jahn, Otto. 1882. *The Life of Mozart* (3 vols.). New York: Kalmus.
Jakobson, R. 1960. 'Closing Statement: Linguistics and Poetics', in T.A. Sebeok (ed.), *Style in Language*. Cambridge, MA: Harvard University Press.
Jay, Martin. 1984. *Adorno*. London: Fontana.
Jones, R.B. and S. Rayner. 1999. 'Music in the Hen House: a Survey of its Incidence and Perceived Benefits.' Paper presented to the Southern Poultry Science Society, Southern Conference on Avian Diseases, Atlanta, Georgia.
Kaminski, J. and W. Hall. 1996. 'The Effect of Soothing Music on Neonatal Behavioral States in the Hospital Newborn Nursery', *Neonatal Network* 16:45–54.
Kellaris, J.J. and R.J. Kent, 1992. 'The Influence of Music on Consumers' Temporal Perceptions: Does Time Fly when you're Having Fun?' *Journal of Consumer Psychology* 1:365–76.
Kingsbury, Henry. 1991. 'Sociological Factors in Musicological Poetics', *Ethnomusicology* 35.
Knorr-Cetina, Karin. 1981. *The Manufacture of Knowledge: An Essay on the Constructivist and Contextual Nature of Science*. Oxford: Pergamon Press.
Kramer, Lawrence. 1990. *Music as Social Practice*. Berkeley, Los Angeles and London: University of California Press.
Krumhansl, Carol and Diana Lynn Schenck. 1997. 'Can Dance Reflect the Structural and Expressive Qualities of Music? A Perceptual Experiment on Balanchine's Choreography of Mozart's Divertimento No. 15', *Musicae Scientiae* 1:63–85.
Kuhn, Thomas. 1970. *The Structure of Scientific Revolutions* (2nd edn). Chicago: Chicago University Press.
Lamont, Michelle. 1992. *Money, Morals, and Manners*. Chicago: University of Chicago Press.
Lanza, Joseph. 1994. *Elevator Music: A Surreal History of Muzak, Easy-listening and other Moodsong*. London: Quartet Books.
Larkin, Philip. 1964. *The Whitsun Weddings*. London: Faber and Faber.

Lash, Scott and John Urry. 1994. *Economies of Signs and Space*. London: Sage.

Latour, Bruno. 1991. 'Where are the Missing Masses? A Sociology of a Few Mundane Artefacts', in W. E. Bijker and J. Law (eds.), *Shaping Technology/ Building Society: Studies in Sociotechnical Change*, pp. 225–58. Cambridge, MA: MIT Press.

Latour, Bruno and Steve Woolgar. 1986 [1979]. *Laboratory Life: The Construction of Scientific Facts*. Princeton: Princeton University Press.

Law, John. 1994. *Organizing Modernity*. Cambridge: Polity.

Lenneberg, Hans. 1988. 'Speculating About Sociology and Social History', *Journal of Musicology* 4(4):409–20.

Leonard, J. 1992. 'Music Therapy: Fertile Ground for Application of Research in practice', *Neonatal Network* 12:47–8.

Lichterman, Paul. 1992. 'Self-help Reading as Thin Culture', *Media, Culture and Society* 14:421–47.

Lomax, A. 1968. *Folksong, Style and Culture*. Washington, DC: American Association for the Advancement of Science.

Lowe, Donald, M. 1995. *The Body in Late Capitalist USA*. Durham, NC and London: Duke University Press.

Lurie, Allison. 1992. *The Language of Clothes* (2nd edn). London: Bloomsbury.

Lury, Celia. 1998. *Prosthetic Culture*. London: Routledge.

Lynch, Michael. 1982. *Art and Artifacts in Laboratory Science*. London: Routledge & Kegan Paul.

MacDonald, Sharon. 1998. *The Politics of Display: Museums, Science, Culture*. Oxford: Berg.

MacInnis, Deborah J. and C. Park. 1991. 'The Differential Role of Characteristics of Music on High- and Low-involvement Consumers' Processing of Ads', *Journal of Consumer Research* 18:161–73.

McClary, Susan. 1991. *Feminine Endings: Music, Gender and Sexuality*. Minneapolis: University of Minnesota Press.

1992. *Georges Bizet's Carmen*. Cambridge: Cambridge University Press.

McElrea, Heather and Lionel Standing. 1992. 'Fast Music Causes Fast Drinking', *Perceptual and Motor Skills* 75:362.

McRobbie, Angela. 1991. 'Dance Narratives and Fantasies of Achievement', in her *Feminism and Youth Culture: From* Jackie *to* Just Seventeen, pp. 189–219. London: Macmillan.

MAIL. 1998. 'Music that Moves the Station Yobs', *The Daily Mail* (January 30), p. 5.

Maranto, Cheryl Dileo 1993. 'Applications of Music in Medicine', in Margaret Heal and Tony Wigram (eds.), *Music Therapy in Health and Education*. London and Philadelphia: Jessica Kingsley Publishers.

Martin, Peter, J. 1995. *Sounds and Society: Themes in the Sociology of Music*. Manchester: Manchester University Press.

Martin, Randy. 1997. 'The Composite Body: Hip Hop Aerobics and the Multicultural Nation', *Journal of Sport and Social Issues* 21(2):120–33.

Mattheson, Johann. 1981 [1739]. *The Complete Capellmeister (Der vollkommene Capellmeister)*. (trans. Ernest Harriss). Ann Arbor, MI: UMI Research Press.

Mauss, Marcel. 1979 [1934]. 'Body Techniques', in his *Sociology and Psychology*, pp. 95–123. London: Routledge.

Mehan, Hugh. 1990. 'Oracular Reasoning in a Psychiatric Exam', in Alan Grimshaw (ed.), *Conflict Talk*. Cambridge: Cambridge University Press.

Melucci, Alberto. 1996a. *Challenging Codes: Collective Action in the Information Age*. Cambridge: Cambridge University Press.

1996b. *The Playing Self: Person and Meaning in the Planetary Society*. Cambridge: Cambridge University Press.

Mestrovic, Stjepan. 1999. *Postemotional Society*. London: Sage.

Middleton, Richard. 1990. *Studying Popular Music*. Milton Keynes: Open University Press.

Milliman, R.E. 1982. 'Using Background Music to Affect the Behaviour of Supermarket Shoppers', *Journal of Marketing* 46:86–91.

1986. 'The Influence of Background Music on the Behaviour of Restaurant Patrons', *Journal of Consumer Research* 13:286–9.

Mills, C. Wright. 1940. 'Situated Actions and Vocabularies of Motive', *American Sociological Review* 5:905–13.

Moore, Lisa Jean. 1997. 'It's Like you Use Pots and Pans to Cook with', *Science, Knowledge and Human Values*.

Moores, Shaun. 1990. *Interpreting Audiences*. London: Sage.

Morgan, David and Liz Stanley. 1990. Special Issue on Biography and Autobiography. *Sociology* 27(1).

Morley, David. 1980. 'Texts, Readers, Subjects', in S. Hall, D. Hobson, A. Lowe and P. Willis (eds.), *Culture, Media, Language: Working Papers in Cultural Studies 1972–79*, pp. 163–73. London: Hutchinson.

Mukerji, Chandra. 1994. 'Toward a Sociology of Material Culture: Science Studies, Cultural Studies and the Meanings of Things', in D. Crane (ed.), *The Sociology of Culture*, pp. 143–62. Oxford: Blackwell.

Mulkay, Michael. 1986. *The Word and the World*. London: Routledge.

Mundy, John. 1999. *Popular Music on Screen: From Hollywood Musical to Music Video*. Manchester: Manchester University Press.

Murry, C.S. 1989. *Crosstown Traffic: Jimi Hendrix and Post-War Pop*. London: Faber.

Negus, Keith. 1996. *Popular Music in Theory: An Introduction*. Cambridge: Polity.

Neilly, L. 1995. 'The Uses of Music in People's Everyday Lives'. Unpublished undergraduate dissertation, Department of Psychology, Keele University.

Nettl, Bruno. 1990. *Folk and Traditional Music of the Western Continents* (3rd edn). Englewood Cliffs, NJ: Prentice-Hall.

Nkeita, J.H.K. 1988. *The Music of Africa*. London: Gollancz.

North, Adrian C. and David. J. Hargreaves. 1997a. 'Experimental Aesthetics and Everyday Music Listening', in D.J. Hargreaves and A.C. North (eds.), *The Social Psychology of Music*, pp. 84–106. Oxford: Oxford University Press.

1997b. 'Music and Consumer Behaviour', in D.J. Hargreaves and A.C. North (eds.), *The Social Psychology of Music*, pp. 268–82. Oxford: Oxford University Press.

1997c. 'The Musical Milieu: Studies of Listening in Everyday Life', *The Psychologist*, July:309–12.

NYT. 1996. 'Playing Classics to Commuters', *New York Times* (6 October), p. 3, section 13, col. 1.

Okwumabua, T.M. et al. 1983. 'Cognitive Strategies and Running Performance: An Exploratory Study', *Cognitive Therapy Research* 7:363–70.

Peterson, Richard (ed.). 1976. *The Production of Culture.* London and Los Angeles: Sage.

Peterson, Richard and Albert Simkus. 1992. 'How Musical Tastes Mark Occupational Status Groups', in M. Lamont and M. Fournier (eds.), *Cultivating Differences: Symbolic Boundaries and the Making of Inequality,* pp. 152–86. Chicago: University of Chicago Press.

Pinch, Trevor and Wiebe Bijker. 1987. 'The Social Construction of Facts and Artifacts: Or How the Sociology of Science and the Sociology of Technology Might Benefit Each Other', in W.E. Bijker, T.P. Hughes and T. Pinch (eds.), *The Social Construction of Technological Systems,* pp. 17–50. Cambridge, MA: MIT Press.

Piron, Francis. 1990. 'Defining Impulse Purchasing', *Advances in Consumer Research* 18:509–14.

1993. 'A Comparison of Emotional Reactions Experienced by Planned, Unplanned and Impulse Purchasers', *Advances in Consumer Research* 20:341–4.

Press, Andrea. 1994. 'The Sociology of Cultural Reception: Notes toward an Emerging Paradigm', in D. Crane (ed.), *The Sociology of Culture,* pp. 221–46. Oxford: Blackwell.

Radley, A. 1990. 'Artefacts, Memory and a Sense of the Past', in D. Middleton and D. Edwards (eds.), *Collective Remembering.* London: Sage.

Radway, Janice. 1988. 'Reception Study: Ethnography and the Problems of Dispersed Audiences and Nomadic Subjects', *Cultural Studies* 2:359–76.

Rahn, John. 1972. 'Review of Coker's Music and Meaning', *Perspectives of New Music* 11:255–7.

Rich, Adrienne. 1994 [1973]. *Diving into the Wreck.* New York: W.W. Norton.

Riesman, David. 1950. *The Lonely Crowd: A Study of the Changing American Character.* New Haven: Yale University Press.

Roballey, T.C., C. McGreevy, R.R. Rongo, M.L. Schwantes, P.J. Steger, M.A. Winninger and E.B. Gardner. 1985. 'The Effect of Music on Eating Behavior', *Bulletin of the Psychonomic Society* 23:221–2.

Rojek, Chris. 1995. *Decentred Leisure.* London: Sage.

Rook, Dennis W. 1987. 'The Buying Impulse', *Journal of Consumer Research* 14:189–99.

Rook, Dennis, W. and Stephen J. Hoch. 1985. 'Consuming Impulses', *Advances in Consumer Research* 12:23–7.

Sacks, Oliver. 1990. *Awakenings* (new revised edn). London: Picador.

Scruton, Roger. 1995. 'Notes on the Meaning of Music', in M. Krausz (ed.), *The Interpretation of Music: Philosophical Essays.* Oxford: Clarendon.

Sharma, Ursula. 1992. *Complementary Medicine Today: Practitioners and Patients* (revised edn). London: Routledge.

Shepherd, John. 1991. *Music as Social Text.* Cambridge: Polity.

Shepherd, John and Peter Wicke. 1997. *Music and Cultural Theory.* Cambridge: Polity.

Sheridan, D. 1998. 'Mass-observation Revived: The Thatcher Years and After', in D. Sheridan, D. Bloome and B. Street (eds.), *Writing Ourselves: Literacy Practices and the Mass-observation Project.* London: Hampton Press.

Shilling, Chris. 1993. *The Body and Social Theory.* London: Sage.

Simmel, Georg. 1917. 'The Metropolis and Mental Life', in D. Levine (ed.), *On*

Individuality and Social Forms, pp. 324–39. Chicago: University of Chicago Press.

Sloboda, John. 1992. 'Empirical Studies of Emotional Response to Music', in M. Riess-Jones and S. Holleran (eds.), *Cognitive Bases of Musical Communication*. Washington, DC: American Psychological Association.

Forthcoming. 'Everyday Uses of Music Listening', *Proceedings of the 5th International Conference on Music Perception and Cognition*. Seoul National University.

Smith, Dorothy. 1987. *The Everyday as Problematic*. London: Routledge.

1992. *Texts, Facts and Femininity: Exploring the Relations of Ruling*. London: Routledge.

Smith, P.C. and R. Curnow. 1966. '"Arousal Hypothesis" and the Effects of Music on Purchasing Behavior', *Journal of Applied Psychology* 50:255–6.

Spink, Kevin and Kelvin Longhurst. 1986. 'Cognitive Strategies and Swimming Performances: An Exploratory Study', *The Australian Journal of Science and Medicine in Sport*, June: 9–13.

Sterne, Jonathan. 1997. 'Sounds Like the Mall of America', *Ethnomusicology* 41:22–50.

STR. 1981 [1960]. *Songs of Two Rebellions: The Jacobite Wars of 1715 and 1745 in Scotland* (sung by Ewan MacColl). Folkways Records, Album No. FW 8756.

Streeck, Jürgen. 1981. 'Speech Acts in Interaction: A Critique of Searle', *Discourse Processes* 4:133–53.

1996. 'How to do Things with Things', *Human Studies*, Spring: 365–84.

Strong, Phil. 1979. *The Ceremonial Order of the Clinic: Parents, Doctors and Medical Bureaucracies*. London: Routledge.

Subotnik, Rose Rosengard. 1976. 'Adorno's Diagnosis of Beethoven's Late Style: Early Symptoms of a Fatal Condition', *Journal of the American Musicological Society* 29:242–75.

1978. 'The Historical Structure: Adorno's "French" Model for the Criticism of Nineteenth-century Music', *19th-century Music* 2:36–60.

1983. 'The Role of Ideology in the Study of Western Music', *Journal of Musicology* 2(1):1–12.

1990. *Developing Variations: Style and Ideology in Western Music*. Minneapolis: University of Minnesota Press.

Tagg, Philip. 1991. *Fernando the Flute: Analyses of Musical Meaning in an ABBA Mega-Hit*. Liverpool: The Institute of Popular Music, University of Liverpool.

TEL. 1998. 'Metro Hooligans Are Sent Packing by Delius', *The Daily Telegraph* (30 January), p. 1.

Thayer, A.W. and Elliot Forbes. 1967. *Thayer's Life of Beethoven*. Princeton: Princeton University Press.

Thoman, E., V. Dennenberg and J. Sievel. 1981. 'State Organization in Neonates: Developmental Inconsistency Indicates Risk for Developmental Dysfunction', *Neuropaediatrics* 12(1):46, 59–75.

Tota, Anna Lisa. 1997a. 'Cases of Non-recognition and the Sociology of Value', *Social Science Information*.

1997b. *Etnografia dell'arte: Per una sociologia dei contesti artistici*. Rome: Logica University Press.

1999. *Sociologie dell'arte: Dal museo tradizionale all'arte multimediale*. Roma: Carocci.

Turner, Bryan S. 1984. *The Body and Society*. Oxford: Blackwell.

Turner, Victor. 1981. 'Social Dramas and Stories about Them', in W.J.T. Mitchell (ed.), *On Narrative*, pp. 137–64. Chicago: University of Chicago Press.

Tyler, M. and Pamela Abbot. 1998. 'Chocs Away: Weight Watching in the Contemporary Airline Industry', *Sociology* 32(3):433–50.

Unyk, A.M., S.E. Trehub, L.H.J. Trainor and E.G. Sellenberg. 1992. 'Lullabies and Simplicity: A Cross-cultural Perspective', *Psychology of Music* 20:15–28.

Urry, John. 1996. 'How Societies Remember the Past', in S. Macdonald and G. Fyfe (eds.), *Theorizing Museums: Representing Identity and Diversity in a Changing World*, pp. 45–68. Sociological Review Monograph. Oxford: Blackwell.

Van Rees, C.J. 1987. 'How Reviewers reach Consensus on the Value of Literary Works', *Poetics* 16:275–94.

Vincent, John. 1995. *Inequality and Old Age*. London: University of London Press.

Wajcman, Judy. 1991. *Feminism Confronts Technology*. Cambridge: Polity.

Walser, Robert. 1993. *Running with the Devil: Power, Gender, and Madness in Heavy Metal Music*. Hanover, NH: Wesleyan University Press.

Weber, Max. 1958 [1921]. *The Rational and Social Foundations of Music*. Carbondale, IL: Southern Illinois University Press.

1970. 'Science as a Vocation', in H. Gerth and C.W. Mills (eds.), *From Max Weber: Essays in Sociology*, pp. 129–56. London: Routledge and Kegan Paul.

Weber, William. 1984. 'The Contemporaneity of Eighteenth-century Musical Taste', *Musical Quarterly* 70:175–94.

1992. *The Rise of the Musical Classics in Eighteenth-century England: A Study in Canon, Ritual and Ideology*. Oxford: Oxford Univeristy Press.

Weizenbaum, Joseph. 1976. *Computer Power and Human Reason*. San Francisco: W.H. Freeman and Co.

Wheelock, Gretchen. 1992. '*Schwarze Gredel* and the Engendered Minor Mode in Mozart's Operas', in R. Solie (ed.), *Musicology and Difference*, pp. 201–44. Berkeley, Los Angeles and London: University of California Press.

Whitson, David. 1994. 'The Embodiment of Gender: Discipline, Domination and Empowerment', in S. Birrel and L. Cheryl (eds.), *Women, Sport and Culture*. Champaign, IL: Human Kinetics.

Wieder, D.L. 1974. *Language and Social Reality*. The Hague: Mouton.

Williams, Raymond. 1965. *The Long Revolution*. Harmondsworth: Penguin.

Williams, Rosalind. 1982. *Dream Worlds: Mass Consumption in Late 19th Century France*. Berkeley, Los Angeles and London: University of California Press.

Williams, Simon J. 1996. 'The "Emotional" Body' (Review Article). *Body & Society* 2(3):125–39.

Willis, Paul. 1978. *Profane Culture*. London: Routledge.

Winner, Langdon. 1980. 'Do Artifacts have Politics?' *Daedalus* 109:120–36.

Winograd, Terry and Fernando Flores. 1986. *Understanding Computers and Cognition: A New Foundation for Design*. New York: Addison-Wesley Publishing Company, Inc.

Wise, Sue. 1990 [1984]. 'Sexing Elvis', reprinted in S. Frith and A. Goodwin (eds.), *On Record: Rock, Pop and the Written Word*, pp. 390–8. London: Routledge.

Witkin, Robert W. 1974. *The Intelligence of Feeling*. London: Heinemann.
  1995. *Art and Social Structure*. Cambridge: Polity.
  1998. *Adorno on Music*. London: Routledge.
Witkin, Robert W. and Tia DeNora. 1997. 'Aesthetic Materials and Aesthetic Action', *Culture: The Newsletter of the American Sociological Association*: 1, 6–7.
Wolff, Janet. 1981. *The Social Production of Art*. London: Macmillan.
Woolgar, Steve. 1997. 'Configuring the User: Inventing New Technologies', in K. Grint and S. Woolgar (eds.), *The Machine at Work*, pp. 65–94. Cambridge: Polity.
  1988. *Science: The Very Idea*. London: Routledge.
Yelanjian, Mary. 1991. 'Rhythms of Consumption', *Cultural Studies*, January: 91–7.
Zolberg, Vera. 1990. *Constructing a Sociology of the Arts*. Cambridge: Cambridge University Press.
  1996. 'Museums as Contexted Sites of Remembrance: The Enola Gay Affair', in S. Macdonald and G. Fyfe (eds.), *Theorizing Museums*, pp. 69–82. Oxford: Blackwell.
Zukin, Sharon. 1992. *Landscapes of Power*. Berkeley, Los Angeles and London: University of California Press.

Index

Adorno, T.W., 1–3, 22, 40, 52, 131, 132, 149, 155, 163
aerobics classes
  components of, 90–1
  cooling off, 101–2
  core, 99–101
  warm-up, 93–6
  music produced for, 91–3
  musical devices in, 96–9
  musical order and disorder, 89–91, 96–7
  research on, 88–9
  role of music in, 92–3, 102–3, 105, 106, 114
aerobics instructors, 95–6
aesthetic agency, 6, 46, 48, 52–3, 58, 64, 65–6, 123
aesthetic reflexivity, 51–3
affordance, 39–40, 99, 106
age
  and attitudes to music, 147–8
  and consumption, 134, 147
agency, 5–6, 20, 27, 40, 54, 76, 122, 129, 153
  see also aesthetic agency
air travel, music during, 11–14
airline passengers
  disciplining, 9–10
  risk perception, 10–11
alchemy, 43, 67
Aldridge, D., 71
Allanbrook, W., 13
Anderson, R., 39–40
animals, 84
appropriation, 31, 33, 36, 43, 47, 67
Areni, C.S., 141–2
Aristotle, 160
Armstrong, L., 158
artefacts, and users, 34–6
Auden, W.H., 158
autonomy, musical, 24

Bach, J.S., 13, 14, 56, 146, 153, *154*
Baez, J., 158

Barlow, G., 55
Barthes, R., 22, 161
Becker, H.S., 4
Beethoven, L. van, 2, 29, 30, 44, 157
Belcher, S., 88–9, 135
Berger, B., 1
Bijker, W., 35
bio-feedback, 161
biography, 41–2, 62, 63–6
Bizet, G. (*Carmen*), 8, *9*, 25–7, 29
body
  interaction with culture, 75–6
  interaction with environment, 75, 87–8
  performative character, 103
  social and medical approaches to, 75–6, 87–8
  see also embodiment and music
Born, G., 7
Brahms, J., 63, 68
breakdowns, 89–90, 95
Butler, J., 153

Cage, J., 148
Callon, M., 39, 94, 100, 160
calm
  music to induce, 16, 41–3
  see also relaxation
Carmen, 8, *9*, 25–7, 29
Cavicchi, D., 18
censorship, 127–8
Cockburn, C., 34
cognitive strategies, 97
Cohen, S., 7
collective occasions, 121–5
communication, music as, 44, 57, 126–8
concentration, 58–61
consciousness, 153, 162
consumer behaviour, 18, 134–5, 138, 142
consumption
  and identity, 131, 134, 147
  see also retail outlets
contrast structure, 98
conversation analysis, 36–8

topoi, 13, 44
Tota, A.I.., 27
transport
  air travel, 9–14
  music in stations, 18
trust, 10–11, 14
Turner, V., 70, 128, 159

Urry, J., 19, 68
users, and artefacts, 34–6

van Rees, K., 27
'venting', 56, 57
verbal meaning, 36–8
Verdi, G., 58
virtual reality, 56, 157
Vivaldi, A., 22, 68, 157

Wagner, R., 150
Wajcman, J., 34
Walkman, 58, 156
Weber, M., 131, 155, 156
Wicke, P., 5, 24, 46
Williams, R., 86–7
Willis, P., 5, 6–7, 27
Winner, L., 34, 35
Witkin, R.W., 2, 129
Woolgar, S., 30, 35
work, music in, 104–5
worship, music in, 146

Zen, 100
Zolberg, V., 1, 131
Zukin, S., 132